Untroubling a
Troubled World

Untroubling a Troubled World

Peace 4 Ever

Dr. J. Knowname

Order this book online at www.trafford.com
or email orders@trafford.com

Most Trafford titles are also available at major online book retailers.

Printed in the United States of America.

ISBN: 978-1-4269-6990-4 (sc)
ISBN: 978-1-4269-6991-1 (e)

Trafford rev. 06/01/2011

 www.trafford.com

North America & International
toll-free: 1 888 232 4444 (USA & Canada)
phone: 250 383 6864 ♦ fax: 812 355 4082

INTRODUCTION TO THE INTRODUCTION

I see a very dangerous world which seems to be on the edge of a cliff, ready for some lunatic to push the self-destruct button. My book UNTROUBLING A TROUBLED WORLD - PEACE 4 EVER is my effort to present some ideas which can bring relief from fear of war, financial ruin, and other serious problems facing our country and the rest of the world. Frankly, I am 79 years old - or as I am apt to say - I am 97 and dyslexic and would like to leave this world knowing I have done something for humanity to make life better for others.

When I was a teacher of a number of foreign languages - I was there for the building of the Tower of Babel - I always told my students that we should start the lesson at the end so that we should know we have finished. Experts later concluded that this is an excellent teaching technique as it lets students know where they are headed!

If you dare to continue reading this pack of brilliance, you will note that I declare that the human race has not yet evolved beyond the stage of childhood – early childhood! I became even more convinced of this truth when I heard that Al Gore received the Nobel Peace Prize! The Committee that made this momentous decision is supposed to be made up of some of the most intelligent humans on our planet earth. From what I have heard, I understand that Mr. Gore has concluded that mankind, kind women or humans have caused the warming of the earth by driving their cars! I wonder if he and the members of the

Nobel Peace Prize Committee ever made a study of how many cars existed when the earth moved away from the Ice Age to our present more accommodating climate. They certainly, beyond a shadow of a doubt, should quickly do so before we all go on "boil" or freeze as the planet has been wont to do since Creation on a rather regular irregular basis without environmentalists trying to control nature.

By the time you digest this entire book, with or without mustard or mayonnaise, you will agree with me that Al Gore should not get the Peace Prize – I should! Why? Simple! This book contains the recipe for achieving world peace and keeping it! May G-d help us do so even if He is too busy with other matters such as dreaming up other deviltries not thought of before!

INTRODUCTION

All religions and all human thinking have gone through an evolutionary process that continues today. I am hoping this book will help us to evolve toward more love and to eradicate hate of any kind. The exclusivity, narrow-mindedness, fear and hatred engendered by many religions over eons of time - even into our present age with the strife in Ireland between Catholics and Protestants in the Christian world must cease. It is indeed tragic that our Muslim brothers are now going through the above calamitous era that most of the world finished with centuries ago. I know I report facts that may be offensive to some Muslims, but these are pointed to with love in mind and a sincere hope that the Muslim world can join the rest of humanity in living according to the above philosophy.

WARNING, THIS BOOK CAN BE OFFENSIVE,
BUT IT IS MEANT TO SAVE YOUR LIFE

Do not let me mislead you; this book is not about religion, but about saving mankind from his own immaturity so that we may all survive. First and foremost, I want to apologize to readers for writing ideas I would never think of expressing if we were living in normal times. But in an age wherein there are extremist groups now having access to weapons of mass extinction that can surely destroy all human life on our planet as we have known it, I feel I must come out with what needs to be said if we are to avoid more human misery and the likely eradication of the human race.

Our basic beliefs are important. We are not made up of groups, we are individuals and one individual is the smallest minority. In all matters, even in the case of religious faith, we have the right to hold on to what is a comfort to us and is of personal help for whatever reason. But, above all, it is best if we can keep our minds open and respect the opinions of others.

I believe that many humans have turned to worshiping religion rather than G-d; that religious leaders who have turned them into businesses have ignored the clear declaration in the Bible that G-d is to have no form, no name and is to remain unknown and that there is only ONE G-d. One who believes in G-d needs to understand that He is in and part of each human being. To "Love the lord thy G-d" requires that we love all of humanity. I believe that all we need to practice is to love one another regardless of differences and that we DO ONLY GOOD AND DO HARM TO NO ONE. This is the roadmap to peace and harmony on earth. I do believe that there had to be a Creative Force of the Universe but whether we understand it, worship it or not worship it is of no consequence as long as we follow the preceding thought.

CONTENTS

FORWARD

Any names mentioned in this book or those who may have contributed in some way toward its completion do not necessarily favor or hold the same views expressed therein. The views expressed are only those of the author and G-d. If Christian, you may wish to hold tight to your cross; if Jewish, it may be safer to wear your yamikah (skull cap as the one worn by the Pope); if Muslim, have your prayer rug handy! If this book is not taken seriously, we will all have to have prayer rugs!

A crazy poor man who hears voices is placed into an asylum for his protection and for the protection of society; a crazy rich man is eccentric. A man of religion who hears voices is said to be a prophet or a God! Oh well, so we live on a Ship of Fools. What else is new?

The "simple"goal of this book is to help create a peaceful and prosperous world in which all peoples can live without fear and enjoy life to the fullest. We are all brothers under G-d, no matter what we may call Him and whether He exists or not; we are all inhabitants of the same planet. It is ours to preserve, not to destroy!

A must reading, IF YOU WANT THIS PLANET TO SURVIVE!

THE FOLLOWING SHOULD GIVE YOU AN IDEA OF THE PURPOSE OF THIS BOOK

I just saw a short part of "GI Jane," a movie about a woman who joined a special unit of the Navy Seals. It almost brought me to tears seeing a woman go through the toughening up program. It was brutal; but she did it. It may be good for the body and brain to withstand a great deal of stress and physical punishment, but it is sad to recognize that all this is to make them better killing machines. I can only hope that some parts of this book may someday make it unnecessary for men or women to train to effectively kill other human beings.

It is also my sincere hope that this book will encourage good Muslims to turn their religion toward respect and love for all human beings no matter what religion or sect of any religion or for those who profess no religion. Let us hope that they can come to realize that we are all temporary tenants of this planet and that it is best for us to live in peace together.

DEDICATION

First, I would like to dedicate this book to the good people of Iraq. May it be a shining example of peace and prosperity for the decent people of the Middle East who deserve to have a chance to live better lives.

It is also dedicated to all the peoples of this world all of whom deserve to live wholesome lives in peace and without fear. It is my hope that this book can help us move forward in our evolution of human thought development so that all these things can be achieved. This is also dedicated to my parents, Mr. and Mrs. Thomas A. and Minerva Morris, who stayed together through thick and thin, good times and bad times. They taught me by example that charity is important, but, most of all, to be good and kind to all people.

DURING THE GOOD TIMES OF THE 1920s

May the philosophy in our lives become:

DO ONLY GOOD
DO HARM TO NO ONE

===

AUTHOR BIOGRAPHY

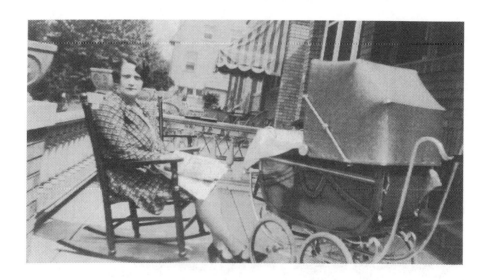

THIS IS THE BEST PICTURE EVER TAKEN OF ME
No, I am in the baby carriage!
The lady is my mother protecting me from paparazzi!

O.K. so here I am a few years later stationed across from
the Liberty Bell in Philadelphia to advocate
free enterprise in education via the voucher system.
He suggests that public school teachers should start their own
small, private, neighborhood schools whose success and
salary would depend upon the success of their students.

KILL THE AUTHOR is the order that went out for the last author of a book expressing such truths as are found in this one. The author is using the pen name of Dr J. Knowname to protect his life. The following biography, however, is correct beyond a shadow of a doubt as far as he can remember.

Dr. J. Knowname was born near his mother in Saint Agnes Hospital in Philadelphia, Pennsylvania on April 7, 1929. After word got around, we had the worst depression in our history! (Did I forget to warn you this author thinks he is Victor Borgia? Watch out for his subtle humor! He stopped thinking he was Napoleon on his seventh birthday.) He graduated kindergarten - after being expelled once - junior and senior high schools, The Wharton School of Economics and Finance at the University of Pennsylvania from which he graduated near the top of his class. He also attended Temple University, Florida State University, Ohio State University and the Faculte de Lyon in France. He was a member of the Modern Language Association of Pennsylvania and speaks some thirty-seven different languages, more or less, mostly less! Oh yes, we almost forgot to point out that he went through Wellesley College - in the front door and out the back.

Dr. J. Knowname spent four years in the Navy, working for a top secret part of naval intelligence which he cannot even disclose today. He had been a public school teacher in Philadelphia for twenty-two years. Dr. Knowname was forced to retire as a result of illnesses caused by his normal efforts to encourage a black child to do homework and to get to school on time. The torment he was put through will be detailed in his web-sites and will, no doubt, cause a real shake-up in our educational system – and legal system! It should put a stop to the "dumbing" down process in education and shake up the corrupt lawyers in the legal profession! It will especially give the shakes to certain Philadelphia lawyers, and I do not think they are either Shakers or Quakers! The web-sites will spell out how to make life better for black Americans. If Top Management allows him to live longer, he also plans to write a book on financial frauds. Our author is now living in Florida and is finally well, more or less as one might say – and I do say His experience in public schools has moved him to advocate a national voucher system to give parents more control over the education of their own children.

PROLOGUE

Through many years of my life, domestic and foreign problems have troubled me. There is no point in describing them without offering some solutions. No doubt I am oversensitive, but I suffer personally when I see so much heartbreak around the world. I believe this book presents some solutions that can alleviate many problems and that can solve most of the dangers facing this country and the rest of the world. There is absolutely no doubt in my mind that once this book sees the light of day, all such problems shall vanish within weeks. Never mind the fact that in over 2000 years Jesus, Mohammad, Buddha and all other Pretenders have not been able to accomplish such a feat. I am sure I cannot, but I know you can! I still remain optimistic as I know my readers will go out and make this a better world in the manner proposed here. You see, it is not up to me, to G-d, to the Tooth Fairy, to Santa Claus, to a string of prayer beads or to the Man in the Moon; it is up to you! Now, if you do not mind, let us get down to the revelation of what needs to be done

Since this book explores deeply into religion,
I believe it fitting to include a prayer:

A DEVOUT ORTHODOX ATHEIST PRAYS TO GOD!

Lo and behold, here are seven PRAYERS OF A DEVOUT ORTHODOX ATHEIST:

Prayer Number One: Holy of Holies and Most Merciful of the Universe, as a replacement for the Dietary Laws, can You please give us one that will help us lose weight and keep it off!

Prayer Number Two: Oh Most Omniscient LORD, if You ever PLAN TO CREATE ANOTHER WORLD, please first examine the many mistakes You made in this one! G-d knows, You made quite a few!

Prayer Number Three: Oh Lord Most High, please do not rest on the Seventh Day until you have made sure You have done everything correctly the first time!

Prayer Number Four: Oh Most Loving Lord, please send us an Angel who can explain what You really meant by "Love thy neighbor."

Prayer Number Five: Oh Blessed One On High and Lord of the Universe, please bring down ten plagues on the heads of those who believe they and they alone know the right way to Your HEAVEN.

Prayer Number Six: Most Beneficent Lord, please rewrite the Good Book - Your Bible and our Bible - so that we will not have to get so many interpretations from those who really have no idea of what they speak, read or write!

Prayer Number Seven: Oh LORD of the Universe; PLEASE protect me from Your followers - all of them!

(Apology for term "atheist." The correct term for me is very likely that I am a Deist because I believe that there had to be a creative force. Nevertheless, I prefer calling myself an atheist for the shock value! I thank God all the time, night and day, that I am an atheist! As you read on – if you do – you will agree that a better label is "Humanist" rather than atheist.) How do I explain the "apology"? Well, it may be psychologically sound or is it cultural conditioning? I am sadly well aware of the sorrows and problems of this world; so I truly am thankful and feel better after expressing this. Even knowing that G-d in the traditionalist sense does not exist, I would still love to be able to ask Him to make this a better, happier and safer world, but I know it is more practical for each of us human beings to do this ourselves as much as is possible. Hence, I am trying to finish this book to encourage people of all faiths and no faith to do so!

Please keep in mind as you read this feeble attempt to save the world that all written here is the Gospel Truth according to Matthew, Mark, Luke, John and Jack … and I am Jack and I swear it on a stack of Bibles of every version known to man!

HOW ABOUT A GOOD LAUGH FOR THE ROAD?

I went to a church the other day during a severe rainstorm. Of course, it was just to deliver something. I said to the secretary that the G-ds must be crying. She admonished me with the statement that there are no G-ds, but just one G-d. I agreed, but added that, unfortunately, He has a multiple personality disorder! She crossed herself and I left! (Sorry, this is meant as comic relief!) The Bible is correct in declaring that there is but one God. This concept was either given to or came from the Jews. Note that on the Passover plate, we must have an egg to remind us of the oneness of the human race, of the universality of life. The story of Jonah and the whale was to point out that the concept of one G-d had to be delivered to the entire world. But Jonah felt he was not up to the job and ran away. It is a whale of a story! As you no doubt know, G-d punished him by having him swallowed by a huge whale and then delivered him to the very place G-d had intended for him to visit and to deliver the message. Do I believe this story? What does it matter? The Bible was written by wise men who told stories that would teach us many things, among them, the need to have love and concern for all human beings. This is all the religions need to teach.

CHAPTER I

BUMPING into the BIBLE or
THE NATURE OF RELIGION

It is written that G-d created this world in six days and rested on the seventh. This sounds like a rushed job in my book; He never should have rested on the seventh day without first checking to see that it was the best of all possible worlds as declared by Jean Jacques Rousseau. From the results, am I being impious to imply He should have taken time at the end of the six days to sit back and see what could have been arranged in a better way?

So who am I to offer a second opinion? Just a non-entity, an old school teacher who has long been sickened by seeing the suffering, the misery, the poverty, injustice, hatred and endless wars and killing in the most beautiful and bountiful world ever created. I am just an unknown, a grain of sand who has been troubled enough to use the brain given to us all by the Creative Force of the Universe to consider ways to "perfectionate" the imperfections of this sad and beautiful world. This is where we should be putting our efforts rather than insisting and trying to prove that our G-d and our G-d alone is the only true and perfect almighty G-d.

I was about to give the O.K. for having this book published when I decided to look up the meaning of "Intelligent Design" which I had long instinctively believed to be a nonsensical argument used by religionists to prove the existence of G-d as most humans understand it. I was astounded to find that the conclusions I put together on my own are right in the "ballpark" with those of Albert Einstein. I fear this sounds presumptuous of me, but I have written or explained a number of times that I feel there must have been a creator of all the wonders and magnificent beauties of life and of the vast universe we know is out there, but that an understanding of all of this is beyond the capability of humans to comprehend. It has always seemed to me to be extremely childish and futile for mankind to try to grasp what is obviously beyond our ken.

One of my main motives in writing this book is that the feeble efforts of mankind to understand the unknowable has led to such horrors, such bloodshed that I am convinced we must come to our senses. Here is the thinking of Albert Einstein and then you may draw your own conclusions, with my permission and blessings. What most people call G-d and I call a Creative Force of the Universe is to Einstein: *"an intelligence of such superiority that, compared with it, all the systematic thinking and acting of human beings is an utterly insignificant reflection."* Albert Einstein

I am just offering this book as a stimulus to all of humanity to start thinking about solutions to our problems rather than wait for a man on a white horse, an imam, a savior or a Moses who brought us the Ten Commandments. I am a Jew who likes and values the story of Moses, but, let us face it, he was a smart Jew! Had he come down from Mount Sinai and declared that he had just written the laws for them to live by, he would have been laughed out of town and, on top of that, they would not have believed a single word of it. Having innate wisdom, he came down from the mountain and declared that these laws to be followed were chiseled by G-d into stone tablets for them to cherish for eternity.

This was a new fangled idea that there was but one G-d! So who said that man did not create G-d? Do not look at me. I may be old and decrepit, but I was not there at the time. The real trouble began when man started creating religions. Here is the rub, for man no longer worships G-d; we worship our own concocted religions.

Am I damning any religion or all of them? Of course not, I am just suggesting that all of mankind needs to grow up, start thinking for ourselves and reinvent religion so that we can all strive together to make this a better world. And now, it is in your loving and capable hands and may G-d bless you whether He exists or not!

RELIGION CAN BE GOOD

By all means, I do not mean to damn religion. It has done some good to mankind. The big question is: does the bad outweigh the good? That is for any remaining readers to determine!

I went to a memorial service the other day for probably the most wonderful person I have ever met. She was my neighbor across the street for about a year. Shortly after she moved in, our "loving G-d" gave her a most painful and hopeless form of cancer. One day, when I asked her how she was feeling, she smiled even though she was in agony and said she was fine and felt good because she knew she would soon be with Jesus! I cried inside but said nothing and just smiled and hugged her. My sincere hope is that she is indeed correct in believing that there is a Jesus in Heaven waiting for kind people such as Carol Kobin. I would never suggest to anyone that they let go of such a beautiful faith no matter which one it may be. If it meets a need and they are happy, I am happy for them and can only say in my heart that G-d should bless them even though I call myself a Devout, Orthodox atheist!

All through the funeral service, I was tormented with the thought of my neighbor's death. On the way out, as I shook the hand of the priest, I barely managed to get out my statement that I thought his faith was beautiful and then completely broke down. I am sure death does not sit well with anyone; I don't know why I so lost control over my emotions! I guess it was the general thought that life is so often cruel and unjust! Also, I am pained over having to say things that may hurt the feelings of decent people of religion.

Through this book I will often refer to my theory of evolution of human thought. It hurts me to suggest that people with strong religious feelings have not yet evolved much beyond the immature thinking of a child, but I am convinced of this. It hurts me to express such a thought, but I am only doing so because the rapid progress in technology has brought this world to a point at which we can self destruct if we do not rapidly grow up. I am happy to report that I see many signs of more rapid progress in the human thinking processes and that this is beginning to move along at a faster clip soon to be in tandem with the progress in making material advancements.

I became very much worried when I realized I may never see this book in print; so I wrote to a very wealthy, clear thinking and prominent business man and wrote the following:

Without help from the Highest Level (Mr. XYZ, in this case), I fear the book will never live to see the light of day. Two publishers have indicated they are afraid to publish it because they fear it would offend Muslims. I believe it goes deeper than this. The book completely pulls the rug out from under ALL religions, ESPECIALLY the Muslim and Christian faiths. I am sure they are offended by my statement that man has created G-d; but man then took a more dangerous step and created various religions. This has resulted in man worshiping RELIGION instead of G-d. They all think they are right and have the only answer and this has resulted in oceans of bloodshed through centuries and can now destroy the world as we know it.

To add a little humor to the book I report on a conversation between me and G-d about these issues. He was very comforted to know that things would be better once my book hit the book shelves and then flew off! I did advise Him though, that the next time He creates a world, He should not rest on the seventh day. Instead, He should make sure everything is right about what was done during the first six days. He again blessed me and saved my life about four times so that

I might finish my book on atheism! Miracles do happen whether we believe them or not!

I wrote the book because I am sick and tired of seeing so much human suffering through the ages. The Bible has a great deal of wisdom in it, but the attention has been given to only what people wanted to accept at the time because it suited their purposes. This Good Book clearly says that G-d is unknowable, is to have no form and no name. This is what I believe, but I know, through logic, that there had to be a creative force of the Universe. Believe me, I am thrilled to see the variety, the wonders, the majesty of creation, but this is not to be worshiped; it is to be enjoyed, safeguarded and shared. It is written that we must love the Lord our G-d with all our heart and all our soul. If this is what is required then why not understand that G-d really exists in all of humanity? This is why I agree with Jesus and all of like mind that we must love one another. G-d is one and the human race is one.

It is the divisiveness of religions that has ruined life on planet earth. All that is necessary is that we do good, care about others and do no harm. I believe that is all we need rather than the magic and hocus pocus of religions that have simply confounded us. I am telling people to stay with their religions if they derive comfort from them or if they are just happy with other aspects of religion. If they are happy, I am happy for them because that is the whole purpose of my book. When I see someone in trouble because of deformity or poor health or economic circumstances, I instinctively want to say "May G-d help them." But I know it is up to me or society in general to try to help because it is the entire human race that is G-d and we are all part of this concept of Deity. But there is no point in worshiping ourselves or an imagined G-d when we know that it is up to us, all members of the human race to work together as brothers to make life better for all of us. I often joke by saying that there is nothing perfect in this world since the "Incident of the Apple" (the Garden of Eden story). If we all work together to attain such a goal, we may not reach perfection, but certainly the world will be better just because of the effort. At any rate this is my idea of being an atheist – a devout orthodox atheist. (Of course, I admit later that I am really a humanist, but that must remain a secret for now.)

MUST HUMANS RELY ON RELIGIONS?

There are ample reasons for us mere humans to rely on religions, especially at the time Jesus brought us His message. Yes, the goodness He taught was cried out for then and valid even today and forever. The land of Israel was under the heavy heel (not heal *) of Roman rule, not known for its sense of moderation or kindness. All around the world, people had a rough life: no TV, remote controls, radios, sitcoms, cell phones, washing machines, hair dryers, vacuum cleaners, decent medical care, dental floss, good cosmetic surgery, clean water, coca cola, massage therapists or anything else modern man takes for granted — at least in parts of the world today. It was one hell of a place! In the world that our merciful G-d created, the entire world was oppressed with fear, fear of one another, fear of death, fear of being killed by war or a neighbor who needed a cup of sugar and fear of the unknown of which there was ample supply. Sadness, stress, struggle just for survival, loneliness, lack of a good public school system and a welfare program with food stamps that could be traded for drugs or alcohol! What a damn world it was and is! Yes, I know the story of the snake tempting Adam and Eve or Steve, one or the other, who seduced Adam into partaking of the forbidden fruit — an apple at that! What I do not know is why He chose the apple! This is the healthiest, most nutritious and delicious fruit we can eat! It makes one wonder if He had a devil may care attitude! Besides, once G-d planted the apple tree, He knew very well what would happen once He commanded that Adam and his significant other would do after He commanded them never to eat thereof! How did He know? Haven't you read the Bible? Are you not aware that He is all seeing, all knowing, is able to see the future and the past and perhaps both at the same time? No doubt Benjamin Franklin must have made a special pair of glasses for Him made of titanium and special crystals! Not crystal meth. I am against all drugs except for the ones I have to take to keep from losing the rest of my mind!

My apologies for treating a subject so serious and sensitive for so many people with levity, but this is the only way I can survive in this still troubled world. Besides, it is amusing for me to think of this when I am half asleep and then get up at 5 A.M., go to the computer and compose it with much mirth. Subconsciously, I may sense that a good shock treatment may be what is needed to pull us up out of our irrational thinking riveted into our minds through ions of brain washing by leaders suffering from their own fears and desires for answers. Even in this modern day and way past the beginning of the Age of Reason, so many people still believe in a supernatural or superior force that supposedly created this enigma that we call life on this earth. This seems, at first thought, to be unbelievable, but I can understand why this is so. We are still subject to death and the vicissitudes of life that can bring such pain, fear and horrors to our doorsteps, often without warning. On top of this, we are constantly bombarded with the balm or glorified advertising for various religions that people are prone to and glad to accept just as children are glad to believe in Santa Claus and the Tooth Fairy. It hurts me to say such things that may hurt individuals who are strongly tied to their religions. I do not make such statements to offend or insult, but only do so because it is necessary for better human understanding so that the human race may survive. We all need to understand that the faith of the faithful is a result of many thousands of years of indoctrination and we must not blame them for their belief in myths and fairy tales.

* If He lets me live, I may write a book on healing the English language! So watch out!

* * * * * * * * *

In reading this book you will understand that the Bible contains much wisdom, but we need to recognize the nonsense when it appears. You will also see a hint that RELIGION CAN BORDER ON INSANITY. Sorry, but the facts are the facts and nothing but the facts, so help me! If my claim that religion can often lead to insanity offends you, type into the search or address line in the computer: "The Witch Hunters of Europe, The Cruelest of Executioners." It is a litany of unbelievable torture inflicted upon victims in the name of religion. The Bible or their interpretation thereof was their inspiration! This is further proof that there is such a thing as the evolution of the human mind. There is no point in going into the multifarious peculiarities. But one more example about the truth that we are evolving: in centuries past, the great sport was to put slaves or Christians or thugs into the arena to make them fight to the death. For the most part we have grown away from this aberration and now even abhor arranging dogs or birds to fight to the death.

I must not forget to tell you that G-d told me He did not write the Bible; it was written by very wise men. They were wise enough to realize that if they told the people that the Bible was full of their own ideas, it never would have become a best seller; especially in an age when gods were "de-rigueur" or the rave of the ages. The Bible is centered on the concept of just one G-d. Prior to this innovation, there were countless Gods of every size, shape, form and whatever primitive man could conjure up. After all, they did not have radio or TV (as far as I can remember at my advanced age); so they had to have something for entertainment and to talk about. And these gods were really something to talk about. Oh, the things they could do and did do! Their deeds were very often X to TRIPLE X rated not proper to relate in this family friendly book.

And now back to the future. Above, I stated that the Bible contains much wisdom. I try to live by that wisdom. Friends often ask why I always wash my hands before eating. I do so because it says in the Bible we must wash our hands before partaking of food. Besides, cleanliness is next to godliness. Imagine how wise these wise men were to know how important this is even before there ever was an idea of microorganisms being in existence!

One day I was talking to a lady about this book and explained that it is about atheism and that G-d saved my life about four times so that I might live to finish it. I also told her that I had G-d talking to me several times. She was amazed and asked how G-d could talk to an atheist. Now it was my turn to be amazed. I said, "How many centuries does it take people to understand we are all G-d's children"? Just think of all the fun we will have with this! As you read below, remember this when I warn later that the Bible may not be an ideal book for children to read since it is so full of sex and violence. The very purpose of this book — or one of many of my aims - is for you to have fun and be happy while expanding your mind! Go to it!

Let us just thank G-d (the Creative Force of the Universe) we have a world, nurture it, care for it and work each day to make life better for ourselves and others. You see, even though I know I am an atheist, I do believe there had to be a creative force that put everything here into place. The big problem is that the human mind has not grown up enough to understand that there is but one creative force, that such a force is unknowable, is to have no name and no form. This is exactly, or nearly so, what is said in the Holy Bible. This force (or God, if we must use the term) is the entire creation including all of mankind. All of the beauty and majesty of this world and universe are here not just for one people, but for all of humankind. This is what I mean by the term "atheism or humanism."

The immature nature of man has caused him to give names to gods, created forms, built upon myths and fairy tales to support his creations which he called religions. The latter is what will destroy the human race if we do not grow up and know that we must consider all humans as being fellow men for whom we must care, have respect, love and never accept violence as acceptable in human affairs. I guess I just hit upon the key idea: man did not only create G-d, he created religions, and there is the curse! Religion was dreamed up as a way of explaining the inexplicable. The trouble is that the explanation is often more incomprehensible and ludicrous than the conundrum we are trying to understand!

I am not a dreamer, but I feel we must have hope and we must all work toward making life more livable. As enlarged upon elsewhere in this tome, I fully believe in the evolution of human thought. Technologically and in material things, we have made unbelievable advances, especially in the last 200 or so years. I know full well that all humans cannot advance at the same pace, just as nations and peoples have never advanced at the same speed. In fact, civilizations have risen only to fall after centuries just to be followed by those considered to be savages who then rose into great civilizations of their own making. This is why I do not advocate that readers suddenly drop their customs and religions like a hot potato, but I do urge them to study the necessities of changing our outlook on life and religion as spelled out here and, yet, continue with things of old that comfort them. This may not seem to be possible, but I guarantee it is. It has been done before. It is well known that much of Christianity adopted pagan ways because it pleased them! See, I told you so! I do not remember them asking me if it would be suitable for them to do this, but they have my blessing as long as they are happy with it. There are some Christians who consider it as giving in to witchcraft, but that is their problem!

Looking through the history books, we see that religions - most of them - have caused more human misery, hatred and bloodshed than any other factor in life. This world has become too dangerous to be reluctant to face this issue. We need to get away from our fantasy world and face life as adults, not as immature children. The last thing I want to do is to insult or hurt people, but to get rid of a cancer it is often necessary to cut or find some way, often very unpleasant or painful, to save the body from this deadly disease. It sounds disrespectful and terrible to label religion as an engine of hate or a disease, but they both kill and in huge numbers! For the sake of all humanity, I urge you to read this book carefully so that you may come to an understanding of what I am trying to impress upon readers. It is not for me or just for you; it is to assure the continuation of the human species. I am asking those who still believe in religious myths – and that is what they are - to open their minds so that they can mature their thinking, enter the Age of Reason and be not afraid.

I was just listening to Paula White, one of the many Christian TV hucksters selling psychology for the simple minded. She is good, very good. I regret feeling compelled to use real names in this scandalous expose, but I sense that I must shock people into understanding what they are falling for. She is a very charming, beautiful woman who may be sincere, but only G-d knows how really sincere she is – and He does not seem to want to talk to me about women. He may be a bit peeved because Eve grabbed that apple and changed the world forever! Of course, you understand this is the reasoning behind religionists placing women in a subservient position! Thank heavens, because of the evolution of human thought some have been moving away from this nonsense taken straight out of the Bible. All these preachers, TV or otherwise, all have their own techniques. Some yell and scream or roll on the floor, some appeal to your sympathies by appealing for money to help the poor in far away places and others put poor souls on the stage and in front of a camera and show how a prayer and a slap on the forehead can cure them of deadly diseases or addictions. Bravo. That was also done in the circus! One thing they all have in common is that they have figured out all possible strategies to reach into your pockets and fill their own!

Why do I declare, with bolts of lightening flashing, that religion is actually a form of psychology? Simple, my dear chap! Religion is all built upon self, to build up one's ego, one's self-image. G-d loves me; I have a friend in Jesus! That's nice (or as they say in Italian, "Datza nice!" And I love Italians)! Jesus can save your soul and give you ever lasting life. He can forgive your sins! Am I wrong in feeling that religion has too often taken the wrong turn in the road? Why do I feel that the emphasis should be on what we can do to make others happy, to give them a feeling of being important, to help those in need, the lame, the elderly, the poor, the sick? I am sorry, but I believe that most religions are too self-centered. It is not important to tell us that Jesus loves us or that Allah will provide us with virgins and plenty of virility; we must love others, care about others and stop just thinking only about "me," the self! When we give love, we are not giving anything away. We are sharing or creating happiness.

But there is more behind the madness or eagerness of preachers to sell their product or products. They feed the watching or listening public with the idea that they can guarantee their personal success in relationships, business or whatever else they want from G-d. Oh G-d, I am sick, infirm, please bless me and cure me! We say: "G-d bless America." Again, this is self-centered; we live in America. Why do we not say: G-d bless this unhappy world"? Just believe in Jesus and pray to G-d - and I still am not sure if they believe that both are one and the same and neither are many avowed Christians - and your supplications will be answered. Notice, they do not give you a money back guarantee. But, of course, to really get help, do not forget the "love gift," the "prayer gift" "the seed money" so that you may reap the harvest or send them a donation so that they can remain on the public airwaves to sell their wares!

Then there is Robb Thompson. He is no "cheapy." He sells wisdom which you can get for $60 or two payments of $30. Using a favorite Madison Ave. technique, it is noted that the regular price was $90. What a bargain or as is said in Yiddish, "Vat a bargen)! I could not "vaite" (I mean wait) to rush over to my check book! And that is NOT the Gospel truth!

They do not stop with selling books and CD's, they build universities, sell cruises and who knows what comes next! How about a reserved seat on the first trip to the moon? At the rate our technology is going, that may soon be attainable. Do they pay taxes on all of these revenue building enterprises? Ask the IRS, ask your Congressman; demand that they be obliged to pay taxes as any other individual or worker who makes his money through the sweat on his brow or corporations that must pay what religions are wrongfully exempted from, thus reducing possible dividends to stockholders! We do not know how much it is costing us to receive all those religious "come-ons" that are so ubiquitous on the TV tube! Would you rather not receive higher dividends than a religious high? The wide spread belief in religions is one of many indications of just how immature most of the human race really is. The number of believers must indeed be high; if it did not bring in the suckers, they would not be on TV.

Why do we allow the tax payers to foot the bill for a major part of the business expenses of religious enterprises? In many cases, religions function as a visit to a psychiatrist. Why should they not pay taxes just as the psychologists must pay on the money they rake in! As matters now stand, the laws are now in violation of the Fourteenth Amendment! To make it more insulting to man's intelligence, these are businesses based upon a product (promises of salvation, forgiveness of sin, eternal life, a bevy of boys or virgin females as a reward for faithfulness, etc.)

whose efficacy can never be proven and are often run by hucksters, charlatans and thieves. Their claims have never been tested by the FDA! Unless you have been living on another planet, you should know that these accusations are absolutely true. To cite one more example of preposterous claims, I point to Saint Matthew's Churches, P.O. Box 22065, Tulsa, OK 74121. They must be very successful as they have been sending me their fables for decades, more or less. I have saved them for years. In fact, as I have been writing this, their mail has been pouring in at your expense! Honest! I wonder if any of their financial statements have ever been checked by any government agency and if they pay any taxes. I have saved some of their advertising and pleas for "Seed money for God" for years because their gimmicks are so outlandish it is hard for me to fathom how people can fall for them. They have sent me pieces of Jesus' robe, prayer rugs, vials of holy water, sands from the Holy Land, a piece of Green and Silver Fleece Prayer Page (Judges 6:37) on which they tell us faithful to sleep, a Ribbon of Blue from the list of seven hindering spirits (NUMBERS 15:38) which we are to keep on our person and place under our pillow at night. I have saved many more like those above. For the "seed money you send them," "the greater the amount, the greater the blessing," they promise you: cure from any disease, salvation, a new car, a new business, relief from any problem plaguing you, whatever you ask for even money that will appear from nowhere! I have one that is really great! "A smiling face blessed with $46,000.00 after using the prayer rug…" and more such you know what! Do not forget, it is our tax money they are spending to send out such mailings. Things must really be good because I have been receiving more than ever, sometimes several a day. One had a packet of seeds, a subtle reminder that we must plant seeds – send money. I believe these were watermelon seeds! Maybe that is why I am so fat around the mid-section. I look as though I swallowed them and they have been growing there for at least nine months!

I am not ridiculing nor am I laughing. I am very sad that so many people are so forlorn, lonely, seemingly without hope that they are moved to fall for most anything. This substantiates my idea that most of the human race is immature.

Oh yes, an attempt was made to remove their tax exempt status because they advocated a certain political position. They were defended by The American Center for Law and Justice, P.O. Box 64429, Virginia Beach, VA 23467, Legal Helpline Phone: 757-226-2489, Radio call-in number:

1-800-684-3110 (from 12-12:30 PM EST/EDT.), Petition call-in number: 1-877-989-2255. For information on broadcasting *Jay Sekulow Live!* or *Jay Sekulow Weekend*: Phone: 770-414-0806. Of course, they asked for money to help defend their fraudulent enterprise! I do not know what happened to the case, but I am sure you can find out from the above information and that law firm is, no doubt, ready and willing to defend any such nonsense that can pay their bills - one way or another. In this case, the suckers pay – we the taxpayers!

The real tragic part is that we, the producers, the workers are being milked to pay higher taxes to make up for religious exemptions. Am I wrong in believing that the money would be better spent on caring for the poor, strengthening social security, better health care, a tax cut, education, curing disease or cutting the national deficit or other such MINOR issues? This is just an idea from a damned atheist who prefers honesty and justice. In conclusion: WE SHOULD TAX RELIGIONS TO GIVE THE WORKING MAN A BREAK and HELP THE POOR and all NORMAL CITIZENS TO HAVE A BETTER LIFE. I am not happy with the religious palaver that "The poor will always be with us!" This "'taint' necessarily so!" But this is up to you, the "we the people" voters! Whatever power created us has obviously given us all brains which we must use to find the "truth." I am merely expressing what I perceive it to be. We all need to consider the thoughts of others, respect them and then decide for ourselves.

Although I say I am an atheist, I pray that whatever force created us or if G-d really exists, that I be given the wisdom to put forth constructive ideas that can be put into play to bring this sad world into widespread happiness. It is not pleasant for me to point out all the harm that religions have done to the world. I understand fully that it is not the fault of religion, but the weakness, greed and immaturity of the human race. But with religions often spouting nonsense and ideas which lead to hate and feelings of superiority, it is enough reason to speak the truth about them. Coupled with the knowledge that our world is too dangerous today to ignore this institution that has caused such misery, fear and death since the idea of religion had first been concocted, it is a matter of survival to understand the foolishness of religions! If you object to the word "foolishness," just go on reading. Talking about reading, once printing was invented by the German inventor Johannes Gutenberg in 1440, people actually began to read the Bible instead of trying to get meaning from the magnificent stained glass windows. Many began to see foolishness in the Bible and this led to the Protestant Reformation. After Martin Luther nailed his 95 theses on the door of the Wittenburg Church on October 31, 1517 and more and more people became literate, more and more Christian sects or denominations developed. (See note 12) As the mind of mankind has matured, many today are recognizing more nonsense and they are becoming agnostics, atheists or humanists! This is just another prime example of the evolution of human thought.

It is gratifying to see that some religious leaders are feeling the necessity and wisdom of concentrating on the essential essence of religion with which I am in total accord. I found a good expression of this in a fine Christian publication, "World News and Prophecy," which is well written and informative. It stresses exactly what this atheist (humanist) feels is necessary for all religious bodies to acknowledge if we are to avoid pushing the self-destruct button. Just type into the address line "World News and Prophecy" to become acquainted with it. I lifted this from their January 2007 publication. You see, I save copies for a long time. Here it is and I could not have said it better myself: "It's time to stoke the fire through our relationships with others. It is time to treat people with respect." It is clear from their writings that they really mean all people, regardless of race, religion or area of the world. Christianity has been moving in this rational direction for some generations. It is my hope that millions of Muslims will start moving toward modernity and join in the Age of Reason. I am glad to see that some Muslims have already done this, but let us hope more will join them so that we can truly live in a world in which there is a universal sense of human brotherhood.

Believe what makes you happy and may He who is - or He who is not bless you! If your faith makes you happy, I am happy for you!

Since the beginning of time and from what I have been reading, the world has had many types of religion all concocted by men. I may be ignorant, but I know of none dreamed up by women! The reason is reasonable: men tend to be the most dominant and religion gives them the means – with a bang! Even with the more modern religions of the Jewish, Christian and Muslim faiths (in order of age) for so many centuries, you see where we are and what good they have done! As an integral part of religion, there has always been a god or some supernatural force or a Great Creative Force which I equate with the term "G-d." It is quite clear that we humans need to believe in something – even if that something is nothing. This primitive need for faith in something is based upon fear of death; fear of the unknown and by the experience of seeing such hardship, injustice and strife in our surroundings. There is obviously an innate need to believe in a life hereafter. Believe it or not, I am human and would like to believe that I would one day see again those I have loved and were near and dear to me. But I am no longer a child and do not believe in Santa Claus or the Tooth Fairy! As G-d said to Moses (straight out of the Bible) "I am who I am!" And I (your author) say unto thee, Life is as it is and that is it! This is more reason why we should be good and kind to all others while they are here on earth!

I am saddened to see, even in this advanced age, killings in the name of various religions all over G-d's earth. Yes, I say G-d, because it is a useful term. Notice that above, I pointed out that I named major modern religions in order of age. We have to be very careful not to offend these narrow minds. Priests of various Christian faiths have been known to battle one another because they could not agree who had the right to go through the church door first – in Jerusalem yet! How rude and stupid can people be! In the Muslim world, the Shiia and the Sunnis kill one another because they cannot determine who is the real heir to the prophet Mohammad! Both the Christians and the Muslims who tolerate this are witness to my claim that religion can lead to insanity. It is like children saying my father is bigger and stronger than your father.

I may have stated that man created G-d, but that is just repeating an oft stated idea. Man created religions and that is what has caused the problems because these exclusive clubs have given names and forms to gods of their own creation or choosing in violation of what is clearly prescribed in the Bible. Is it not clear that these overzealous, pompous, self-centered religionists pick from the Bible what serves their interests, what they want to choose and have overlooked this clear message even though they say that the Bible is the very word of the Lord and is never changing unless they want it to, of course? They often set themselves apart from others by wearing peculiar garb, hats, long robes – adorned and plain – all of which say to those not in that club: "See how pious, religious and special I am."

Religions have set up a maze separating humans from one another. The walls of hedges need to be clipped down with love and patience until we come to the realization that we are but one. It is up to Christians, Jews, Hindus, Muslims, atheists and all members of the human race to reach over the hedge and to have compassion, concern and love for all no matter how different we may be. It bears repeating. This is no joke. The world is in one hell of a mess; so let us get down to the basics as stated above and make it better! It does not matter that I say man created G-d to lessen his fears and to control others. Perhaps wiser men hold the view that G-d created man in His own image. I would be pleased with that view also. More importantly, it is said that G-d is love and that we must love G-d with all our might and with all our soul. Why not understand all of this to mean that mankind and G-d (the creative force of the universe) are one and the same and therefore we should love and care about the lives and welfare of all human beings and do no harm to any man no matter what our differences? This is where I stand as an atheist or humanist.

SO THE BIBLE IS THE FINAL DEFINITIVE
WORD OF THE LORD?

Of course the world is flat! The Bible clearly refers to the "four corners of the earth." How can a globe have four corners? It must be flat if it has four corners! How stupid can you be? You must be an imbecile not to believe this! Besides, everyone knows that if one goes too far out to sea, he must fall off the edge of the earth! Here is a good example of "evolution of human thought, mentioned several times in this book which sometimes questions the authenticity of the Bible and on other occasions accepts the wisdom of the Bible. .

May we take out of the Bible what we wish or is it the unchangeable word of God? Consider this situation: "An engineering professor is treating her husband, a loan officer, to dinner for finally giving in to her pleas to shave off the scraggly beard he grew on vacation. His favorite restaurant is a casual place where they both feel comfortable in slacks and cotton/polyester-blend golf shirts. But, as always, she wears the gold and pearly pendant he gave her the day her divorce decree was final. They're laughing over their menus because they know he always ends up diving into a giant plate of ribs but she won't be talked into anything more fattening than shrimp.

"Quiz: How many biblical prohibitions are they violating?
Well, wives are supposed to be 'submissive' to their husbands (I Peter3:1).
And all women are forbidden to teach men (I Timothy 2:12), wear gold or pearls (I Timothy 2:9), or dress in clothing that 'pertains to a man' (Deuteronomy 22:5). Shellfish and pork are definitely out (Leviticus 11:7, 10) as are usury (Deuteronomy 23:19), shaving (Leviticus 19:27) and clothes of more than one fabric (Leviticus 19:19).
And since the Bible rarely recognizes divorce, they're committing adultery, which carries the rather harsh penalty of death by stoning (Deuteronomy 22:22). So why are they having such a good time? Probably because they wouldn't think of worrying about rules that seem absurd, anachronistic or – at best – unrealistic. Yet this same modern

day couple could easily be among the millions of Americans who never hesitate to lean on the Bible to justify their own anti-gay attitudes." Source: From lesbian columnist Deb Price's book, "And Say Hi To Joyce."

PAGANISM and CHRISTIANITY

The Pagan History of Christmas (by the way, I like the ideas behind Christmas and do not believe it should be brushed aside. It brings happiness to millions of people, especially children. Happiness is what the world needs. jk)

By Dr. Joel Ehrlich *of* Hebraic Renewal

The Church and much of Judaism is entrenched deep in the ancient Babylonian mystery religion, only today it is referred to as 'culture' or 'traditions.' The seventeenth chapter of the book of Revelation speaks of a mysterious woman who rides a beast. It shows that at the end of the age, most of the earth would be drinking out of her hand. With the excessive compromise that has taken place in Judaism and Christianity, that time has arrived. Her method of intoxication is merriment, festivity, drink, and most of all, materialism. This materialism is the free enterprise, or capitalistic system. (In spite of this, I must admit I believe fully in the free enterprise capitalistic system with some modifications as explained in CHAPTER 10 of this book. (jk)

Revelation 17:1-2
1 And there came one of the seven angels which had the seven vials, and talked with me, saying unto me, come hither; I will show unto thee the judgment of the great whore that sitteth upon many waters;
2 With whom the kings of the earth have committed fornication, and the inhabitants of the earth have been made drunk with the wine of her fornication. (I do not think I would like to explain the word "fornication" to a child! I fear taking too much out of the Bible since I would like this book to be appropriate for any member of the family. (jk)

PAGAN CHRISTIANITY

Socrates was killed as a result of him pelting people with searching questions and dragging them into critical dialogues about their accepted customs. The "establishment" wanted to send a clear message to other Athenians: All who question the established customs will meet the same end!

Other philosophers received the same loving treatment: Aristotle was exiled, Spinoza was excommunicated and Bruno was fried, boiled and baked alive...O.K. just burned alive! As I am sure most know that thousands of Christians received the same loving treatment. Since there was not much on the TV in those days to entertain the masses, executions became a sport, and adding a little torture to the mix made it more entertaining. The institutional church at that time did not like having its basic teachings challenged. Sadly this has been true through the ages and was done even in civilized (Christian) countries. The fault does not lie with the religion, but with the ignorance of the masses.

I may have said before that life is change, the world is always changing and religions have changed, transformed themselves to their liking. If I did not write this before, I should have. Many hundreds of years ago, the pagan cults, corrupt priests and the Church changed the Bible. The adorning of Christmas trees, decorating with pine branches, holly, mistletoe, yule logs and exchange of gifts all originated in ancient forms of idol-worship, including the Egyptian cult of Isis, the Syrian and Babylonian cults of Astarte (or "Ishtar"), the Greek cult of Dionysus, the Roman festivals of Saturnalia and the sun Gods, the cults of the Druids in England, and others. So what! Christmas is tradition and enjoyed by all. It is a happy holiday and should be practiced by anyone who wishes to follow this tradition.

The cults mentioned above were known for practicing witchcraft, forced prostitution, self-mutilation, human sacrifice to false gods, and even the burning of children alive. These, too, were traditions, but the evolution of human thought has thankfully led most humans away from them. Many of these practices were condemned by such Biblical prophets as Jeremiah, Ezekiel, and Daniel for their wickedness.

The so-called priests came up with the idea that we need a mediator between G-d and man. These mediators became the idols and false gods worshipped by the deceived masses. They were even led to believe that G-d dresses Himself in the body of a man, such as the Pharaoh of Egypt or any king. This put the priests at the service of the kings, one supporting the other! Thus started the greatest business on earth besides prostitution – religions.

These cults were attached to the idea that blood was needed for salvation. This led the new Christian faith to the belief that the blood of Jesus is all that is needed for salvation and eternal life. On top of this they proclaimed that there was not one G-d, but three, the Trinity as in Egyptian cults. If you doubt the above, just type into the address line on your monitor screen the words: "Christmas pagan customs" or "Pagan customs in Christianity". I can't believe you would think all this ancient knowledge came out of my little head!   This is not intended to belittle or ridicule any one religion. All of them are guilty of similar nonsense. If we say we believe in something, we need to know exactly what that something really is! What words of profound wisdom I come up with!

SLAVERY IN THE BIBLE

And Reverend D. James Kennedy and his ilk persist in demanding that America is a Christian country. They want to bring America back to Jesus. Really? It was the Christian America that almost wiped out all the native Indians, gave us Jim Crow, enslaved black Africans, perfected it, maintained it by using the most cruel, inhuman and despicable means. If these Christian zealots take over, what do we have to look forward to? Just look at the source of their wisdom! Read on!

Quotations by learned men from the 19th century:

"[Slavery] was established by decree of Almighty God...it is sanctioned in the Bible, in both Testaments, from Genesis to Revelation...it has existed in all ages, has been found among the people of the highest civilization, and in nations of the highest proficiency in the arts." Jefferson Davis, President of the Confederate States of America.

"There is not one verse in the Bible inhibiting slavery, but many regulating it. It is not then, we conclude, immoral." Rev. Alexander Campbell

"The right of holding slaves is clearly established in the Holy Scriptures, both by precept and example." Rev. R. Furman, D.D., Baptist, of South Carolina

"The hope of civilization itself hangs on the defeat of Negro suffrage." A statement by a prominent 19th-century southern Presbyterian pastor, cited by Rev. Jack Rogers, moderator of the Presbyterian Church (USA).

"The doom of Ham has been branded on the form and features of his African descendants. The hand of fate has united his color and destiny. Man cannot separate what God hath joined." United States Senator James Henry Hammond. 3

Overview:
The quotation by Jefferson Davis, listed above, reflected the beliefs of many Americans in the 19th century. Slavery was seen as having been "sanctioned in the Bible." They argued that:

Biblical passages recognized, controlled, and regulated the practice.

The Bible permitted owners to beat their slaves severely, even to the point of killing them. However, as long as the slave lingered longer than 24 hours before dying of the abuse, the owner was not regarded as having committed a crime, because -- after all -- the slave was his property.

Paul had every opportunity to write in one of his Epistles that human slavery -- the owning of one person as a piece of property by another -- is profoundly evil. His letter to Philemon would have been an ideal opportunity to vilify slavery. But he wrote not one word of criticism.

Jesus could have condemned the practice. He might have done so. But there is no record of him having said anything negative about the institution. Eventually, the abolitionists gained sufficient power to eradicate slavery in most areas of the world by the end of the 19th century. Slavery was eventually recognized as an extreme evil. But this paradigm shift in understanding came at a cost. Christians wondered why the Bible was so supportive of such an immoral practice. They questioned whether the Bible was entirely reliable. Perhaps there were other practices that it accepted as normal which were profoundly evil -- like genocide, torturing prisoners, raping female prisoners of war, executing religious minorities, burning some hookers alive, etc. The innocent faith that Christians had in "the Good Book" was lost -- never to be fully regained.

Passages from the Christian Scriptures which Sanction Slavery:
Neither Jesus nor St. Paul, nor any other Biblical figure is recorded as saying anything in opposition to the institution of slavery. Slavery was very much a part of life in Palestine and in the rest of the Roman Empire during New Testament times. Quoting Rabbi M.J. Raphall, circa 1861, "Receiving slavery as one of the conditions of society, the New Testament nowhere interferes with or contradicts the slave code of Moses; it even preserves a letter [to Philemon] written by one of the most eminent Christian teachers [St. Paul] to a slave owner on sending back to him his runaway slave."

People in debt (and their children) were still being sold into slavery in New Testament times:

Matthew 18:25: "But forasmuch as he had not to pay, his lord commanded him to be sold, and his wife, and children, and all that he had, and payment to be made."
Priests still owned slaves:

Mark 14:66: "And as Peter was beneath in the palace, there cometh one of the maids of the high priest:"

Jesus is recorded as mentioning slaves in one of his parables. It is important to realize that the term "servant" in the King James Version of the Bible refers to slaves, not employees like a butler, cook, or maid. Here, a slave which did not follow his owner's will would be beaten with many lashes of a whip. A slave who was unaware of his owner's will, but who did not behave properly, would also be beaten, but with fewer stripes. This would have been a marvelous opportunity for Jesus to condemn the institution of slavery and its abuse of slaves. But he is not recorded of having taken it:

Luke 12:45-48: "The lord [owner] of that servant will come in a day when he looketh not for him, and at an hour when he is not aware, and will cut him in sunder, and will appoint him his portion with the unbelievers. And that servant, which knew his lord's will, and prepared not himself, neither did according to his will, shall be beaten with many stripes. But he that knew not, and did commit things worthy of stripes, shall be beaten with few stripes. For unto whomsoever much is given, of him shall be much required: and to whom men have committed much, of him they will ask the more."

One of the favorite passages of slave-owning Christians was St. Paul's infamous instruction that slaves to obey their owners in the same way that they obey Christ:

Ephesians 6:5-9: "Servants, be obedient to them that are your masters according to the flesh, with fear and trembling, in singleness of your heart, as unto Christ; Not with eyeservice, as menpleasers; but as the servants of Christ, doing the will of God from the heart; With good will doing service, as to the Lord, and not to men: Knowing that whatsoever good thing any man doeth, the same shall he receive of the Lord, whether he be bond or free. And, ye masters, do the same things unto them, forbearing threatening: knowing that your Master also is in heaven; neither is there respect of persons with him."

Other passages instructing slaves and slave owners in proper behavior are:

Colossians 4:1: "Masters, give unto your servants that which is just and equal; knowing that ye also have a Master in heaven."

1 Timothy 6:1-3 "Let as many servants as are under the yoke count their own masters worthy of all honor, that the name of God and his doctrine be not blasphemed. And they that have believing masters, let them not despise them, because they are brethren; but rather do them service, because they are faithful and beloved, partakers of the benefit. These things teach and exhort. If any man teach otherwise, and consent not to wholesome words, even the words of our Lord Jesus Christ, and to the doctrine which is according to godliness;"

In his defense, St. Paul incorrectly expected that Jesus would return in the very near future. This might have side tracked him from speaking out against slavery or other social evils in the Roman Empire. Also he regarded slaves as persons of worth whom at least God considers of importance. St. Paul mentioned that both slaves and free persons are sons of God, and thus all part of the body of Christ and spiritually equal.

1 Corinthians 12:13: "For by one Spirit are we all baptized into one body, whether we be Jews or Gentiles, whether we be bond or free; and have been all made to drink into one Spirit."

Galatians 3:28: "There is neither Jew nor Greek, there is neither bond nor free, there is neither male nor female: for ye are all one in Christ Jesus." (Then why are women not allowed to be priests in the Catholic Church? jk)

Colossians 3:11: "Where there is neither Greek nor Jew, circumcision nor uncircumsicion, Barbarian, Scythian, bond nor free: but Christ is all, and in all."

St. Paul apparently saw no evil in the concept of one person owning another as a piece of property. In his Letter to Philemon, he had every opportunity to discuss the immorality of slave-owning, but declined to do so.

Deuteronomy 23:15-16, cited above, requires a Jew to protect a runaway slave, and to not return him/her to their owner. However, St. Paul violated the law. While in prison, he met a runaway slave, Onesimus, the slave of a Christian. He was presumably owned by Philemon. Rather than give the slave sanctuary, he returned him to his owner. Paul seems to hint that he would like Pheliemon to give Onesimus his freedom, but does not actually request it. See the Letter to Philemon in the Christian Scriptures.

TAKEN FROM GOVERNMENT RECORDS:

"Slavery was declared illegal in the West in the 19th century, but in Somalia and the rest of the Arab world, slavery of Africans has continued unabated. It's a world in which history rests on a pillow of oblivion. As to the widely reported slavery in the Sudan, the world community has done precious little beyond plucking a small group of boys from the dry and dusty camps of northern Kenya.

"Although as dark as the majority Somali, the Somali Bantu were called jarer, because of their strong curly hair. It's also a term of denigration. Historically, some Bantus were displaced by Arabs who moved into Somalia from the north. Others were captured and enslaved from further south along the eastern coast of Africa. These people were called habash, or servants, by the Arabized Somalis, who regard themselves as superior people.

"Over time there has been some intermarriage, but the Negroid-Arab children are not accepted. It's something one sees all across the Arab world: The dark, Negroid people are never accepted as equal to the Semitic-featured Arabs.

"I've talked to friends whose forefathers were slaves and many have no concept that the black world is still brutalized by slavery. Many have no idea of what's happening beyond America's shores. So few know anything about the lost boys of the Sudan, the Bantus of Somalia, the slavery of girls and boys in West Africa. Few know that the system that killed millions of their forefathers in the Middle Passage is still alive and well."

UNDER GOD

This is just a one-paragraph excerpt from a letter sent to me from my Christian Right friend (he thinks he is right, but he is wrong). I like him anyway. He cannot help it. After centuries of brainwashing which is the same as cult indoctrination, his views are quite understandable! It may be very tough to overcome this impediment to adjustment into a world of reason.

"Everyone is talking about the growing red state/blue state divide in America. The words 'parallel universe' have even been used to describe the two ethics that dominate our political scene. To put it simply, the red side believes in 'one nation, under God,' and the blue side doesn't. We think rights come from our Creator -- they think rights come from our government. We think there are moral absolutes. They think everything is relative, including the Constitution."
SOURCE: -- Excerpts from "My Un-American Democratic Party," by Bob Just, Whistleblower, May 2004, pages 40-41. Address: PO Box 2450, Fair Oaks, California 95628. Phone: 916-852-6300. Fax: 916-852-6302.

My response to the above for what it is worth!

As usual, I largely agree with you. I voted for Bush, but I believe in "one nation with life liberty and the pursuit of happiness for all, and that rights come from an alert public that will not allow itself to be hoodwinked by such things as prohibition, anti-drug laws, allowing the government into the bedroom and telling citizens who can be married. If rights came from G-d, what took him so long? And where was He, until recently, when very few people had rights in any country other than the U.S.A. and that was not so until after slavery was abolished? Where was He when there were millions of "Untouchables" in India for so many centuries? The world is millions of years old, perhaps billions, but I cannot remember that far back! I strongly question 'moral absolutes.' If they come from the Bible, they are often from errors in translating, misinterpretations and depend on what the big shots in the sect want them to be.

I think the Constitution is a great step forward for human governance, but it has been wrong. Slavery should never have been accepted, even though it was acceptable in the Bible! Taking it out of our Constitution was a step forward in the evolutionary process of human understanding.

SHOULD PARENTS BE NOTIFIED BEFORE A CHILD CAN LEGALLY HAVE AN ABORTION?

I was fortunately tuned in to a program on TV presenting a debate in Congress on this very issue. As usual, the religious right folk, usually Republicans – and I usually vote Republican - were extolling the virtues of upholding family values. I agree, but "the family" is an ideal that does not always exist. If the pregnancy is a result of incest, how can the child point a finger against a brother, a father, a step-father? Somehow, the ideal of "family" went out the window! The fresh air of logic is shut out once religion is accepted. These poor religious right folk cannot think beyond the ends of their noses! I forgive them as it is not their fault. This lunacy, lack of logic on the part of the religious "thinkers," is more proof that my belief that once religion corrupts a mind, all reason flies out the window. G-d bless them and keep them away from making decisions about the lives and well being of our children!

I attended a Quaker school and I know they would never accept or teach some of the nonsense found in the Bible. They were well ahead of the rest of the world centuries ago. This is why they were so persecuted. This is an example of what I mean by saying that different groups or nations do not evolve as fast or in the same way as others. This by no means is an excuse to treat those who are less advanced with less respect, care or love. It is only a matter of chance that any one of us has been born into a group or nation that is more or less advanced along the path of evolutionary growth in social thinking. Sound non-sectarian or secular schools may help for the future. Does anyone really believe that many preachers of the gospel understand that government cannot mandate the ideal of "family" any more than dictatorial government could stop people from drinking alcohol or using drugs of their choice or from sleeping with a lady of the night? How many citizens realize that our George W. Bush has gone from his drug of choice – alcohol – to the drug of religion?

How many people still believe that the world is flat, that the heavenly bodies revolve around the earth, that evil doers should be stoned to death? Remember my brilliant conclusion that religion tosses out reason? Of course you do, and this is about to confirm my theory (or someone's theory) of the evolution of human thought. Along came Copernicus who threw a monkey wrench into the teaching of the theologians that the universe revolved around the earth which fit so well with their doctrine that G-d created man and all revolved around him. Copernicus contradicted the theory of Aristotle and of the Bible. His theory set in motion a chain of events that would eventually (long after his lifetime) produce the greatest revolution in thinking that Western civilization has seen. His ideas remained rather obscure for about 100 years after his death. But, in the 17th century the work of Kepler, Galileo, and Newton would build on the heliocentric Universe of Copernicus and produce the revolution that would sweep away completely the ideas of Aristotle and replace them with the modern view of astronomy and natural science. This sequence is commonly called the ***Copernican Revolution which demonstrates that the earth revolves around the sun. I guess the Church objected because this seems to give credence to the validity of a Sun God or Goddess, whichever your preference!***

Giordano Bruno had the audacity to even go beyond Copernicus, and, dared to suggest, that space was boundless and that the sun was and its planets were but one of any number of similar systems: Why! -- there even might be other inhabited worlds with rational beings equal or possibly superior to us. For such blasphemy, Bruno was tried before the Inquisition, condemned and burned at the stake in 1600. Galileo was brought forward in 1633, and, there, in front of his "betters," he was, under the threat of torture and death, forced to his knees to renounce all belief in Copernican theories, and was thereafter sentenced to imprisonment for the remainder of his days.

"Of all discoveries and opinions, none may have exerted a greater effect on the human spirit than the doctrine of Copernicus. The world had scarcely become known as round and complete in itself when it was asked to waive the tremendous privilege of being the center of the universe. Never, perhaps, was a greater demand made on mankind - for by this admission so many things vanished in mist and smoke! What became of our Eden, our world of innocence, piety and poetry; the testimony of the senses; the conviction of a poetic - religious faith? No wonder his contemporaries did not wish to let all this go and offered every possible resistance to a doctrine which in its converts authorized and demanded a freedom of view and greatness of thought so far unknown, indeed not even dreamed of." [Goethe.]

In a democracy, all must have the right to vote, but we need to be very vigilant when it comes to those with closed minds as is found in many religions. No I am not advocating that the right to vote should be taken from them, but we need to be aware of where they stand on the continuum of evolution of human thought. Notice below where the Evangelical Protestants and the Republicans stand on the "closed mind" idea that grows out of exaggerated and distorted religious convictions. Evangelicals I think we may agree are likely "born again Christians," a nonsensical term in itself. I have little doubt that many of them are part of the religious right that supports the Republicans. Read the results of the poll presented below and draw your own conclusions. My own conclusion is that we need to improve our educational system, have secular education privately managed. Humanist schools would have my profound blessings!

A new poll indicates more than nine in 10 American adults say they believe in G-d, and 87 percent identify with a specific religion. The Newsweek poll of more than 1,000 adults also found that nearly half — 48 percent — reject the scientific notion of evolution. Perhaps even more surprising, 34 percent of college graduates say they reject evolution and accept the biblical account of creation as fact.

Other findings of the poll include:

73 percent of Evangelical Protestants believe G-d created humans in their present form within the last 10,000 years, compared with 39 percent of non-Evangelicals and 41 percent of Catholics. (I just heard on TV a preacher saying that the dirty deed done in the Garden of Eden was just a few thousand years ago! jk)

More than six in 10 registered voters say they would not vote for a candidate who is an atheist. That leaves me out! But I am not running; however, I may be running for my life once this book makes the rounds if I find a publisher with the guts to print it!

42 percent of Democrats say that religion has too much influence on American politics, while only 14 percent of Republicans agree. I remind my reader that I normally voted Republican – notice use of the past tense in "voted."

I also conclude that the very high percentage of Americans believing in G-d is a result of the proliferation of religious brainwashing on TV, a medium of communication that must cost them a mint! Obviously, they must be making a pile of money on this Hocus Pocus Dominocus or they would not continue with it. It would help the intelligence of the American public if we were to tax all religion based business – churches – in the same way all other Americans are taxed. Religion itself is a business and has grown at taxpayer expense! It is only right and just that they all pay taxes as we are now living with a violation of the Fourteenth Amendment of the Constitution which requires that all Americans be treated equally. The business of religion is set up as one to get special privileges! This is a direct violation of the U.S. Constitution. Besides, isn't their product or business really a fraud? A pharmaceutical company cannot market a drug without proving that it has some usefulness, that it fulfills what is promised. The claim of the saving of a soul, the remission of sins or the granting of eternal life can never be proven. How then, logically, can we allow this fraud to continue and continue at public expense! It is especially hurtful to the working people who barely make a living and to corporations whose stockholders would be better off if that burden were lifted from corporations so that they could pay more in dividends.

I am very much concerned that so many running for the presidency in 2008 had very narrow religious views. I saw Senator Mike Huckabee on TV and liked him as a person even though I knew his views could be somewhat twisted from centuries of cult-like indoctrination. But on the same day I read that this Republican presidential hopeful supports a measure that would make it a crime for Americans with dual citizenship to vote in foreign elections, perform military service in other nations, or even use a foreign passport. Does he not consider that other countries should have a say in this individual exercise in freedom? The same was tried in 2005 by John Hayworth who was then a Republican congressman from Arizona, introduced a bill that would have imposed jail time for such "crimes." The bill never made it out of committee. Only dictatorial minded Republicans could come up with such a fascistic idea! It is not enough for them that they have been condemning homosexuals now more than ever after it became unpopular to demonize blacks and Jews; they now seem to be looking for other groups to step on!

It is too apparent that Republicans (Republirats) are in the clutches of the narrow minds of the religious right. They may not wear checkered towels on their heads, but they are no different from the Mullahs, Mammas, Pappas and extremists of the Muslim world who wish to impose their religious dogma on all citizens. Following their twisted reasoning, the French should have condemned General Lafayette to jail for helping us gain independence from England. Don't these brain dead religionists know that there were Americans who fought in both World War I and II against tyranny long before this country was officially at war? American citizens also fought to protect Spain from fascism. Should these men now be considered criminals? If I were prone to say a prayer, I would pray: "Jesus, save me from your followers!"

THE JESUS STORY

I like the story of Jesus, the tale of Cinderella and that of "Hansel und Gretel" and more than I can now remember at my age! The story of Jesus is probably the most beautiful story ever told. I do not intend to demean Jesus in any way as I feel he was a very good man who repeated some very sound and good ideas of other great prophets in the Bible. Among them I believe would be included Amos and Mica. I am confident there are others, but as you probably understand by now that I am not an expert on the Bible. If we were to all follow the sensible words of their philosophies, the world would be much better today. I just do not believe that one needs to get ideas from a supposed deity or from a religion to feel and understand what is right and to do good in this world nor do I feel we should expect or accept a reward for doing what we know in our heart is good. In other words, we need not expect a lollypop from an imagined G-d, the tooth fairy or Santa Claus just as a child may expect a reward from parents when he is good.

I understand that Jesus is considered to be G-d. This is difficult to understand considering that, while He was on the cross, He looked up to heaven and said: "My G-d, my G-d, why hast thou forsaken me?" This can take a lot of explaining and is almost as bad as "Which came first, the chicken or the egg?" story!

Jesus is also said to be the Son of G-d. Is this not a throwback to heathen religions in which their various Gods had sons, fathers, mothers, maybe even godfathers? It seems that they were also in family disputes as well. In other words, the authors of the tales were just playing up on an old successful theme much as they do in Hollywood! It really went over like a bang, especially after the Roman Emperor Constantine converted to Christianity and made all Romans do likewise – if they did not want to be fed to the lions as had been done to the earlier Christians. What an age they lived in! This is another example of my theory of the evolution of human thought. The truth is any religion could have instantly become a world religion once an Emperor of Rome embraced it!

What is also difficult to understand is why so many Christians have blamed and, as a result, slaughtered Jews through the ages because they claimed that the Jews killed Christ. Now that more people can read, I trust they understand that, according to the Bible their source of all wisdom, G-d himself set up the entire sequence of events! After all, how could He have risen from the dead if He had not been killed? It was a dirty job, but someone had to do it! In my humble opinion, it seems to me that a loving G-d could surely have thought of a better way. Jesus was a nice Jewish boy. Why did He have to kill Him in such a horrible way? This is one reason I have a bumper sticker on the back of my car which reads: MAKE ROOM FOR GOD IN THE CLASSROOM. It has now come to mean for me that He needs to go back to school to learn of more merciful means of controlling His creation!

I am happy to note that in our time there are more and more Christians who are beginning to think as Christians should. To my thinking, Christ or Jesus represents love. As a result, more and more Christians are beginning to recognize their Jewish roots and that Jesus, Mary and Joseph and most all early Christians were Jews. It is not strange to me why the world has always hated Jews. It is the fault of Moses who came down from Mount Sinai with the Ten Commandments and all those "thou shalt not" admonitions. These were bound to spoil everybody's fun. Who does not covet and have thoughts best not expressed toward his neighbor's wife? Stealing and killing were common! How else could a man have some excitement and fun?

As you may have noticed, G-d and I (whether He exists or not) do not always see eye to eye on all matters. I was never really happy with the way in which G-d got the Israelites out of Egypt. You understand, of course, that He never sought my advice. Sending ten plagues to convince the Egyptians to let His People go was not exactly my idea of a loving God! The suffering and deaths of so many Egyptians never made me happy. In fact, it was the drowning of so many handsome, strong Egyptian soldiers that really angered me and made me question the sanity of "Top Management"! A truly loving G-d would have softened the heart of Pharaoh and made him send off the Israelites with gifts and good wishes and promised that they would always be good neighbors who could help one another when in need! But after all, these were stories that had to play well on Broadway; they needed plenty of magic, blood and violence if people were to listen just as our TV must have the same today if people are to turn on the tube! These are, after all, just stories, not the direct word of G-d! Sorry, but this is the Gospel truth, guaranteed!

My reason for my non-belief in G-d may be because I look 'round at the world and feel anger. I am angry because it is known that He is all-powerful, all knowing and present all around and in everything. Since He knows all that will take place in the future, why did he plant the apple tree in the Garden Of Eden and tell Adam and Steve - sorry, I mean Adam and Eve - not to partake thereof? Is He the Devil or just toying with His creation? Jokingly, I often say that if there is a G-d, He should be sued for mismanagement at the Highest Level! But do you really believe there are lawyers in heaven to file the suit? Unfortunately, if G-d does indeed exist, I doubt if I ever could find a lawyer good enough or honest enough to try such a case even if one slipped through the pearly gates! G-d knows I have had nothing but bad experiences with most lawyers!

As you can see, my doubts about the existence of G-d came long before the Holocaust. After that tragedy, who could not wonder about the upper management of this universe! Our answer to such horrors is the need for all humans to understand the need for forgiveness and love of all human beings. Even during the Nazi years my family always had good Christian German friends and neighbors. When I became older but young enough to travel to Europe and not break my bank account, I went to Germany and made friends with Germans. I remember one who wondered how I could even talk to him when he found out I was Jewish. I will not explain how he found out I was Jewish; I just let it slip out – the fact, I mean – as we were talking about things in general. He seemed to be embarrassed over what had happened. I refer, of course to Germany's deeds under Hitler also affectionately called "Dolphy" or "Dolfy". I explained that I felt it would be wrong for me or anyone to blame an entire group for what happened in years past and that I sensed he was a good person – I refer, of course to my new German friend, not to Dolphy! It is my sincere hope that all peoples who have been in conflict will accept this attitude. To go on hating and to seek revenge is to assure ourselves of perpetual enmity for the future. We must move ourselves beyond the tribal state of mind. How wonderful it would be if the Muslims in Iraq were to accept this thought! In the above passage in which I wrote "…I just let it slip out", there is a line that may bring forth an X rated thought in your mind. I want you to know that it could never have entered into my mind as it is forbidden by my non-religion religion! Not really because there is no dogma, but it is fun to say so. You had best confess your evil thoughts, maybe! Understand, however, that those who follow a religion or a non-religion may at times break the taboos! Man in his ignorance has created this taboo, but G-d has given it His blessing as is explained in this book you dare to read.

Religion is a throwback to the concept of "Tribe." Note that many Muslim groups or nations still live in a tribal state. Assigning god-like attributes to an object or an idea was a way of controlling the tribe, of giving a sense of power in a world in which humans are really just about powerless! It is used as a rallying point to help in the waging of war against other tribes. In our so-called modern world this continues to a great degree, but it is used to impose the views of some over those of others, it is used to gain money and power over poor souls who have not evolved far enough to think for themselves. I would like to point out that the Protestant Reformation was a part of the evolution of human thought. People who started to read and think for themselves, refused to knuckle under the thumb of Rome. Do not worry. Some of my best friends are Catholics!

IT IS STRANGE HOW THE MIND WORKS

Here is something for the U.N. or any other organization to do. Do not use my real name. My pseudonym is Dr. J. Knowname, but there is no need to even use that. I hope this can be circulated in any country on earth where there is tension between peoples or actual fighting. This is something any reader can do on his or her own to promote world peace. Yes, it is strange that I do most of my thinking just as I am beginning to arise from sleep to the realization that I have lived for yet another day. The joy is not for myself, but for the hope that somehow, by some miracle, I may get the message to others that we must move man's thinking from hate to love. Strange, since I know I am just a nobody, another soul moving through the experience of life on this troubled planet. Why do I even bother to write this? I do it because I feel such pain when I daily see the horrific suffering of so much of mankind throughout the world. I can only hope that I can convince - perhaps even religious leaders - and individuals like you to replace hate with love and to think of ways to make this a happier world. Stranger still is that I even thank G-d for the dawning of each new day – a gift. Stranger yet since I do not believe in a G-d of a physical or ethereal nature who can control or alter anything in this suffering world. I harbor a vain hope that by speaking my mind I may move others to the realization that life can be better if each individual strives to make it so. In my mind I feel that Jesus the Jew who embodied thoughts of the prophets brought us the message that love must overcome hate. It is always possible (but not very likely) that I may be wrong in not accepting Him as Savior and G-d or a Son of G-d, but what does that matter? What is important is the message!

I believe that Jesus, and other good souls or men were part of the evolution of human thinking, a progression of thought that can improve the lot of mankind and save him from pushing the self-destruct button. The incredible advances in technology take away the luxury of time. For the survival of this planet, all of us must strive to eliminate recriminations and violence or thoughts of hurting others and replace these negatives with working toward mutual understanding, positive thoughts of working toward making this world better for all of human kind no matter what their religion or non-religion or region in which they happen to live. It may be that I was moved to write this because of what I read yesterday about killings in Sri Lanka. I was thrown into deep grief envisioning the too oft repeated scenes of brutality brought on by illogical hate that in yet another region of this world has overcome reason and logic and fomented acts of violence that should never happen and need not ever happen! I was reading of the recent upsurge of fighting in Sri Lanka, an area near India. The Liberation Tigers of Tamil Eelam (LTTE) are fighting for an independent state in north and east Sri Lanka. Since 1983 there have been nearly 70,000 people killed, an estimated 4,500 people since last year alone. For those who are dead, a war is never really won! Would it not be better for all concerned if we could learn to live in peace and harmony together, forget old grievances and instead love and respect all humankind no matter how different we may be? If all nations were to stop wasting time, money and resources on war and killing, just think how much would be available for creating a better world for us all! We have the technology to create a paradise on earth, to have a pie of plenty enough for all of us to share. Why not concentrate on building this together for the happiness of all! I believe the creation of the WPA (World Peace Association) can help us reach this goal.

As I said, I like the story of Jesus. Here is an old one you probably never heard before. I know this for sure, beyond a shadow of a doubt, because I just made it up!

A NEW GARMENT FOR JESUS

One day, Jesus came riding into Jerusalem on his ass, his face strained as though in heavy thought. Already, I do not like what I am writing, but my hands are tied by the bizarre nature of the English language. You see, I was a language teacher when I was alive; so words can bother me. What can I do? "… on his ass…" is a perfect translation from the Hebrew and even from Aramaic, but in English, it sounds disrespectful or as though I might be joking. Frankly, I see nothing wrong with "donkey" no matter how you spell it, bake it, broil it or fry it! That was the mode of transport in that part of the world before Henry Ford (that anti-Semite) invented the motorcar! If we try to substitute "donkey" for "ass," the spelling of "donkey" then troubles me. Why not "DUNKEY"? Consider the sound of "du" in the words: junk, sunk, bunk, hung, hunk or dunk as in "Dunkin Donuts." Now there is food for thought, but I am concerned about my waist not my waste. But I love them! One day, if I live again, I may write a book on the idiosyncrasies of the English language!

O.K. already, we will accept, "…Jesus came riding into Jerusalem on his donkey…" and forget about the peculiarities of the English language! His face looked strained because he had a premonition that he would soon be attending a very important supper that would be remembered through eternity. Jesus was not a vain man, but after much thought, he realized he would need a new garment for such a serious occasion. He had not the foggiest notion of where he should go, but God led him to an ordinary tailor in a not so "shee shee or chee chee" or swanky part of town. In fact, and to put it bluntly, it was the kind of street (and G-d forgive me for saying this) on which a man would not normally walk after dark! And in Jerusalem, yet!

The plain tailor, a little old Jewish man, was sitting at his front door as though he had been waiting there for Jesus for an eternity! The old man greeted Jesus with warmth and respect as though he were G-d Almighty. After all, he was his first customer of the day and the sun was getting ready to set! He showed him bolt after bolt of the finest cloth in the land, but Jesus, not knowing much about such matters, asked the tailor to choose one for him. This little old Jewish man was so taken by the gleam of purity and kindness in the eyes of Jesus that he chose for him the finest, pure white cloth that he felt would be perfect for this pensive stranger. The tailor took all necessary measurements and told him to return in three days.

In three days, Jesus returned with great expectations. This time, the tailor was there with his assistant. They fitted the garment on the slender Jesus and sat back in awe! They both exclaimed – almost at the same time – that he indeed looked heavenly! Jesus paid the modest sum and walked meekly back to his home, but felt that the world was staring at him. Finally, someone had asked him where he had purchased such a fine garment. The word was now all over town. There were soon long lines waiting to see the tailor who had created such a wonder. Everyone, but everyone wanted one like it! The poor tailor was so busy sewing that it took a customer to point out to him that he needed a much bigger shop with many more workers.

When the work had to stop for Friday night Sabbath, the tailor and helper, both exhausted but pleased, discussed the problem. It was apparent that a much larger shop was needed, but such a shop had to have a catchy name. One could not continue to call it the "tailor shop around the corner"! The exhausted tailor and his much younger helper discussed the yeas and nays of name after name for hour after hour and then some! Finally, as though it were from a bolt of lightening, the young helper blurted out the name "Lord and Taylor." At once they both knew that was it and the name has hung around ever since! And that is it, my friend! Truth is stranger than fiction and this is the truth according to the Gospel of Matthew, Mark, Luke, John and Jack, and I am Jack, the final and last of the Gospel writers!

RELIGION, SHAPE UP OR SHIP OUT! NOT NECESSARILY A MUST.

I implore people of this world to help us move toward reason in the realm of religion. I just saw a film about Karbala, a religious symbol for a good part of the Muslim faith. I advise readers to look up Karbala and the religious wars (in Europe) and you may understand why I say that too often religions border on insanity. The battle of Karbala in 680 CE is a perfect example of how religion can give rise to murderous rampages that make no sense. **This story is very central for Shi'is today and not too different from the crucifixion of Jesus in Christianity. It marked the division of Islam into the Shia and Sunni branches and killings that go on into our present era.**

In our present age with weapons of mass extinction so readily available, we had best remind ourselves that there are two sides of the moon – the light side and the dark side! There is the light or good side of religion which teaches respect and compassion for all humankind, even those with differing faiths; and the dark side which has soaked the pages of history, from the dim dark past into the present, with the blood of senseless killings in the name of religion or tribal differences. It would be best if a miracle could quickly make the entire human race evolve over night to the point of understanding that religion has been used as a means of grasping power for those who promote it and too often death and ruin to those who are brain-washed into defending it. Better and wider spread education in the world and books which reinforce the absolute need to love and care for all human beings regardless of belief or any other differences can help. But I do not expect a miracle. It is for this reason that I promote the idea of the World Peace Alliance (WPA) to control irrational human passions.

I have no intention of trying to wipe out all religions, even if that were possible, but it is necessary that most must change to accept the realities of what religion is all about. To convince people who need a faith to lean on is not unlike telling a child – a young child – that there is no Santa Claus or Tooth Fairy! Until they really grow up, they may need a light in the room when they try to sleep in peace. We should not look down upon those who need to continue with their various faiths, if they must, but all must acknowledge that it is wrong to insist that their religion or brand thereof is the only way to heaven. Yet in what we thought was our age of enlightenment, we have the statement below of our present Pope.

POPE PUREE

The Pope has just implied that if one does not belong to the Roman Catholic Church, he is attending a defective church. Recently our Pope declared that it is only through the Roman Catholic Church that there can be remission of sins or a free ticket to heaven. This is new? What else have they been teaching since they found this way to grow their business? Evidently, the Pope has not progressed much beyond the Middle Ages! His statement made absolutely no sense in view of the fact that most religions have been making efforts to accommodate to one another and to erase old dogma that caused so much tension. This is all part of my theory of the mental evolution of the human mind. Even the Catholic Church gave lip service to accommodation with others. His attitude is the same as the conviction of Sunnis that Shiites are apostates and infidels! Has he forgotten the bloodshed for centuries between Catholics and Protestants? This Pope has no perspective and is lacking in rationality, to say the least! But his view is no reason to hate him or Catholics. We all need to understand that persons with such narrow views are just not mature enough to understand the implications of what they are proclaiming. As Jesus, said, "Forgive them for they know not what they do"!

I very much regret having to state that the recent position of our present pope takes us straight back to the mentality that brought on the religious wars in Europe. The latter dragged on for centuries in its murderous ways. My saintly Catholic stepmother never would have agreed with him and I am confident that there are now enough "evolved" Catholics so that it will not presently lead to violence, but it is indeed sorrowful that such medieval insanity would still be coming out of the Vatican. I cannot say that I do not know why the Pope suddenly, even in the twenty-first century, took the trouble to repeat this point of dissension that has caused so much turmoil and death for centuries. The reason is quite clear to me: Once religion clouds the brain, all logic flies out the window. The Church must agree with me since they admit that belief can only grow with faith. This is an admission that religion must flush reason down the toilet! No, erase that tape! On the contrary, put it back! It may be that these relics, minds that are set in the Dark Ages, need shock treatments of one kind or another to bring them down off their clouds, back to their senses, back to reason! I know my saintly Catholic step mother never would have agreed with him! She made my father follow our Jewish faith more than he ever did! I have always equated Christianity with love and kindness. Does this prove again that I have been naïve? I am confident that most Catholics pay no attention to the Pope in this matter, just as they ignore other demands of the religion which make no sense. But, this is a matter of personal choice. Whatever they may believe, we must still love them. This is the cornerstone of my non-religion religion - call it atheism or humanism if you like.

Could it be that there is too much lead in all those heavy crowns of glory he wears? We all know what lead can do to the brain! Is this insulting? His proclamation is insulting to any intelligent person!

I remember the words of a Protestant naval officer said to me as we toured the Vatican while I was on leave in Europe. I will never forget his remark that all the poor in the world could be taken care of if the Church were to sell some of the magnificent baubles lying around in protected cages. But it gets worse! He constantly maligned the Church and the Papacy, using language I could never imagine as I was a very sheltered Jewish boy.*   I would not even think of repeating them here since this is a family friendly book. Talk about four letter words! That naval officer knew them all and how to embellish them!

*   I had never heard such raw words and never even knew about sex until I was 24. One might say I was deprived! Just joking – about being deprived, that is!

I found this naval officer's raving and ranting to be so outrageous, I felt compelled to say something. I spoke up and said: "Sir, you may think it strange that me, being a Jew, would stand up for the Church, but what you are saying does not seem appropriate for a U.S. Naval Officer to be saying such hateful things about the Pope who is a fellow Christian!" He hardly said a word about anything after that! Well, we win some, we lose some!

I have no doubt some will take offense to what I say here, but what could be more offensive than the Pope's proclamation that all other religions are defective!

* * * * * * * * * *

Proselytizing is an insult to others and is dead wrong! The two most guilty are the fundamentalists or extremists in the Christian and Muslim faiths. They seem to be oblivious to the fact that by insisting that their faith or their version of it is the only way to salvation is a slap in the face, an insult to all other thinking people. This change of thinking I am asking for – no, pleading for - if the world is not to push the self-destruct button should not be difficult to do if we but reason together. This change is not unlike the change in medicine through the ages. This is yet another example of evolution in human thought. Long ago and far away, the accepted cure for most ailments was to use leaches or bloodletting! We knew nothing about microorganisms, germs or the need for vitamins. Why not understand the need for evolution in human thought in the realm of religion! The leaders of these extreme views who make money from selling their snake oil will most likely never accept this; so it is up to the congregations to insist that their religious leaders grow up and stop acting like little, spoiled children. This will not be easy as this is how religious leaders fill and overload their pockets! Religion is the best and worst business on earth! Best because it is adept at bringing in the suckers; worst because it practices false advertising and fraud in its claim of everlasting life and remission of sin with "sin" rarely being defined other than by the prelates who have the balm to make the sin go away – in a huff and a puff if they say the correct prayers, sprinkle a bit of holy water and send in the "seed money" so that the false advertising can continue! After all, having the means of forgiving sin is the basis of their business! But where is the guarantee from G-d that their sins have really been forgiven?

Little old me says: Do no wrong in the first place and you will not need forgiveness. Also, if sin is so easily forgiven, why not enjoy sinning again and then do the usual hocus pocus to have the sin removed again? After all, I know of no notice from G-d that there is a limit to the number of times a sinner can be forgiven! Why should G-d do that? Just think how many poor souls may be discouraged from ever returning to Church! That would be bad for business! Go sin to your heart's content. It will give the Priest a thrill and something to do in the confession booth! If you feel it is wrong to express the facts in this way, just think of the many priests who have been uncovered in the sin of molesting young boys and how many Popes and priests had horizontal recreation with women. With all the cover-ups one can only imagine how many present and past indiscretions were never brought to the light of day?

Who am I to criticize the Catholic Church, but in my humble opinion the fault for molestation lies with their rule that makes men live as eunuchs when they are not. So much for the celibacy rule! It does not make me happy to point this out, but the truth is the truth. We should be adult enough to face up to it and not bury our heads in the sand! If people of faith take offense to this, how else do they propose we bring them into the age of reason! It is the twenty-first century, for heavens sake! See, I will not take the name of the Lord in vain, whether He minds or not!

OUR MERCIFUL GOD

As you dare to read through this, I am sure you will understand why I would never ask G-d to bless you with His mercy!

To believe that God is merciful has to be one of the most ridiculous, ludicrous and infantile ideas ever heard! To believe this can only come from being brain dead, or from cultural conditioning to believe anything our religious leaders tell us is a sign of mental illness or deficiency. I am sorry to be so rough, but we need to drive home the point that the human race must start to think. Religion usually fears this (the right to think) and expects the sheep to take their nonsense on faith! Just consider the many deformities we can have, the horrible diseases that have plagued mankind, the thousands killed at the World Trade Towers on September 11, the some 216,000 killed by the Tsunami across Asia. Were all of these sinners? Were they all homosexuals? Of course, the religious hucksters tell us we are all sinners from the time we were born - a good line perfected by the Madison Avenue advertising boys to bring in the suckers! They opened wide a huge market! After all, who would not want to be saved! It is said that Jesus saves. I say we should all save, especially for retirement.

When something goes wrong or there is illness or a problem, I get a kick out of saying that I do not worry about a thing. I know that God takes care of everything just as He did with the poor souls on the Titanic, the victims of drive by shootings, the thousands at the World Trade Center, the victims of the Tsunami across Asia and the devastation and unknown number of deaths in New Orleans, Louisiana and neighboring states and the countless millions killed in the two world wars. No doubt, God was with them to the very end! Strikingly, the millions of deaths caused by the First World War were not enough for Him. He had to take more millions of lives with the flu epidemic at the end of the war in 1918. Hallelujah! It is an old tradition that blood always appeases the Gods! Such mercy, we do not need! Looking at the world today, it seems that He thirsts for more blood to appease Him!

Many surely have an excuse for G-d for allowing the above tragedies by proclaiming that all troubles in the world are due to man's sin in the Garden of Eden. When Adam and Eve partook of the forbidden fruit of the apple tree, they committed the first sin and that was the beginning of evil. Didn't G-d know that to leave bars of gold on the front seat of the car with the door unlocked was inviting theft? Anyone who accepts this excuse and believes in the Garden of Eden fairy tale must also believe that Cinderella's fairy godmother turned a pumpkin into a carriage to carry Cinderella to the ball where she would meet her young prince. You may recall that Cinderella had to leave the ball before her carriage could turn back into a pumpkin. Any reasonable adult should conclude that lending credence to either of these tales indicates that adult must have the brain of a child – a very young child.

But go on and believe whatever makes you happy until you come to your senses and understand that religion is not necessary for a man to realize that to do good and be kind to others does not require the fear of hell fire; doing what is right and just produces its own reward. (Being a devout, orthodox, homosexual atheist, I approve of this message. jk)

HOW WOULD BIN LADEN VOTE,
and what car would he drive?

Before getting into the subject of "death," let us visit that lively fellow, Osama Bin Laden.

First, let us overcome a technical problem. We will be dealing with people of the cloth - not necessarily checkered towels - but people of religion. They are quite versed in the Good Book that is overloaded with bad happenings that should not be witnessed or brought before children, but these erudite zealots have a bedeviling problem with spelling. Some think his name is Ben Laden, Bin, Ben or Ban as in the deodorant. We will let them express themselves as they wish and G-d Bless them anyway! Our Modus Operandi has been to send a cadre of religious leaders of all faiths to Bin Laden to ask him personal questions about how he would vote on various matters and what kind of a car he would prefer driving.

The first person to come forward was not even a religious leader. He was a layperson of the Society of Friends and they are, generally speaking, pacifists. They are also known as Quakers, but they fear nothing, as they know for sure, beyond any shadow of a doubt, that God is with them! Unlike most other religions, they do not insist that their religion is the only road to Rome (roam?) OK, salvation. Perhaps that is not the best way to express this. Unlike most other sects of all religions, they do not insist that their path is the only one that will reward them with everlasting life plus a harp, fairy wings and a cloud beside G-d to float around Heaven all day. Each individual is allowed to use his own brain, a rarity in religious thought!

Sorry, I did not intend to go so far off the path! One of these good Quakers came forward immediately, looked into the somber and yet glaring eyes of Bin Laden and said: "Ben, my good chap, it is said around the world that you are a man of great wisdom, much wiser even than Bush. If you had the right to vote in the upcoming U.S. election in November, for which candidate would you vote?" "Well," began Mr. Laden, "I forgive you for addressing me as 'Ben, my good chap' because I am very erudite and know that Quakers originated in England. As a matter of fact, my good man, I was hoping another Chamberlain would appear out of the woodwork, but no such luck. Bush came out of the bushes – trees – that is! I do not know for sure that 'What's His Name' Kerry would be as good as Chamberlain, but I know he prefers peace and is very sensitive to the feelings of killers. I would vote for Kerry and once he gets into office, I would send my towel men into all the States of the Union and then take a piece of Pennsylvania, a piece of Maine, a piece of California, a piece of Nevada after bombing all of the casinos and collecting all of the money, a piece of North Carolina, etc, etc., etc. Kansas, Nebraska and all the rest of them would never be the same! Most of all, and perhaps first of all, we would take a piece of Texas and try George W. Bush for war crimes!

Our next interlocutor broke in before any more could be said because he was most eager to get in his question. He was a Methodist and there was a method to his madness! His particular sect latched onto the idea that human kind must nurture and preserve the earth, in other words, their concern is very much with the environment. He asked if Bin Laden would consider voting for Ralph Nader.

Bin Laden pulled his beard a few times and replied that his first choice would be Kerry, but he would certainly consider Nader. The Great One (Bin Laden, of course) assured the Methodist minister that there would no longer be a problem with the environment with Nader in the White House because the White House and all else on the American continent would no longer have an environment to worry about – all would be blown to smithereens!

The next one to gather wisdom from the All Wise One (Bin Laden, who else?) was a Christian Coalition minister. These particular types had made so much money selling their malarkey on TV that this man of the cloth was more interested in cars than anything else. He asked the Devout Bin Laden what kind of a car he would drive, hoping to High Heaven that he would pick out the biggest, gold plated, most expensive gas-guzzler luxury Alexis Pick-Up-Van available!

Bin Laden looked stunned, but replied, "Let me take this up with the Greatest Thinker of All Times, Allah Ishbad Mohamad Maharaja Khamenei Mesbahuddin Ben Ibraiham Siraj Abu Babaloo Smith better known as ALLAH! Come back in three days and I will tell the whole truth and nothing but the truth or I will never again eat my challah, a famous and delicious Jewish bread. I bet you didn't know bread can be Jewish! Rightfully so, it is a matter of equal opportunity to make dough.)

Three days later, and after considerable prayer and reading of the New Testament, the Christian Coalition minister returned to the cave of Bin Laden. The minister waited and waited and waited. Finally, Bin Laden appeared at the mouth of the cave, sitting on his donkey. Bin Laden looked at the poor minister whose face was glowing with pride and declared with a fatwa heard 'round the world. Bin, Ben or Ban declared that G-d (meaning Allah) "was stunned that a Christian should pose such a stupid question." Allah said to him (Bin, Ben or Ban), "Does he not see that you can get anyplace in the world by just sitting on your ass!"

Next questioner was a Jewish Rabbi (did you ever know a rabbi who was not Jewish?). The rabbi came forward, wearing his large, black hat, long black coat almost down to the ground, all of which was so stylish in the Polish ghetto centuries ago. Amazingly, The Good Man (the rabbi) seemed totally impervious to the torrid heat of 110 degrees. He came forward, timidly, and asked his question: "My dear Miester Osama Ben Laden, please tell us vhat you vood drive considering the decline in oil reserves 'round ze verld?" Bin Laden did not have to think very long. He was furious that a Jew should ask any question, let alone one so stupid! He furiously pulled on his long gray beard until it almost came off and then spit out: "Jew, I do not have to go away for three days to consult with Allah for this one! I remember clearly that Allah has written that Jews are a wonderful people and that every Devout Muslim should own one. Three times a day they should be faced with their heads toward Mecca and they should be beaten so that they will no longer make so many of those damn hard matzo balls. After one hundred years of servitude, we should DRIVE all Jews out of Muslim countries and bless Allah from every Minaret in town! Besides, why do you ask about cars? Are you so stupid that you do not realize that once we take over, all cars will be banned?

BIG DADDY

By way of introduction to BIG DADDY, I feel I must include in this epistle the statement below which I sent to my many liberal friends:

Here it is; so fasten your seat belt!

Of course, I am sure you understand I am getting ready to tell George (W. Bush) to come off his religious cloud, come down to earth and understand religion and the Bible are very much subject to interpretation and for the most part represent the "greatest consumer fraud ever perpetrated upon the gullible public" You may quote me on this!

"There is no God but Allah and Muhammad is his messenger." "There is no road to heaven other than through Jesus Christ who is the messenger of God." I would say these are not unlike little children bragging that "My daddy is bigger and stronger than your daddy, so there!" Are we going to still scrap in the playground called "earth" or are we going to come to our senses and grow up! It is going to be a tough job to convince all the mullahs, imams, mammas, papas (Pope), priests, ministers, etc. to give up the malarkey that has brought in the customers, but it must be done if the planet is to survive.

The HUMAN RACE NEEDS TO GROW UP – AND FAST! I suggest that the parishioners, congregations, and all the participants of religion insist upon brotherhood, concern and love for all of earth's children no matter how different we may be!

Notice I left out the term "rabbi" when listing the names of religious leaders. I did so because they never went out of their way to find converts and made no promises of salvation if only the person were to accept their brand! I believe about the same can be said for some Christian sects such as the Quakers, Unitarians or Mennonites, but I am not sure. Of course, there may be others and I devoutly hope there will be more! I truly love many of these people of religion! Yes, I do mean it. Unfortunately, we are faced with religious hucksters, charlatans, power hungry prelates who are determined to control the lives of others and then ask for donations so that they can continue to spread their snake oil and continue with their luxurious life style. The greatest danger to this planet is the religious extremists, radicals or fundamentalists of the Christian and Muslim persuasions. It is the teaching of these opportunistic and conniving brain dead idiots that has led to and will always lead to bloodshed. If they continue to preach that their brand of religion is the only way to salvation, the only way to sit on a cloud for eternity next to G-d, then we are doomed! Again, because of the rapid growth in technology, we must not allow these views to persist. Such a mentality is as explosive and dangerous to the world as allowing a maniac regime such as the one in Iran today to possess nuclear weapons. In this age, IT IS A MATTER OF SURVIVAL OF THE HUMAN RACE!

You will find through this book stories of how religions have brought so much death and misery into the world. This is to drive home the urgency of bringing all religions into accepting change so that the world will have a better chance of living in peace. I am not condemning most religions. I am just trying to get their leaders to understand that they must make some changes in their thinking and their teachings if our planet is to survive THIS AGE IN WHICH WE CAN INDEED DESTROY THE PLANET! All is not lost. I do have some faith that there are some sincere religious leaders who can do this with ease. Some are already speaking up on the matter.

All is not lost! Thank G-d the last Pope seemed to be heading in the right direction. Let us hope his successor will evolve to this point.

Take some comfort by reading this:

Pope Condemns Use of Religion for Violence
Published: 11/18/04

VATICAN CITY (AP) - Pope John Paul II received Muslim, Orthodox Christian and Jewish religious leaders from Azerbaijan, calling their visit Thursday a symbol of tolerance and declaring that religion must never be used for violent aims.

"No one has the right to present or use religion as an instrument of intolerance, as a means of aggression, of violence, of death," the Pope told the group.

Christians, Muslims and Jews must appeal together for an end to violence in the world "with justice for all," he said. "This is the way of religions," he said.

The audience was scheduled to repay the Pope's 2002 trip to Azerbaijan, a former Soviet republic and mainly Muslim nation with a Roman Catholic population of only 300 people.

The Vatican said the Pope wanted to hold up Azerbaijan as an example of coexistence and cooperation among religions and express hope that "a full peace in the spirit of reconciliation" may be achieved in the region - a reference to the country's conflict with Armenia over Nagorno-Karabakh, an ethnic Armenian enclave.

A cease-fire ended fighting in 1994 after some 30,000 people were killed and more than 1 million people fled their homes. The area of the world in which this happened is about the size of a postage stamp and yet 30,000 people were killed. No wonder G-d wonders about the imbeciles He created!

I'M JUST AN ORDINARY GUY!
(Another good title for a song?)

You can have no doubt that I am just an ordinary human being, but I have set myself a goal of changing the mindset, the thinking of the entire human race! So far, I see little change for the better. Oh well, it may take another week or so! All joking aside, we may not have very long considering the rapid growth in technology, especially those that can vaporize millions of people or eradicate them with chemical weapons or radiation from dirty bombs! Frankly, who cares if it is a dirty bomb or a clean one! Dead is dead! Increasingly, these dooms-day weapons are getting into the hands of the wrong people! Time is definitely not on our side!

Why do I say so much about religions and G-d when I freely declare I am an atheist? First of all, it is a matter of cultural conditioning and it is more convenient to use the term "G-d" rather than say "the universal creative force." I do so because I have a sense of great pity for the human race. As I never tire of saying, the human race is always evolving, but, tragically, we do not all evolve at the same rate. Have the aborigines of Borneo evolved as much as the Scandinavian peoples?

(My apologies to the "Borneoeans") The question answers itself! Advanced cultures have arisen only to falter and die, being replaced with more primitive humans. The Christian and Muslim worlds have obviously had their ups and downs. When Europe was in the Dark Ages, Muslims were preserving the knowledge of the ages, of the Greek and Roman cultures, for future generations. We need to be thankful to them for that. Tragically, as the west advanced through the industrial revolution, the Muslim world slid back into a state close to oblivion as far as education and technological advances were concerned. They exist now in a time warp!

I recognize that every human being is not evolving at the same rate, that many individuals are devoted to their religions because they need to have faith and there is a great deal of beauty in much of it. Eventually, I am confident that most people in the world, if it is still around, will come to understand what I am saying in this poor attempt at a book! I am struggling to write this, in spite of my poor health, because I love the human race and fear for its extinction by its own hands.

If it makes people happy, I encourage readers to go on believing what they wish as long as they understand and accept that we all must have concern for and love for the entire human race no matter how different we may be. Do unto others as you would have them do unto you. This is all that we really need to emphasize and bears repeating.

The statement below was made by Rabbi Hillel:

> *That which is hateful to you, do not do to your fellow. That is the whole Torah; the rest is the explanation; go and learn.* (Babylonian Talmud, tractate Shabbat 31a. See the ethic of reciprocity or "The Golden rule")

The Golden Rule

"Therefore all things whatsoever ye would that men should do to you, do ye even so to them: for this is the law and the prophets."

Matthew 7:12

As I have said before, there is wisdom in the Bible. (jk)

The idea of the evolution of human thought comes from observation and simple logic. I might also say from common sense, but common sense is not so common! Just a few facts: In our early stages of development, mankind believed in witches, demons, devils, human sacrifice (the latter of which G-d ended by telling the story of Abraham and his son Isaac who was to be a blood sacrifice to G-d), the saving grace of blood, in the killing of chickens (not necessarily Purdue) and the sacrifice of animals, etc. We believed that the chief or King was appointed by G-d to lord it over us, that the earth is flat, that the sun, moon and all other heavenly bodies revolved around the earth, that the woman should be subservient to the husband – usually a man. It is interesting to note that the last king to be considered a god was the Emperor of Japan. Just another example of how different peoples evolve at different rates. What is wonderful to report, and I am glad to do so, is how Japan has so rapidly evolved into one of the most advanced nations on earth in such a short time after the retirement of their god! No disrespect is intended toward the Emperor of Japan and his family. I am sure they are very fine people and I wish them great happiness.

Consider the wonderful transformation of Japan and compare the evolutionary development they went through with the lack of progress in such countries as Haiti and much of central and South America which are largely Catholic. I explain this by the fact that Catholicism is more concerned with the "after life" than with life here on earth. No offense is meant, but listen to or read the latest proclamations of our present pope and you will read and hear the same medieval nonsense they have stuck to for centuries. No place for women in the clergy, no abortions for any reason, homosexuals are an abomination to G-d and priests not allowed to marry. Nuns have practically vanished from our hospitals. One day soon, they will have no one to lead the prayers! How can they think that priests should not marry and that homosexuals are unacceptable? The latter is one of the variations of life that abounds in nature, but for priests not to marry is contrary to all that is normal in human life! Don't these men in long black robes see the wonderful variations in all sorts of life that have been created by our unknowable creator? Can they not understand that sexuality also has natural variations? Did I say yet that religion is often irrational? Well, you decide!

Yes, I thank G-d I am an atheist and thank Him many times during the day or night for all the good I have had in my life. Oh, I have had my share of grief, but I do not blame G-d for them. I just thank him for everything. Why not? If religion can be totally irrational, why should not a non-religion be just as irrational! I know He is a figment of our imagination and a product of our desires and needs and that man created G-d to explain what cannot be explained! I say, just keep it simple! If one feels better by thanking G-d for everything - it would take too long to list all the blessings - why not! It is most likely cultural conditioning. I think I said that before, but remember, I am older than I used to be! I cannot emphasize it enough that I do not pretend to have all the answers nor do I expect people to accept the idea of being an atheist or a humanist in droves just because of what I am writing here. After all I am really just a no-body. I have no degrees in religious studies or psychology. I simply do my own thinking. I just hope you will open your mind and decide for yourself. If you are happy with your present established religion, by all means stay with it and may He who is or He who is not bless you!

I am sure there had to be a creative force way beyond our ken – the ability of humans to understand - who or what force has created such myriad variety in every form of material or human or animal life. It is for convenience that I use the term G-d for what I understand to be the Creative Force of the Universe. This can be confusing, but I believe in the latter, not the former. I ask nothing of G-d or of the Creative Force of the Universe because I understand that things happen because they happen and it is foolish to try to explain them with nonsense and it is useless to try to understand them! It is also childish to accept any kind of nonsensical story, circulated through the centuries, to explain the inexplicable!

The sad truth is that I feel religion has been the worst plague leveled upon the human race! For one religion to insist that their religion and theirs alone will give them a chance for everlasting life, forgive their sins and get the believer to heaven or to a cloud floating around heaven all day next to G-d and all the angels is the greatest consumer fraud ever perpetrated upon a gullible public! Am I repeating myself? Good, it needs to be remembered!

This eternal life line is about as ridiculous as the hucksters who sell pills to reverse aging. "Take our pills and you will see and feel the years float away!" They are simply sales pitches to drag in the gullible customers! G-d knows, I may have tried them all! So, I am guilty; so sue me! I have been taking so many pills to bring back my youth, I must now be in my third childhood! To tell the truth, and that is a requirement of being a Devout Orthodox atheist, I am now taking another pill that is guaranteed to extend life for fifty years. I will hold them to it. If I do not live 50 years beyond my present age of 78, I will sue them! I have proclaimed it, so let it be written so let it be done!

ORIGINAL SIN

Religious leaders made up the concept of original sin. Naturally, it comes from the story of the Garden of Eden to give it legitimacy. No need to repeat this story since it is an age-old fairy tale from the Best Book Ever Written, the Bible. And we all know that if it is in the Bible, it must be the Gospel truth and can never be doubted! I do not ridicule the Good Book. I find it to be incredible and the First Wonder of the World that such excellence in writing, imagination and creativity could have existed at that stage of development of the human race.

Guess what? Lo and behold, the religious salesmen who created the concept of original sin just happen to have the cure for that sin – as long as you adhere to the one and only true religion – the one for which that particular spinster happens to be seeking new members, new believers to join his club. As Barnum said, there is a sucker born every day and they come forward in droves to be blessed, sprinkled, partially dunked, fully-dunked in water or whatever magic potion or motion they have devised to admit those poor souls into their magical club. That magic motion, the pouring on of water, has now become a magical moment. Now, as a full-fledged member, all you need to do is confess that sin and you will immediately be pure as snow. Sins forgiven because of the sacrifice of a burnt offering or the blood of a human being or of an animal, depending upon which brand of religion you have been suckered into. And then someone wrote that song: OH MAGIC MOMENTS...! I like it, I like it, I like it.

Wait, there is more. Now that you are saved, you will also never die. You assuredly are blessed with eternal life! What a club! Since these practitioners are taking away the fear of death, they usually wear basic black or some wear pure white to let the world know this is the club in which you find purity. Am I being sarcastic? Yes, but isn't it the truth! But as I always declare, if your faith makes you happy, stay with it! We love you anyway.

I received the following from a good Christian friend:

Europe's Future

"[After] Europeans stopped going to church, they stopped having children, having lost the spiritual impetus for procreation. Demographic winter set in. Then the Muslims moved in. [. . .] A glimpse of Europe's future may be seen in the recent Muslim riots around Paris. Besides burning cars, the rioters firebombed churches and synagogues.

"For the past five years, Europe has experienced a wave of anti-Semitism not seen since the Second World War. It's not evangelicals beating Jews in the streets of Paris, attacking Jewish day schools and kosher restaurants, and vandalizing Jewish cemeteries.

"Twenty years ago, Joshua O. Haberman, a reform rabbi, wrote an article entitled, 'The Bible Belt Is America's Safety Belt.' It's what keeps us from careening into a moral abyss of death-on-demand, sex divorced from values, a Roman orgy and demolition derby passing as entertainment, drugs used to fill lives devoid of meaning, and a generation of strutting savages in Calvin Kleins."

-- Excerpts from "The Anti-Christian League," December 13, 2005 in, as quoted in "Kristallnacht II," Culture, etc., *The Washington Times National Weekly Edition,* December 26, 2005 - January 1, 2006, page 28. Address: 3600 New York Avenue, NE, Washington, DC 20002.

My response to the above:
My first impulse is to want to say: "Thank G-d for the Bible Belt!" I know that children need guidance, but I feel it can best be done through humanist private schools teaching the need to have love and compassion for all people regardless of who they may be.

A THOUGHT FOR THE DAY FROM
A NON-RELIGION RELIGIOUS VIEWPOINT

Let us start each day by smelling the roses, by noticing the blue sky, the artful floating clouds, the mountains, streams, magnificent oceans, the endless varieties of every form of life created by the Creative Force of the Universe. Intended or not, we are blessed to be able to live on such a planet. Spread the joy, by being good to one another, give a pleasant greeting to a friend or neighbor and, if you have one, turn an enemy into a friend! I am sure this was the purpose of religion, but, sadly, the human race has distorted it into something hateful! Let us all work together to turn them all toward love and understanding for the entire human race. In a way, I am hopeful because I know many men of the cloth are beginning to understand what I am saying here – certainly it was the very foundation of the teaching of the Rabbi Jesus. I am also confident that there are millions of people who realize that religions need to reinvent themselves. We will explore this if you read on or you may figure it out on your own. (And I approve of this message. jk)

* * * * * * * * * *

Oxford Professor Richard Dawkins is perhaps the world's foremost apostle of atheism. British author Roger Scruton wrote that Richard Dawkins believes that faith is an infectious disease which spreads intolerance and conflict. History proves he is correct, but according to "The Spectator, Jan. 14, 2006, p.24, it claims it (faith or religion) is our principal source of love and peace. (I guess the Irish Catholics and Protestants loved one another to death right on into the twenty-first century! jk)

Out of "WORLD NEWS & PROPHECY Biblical Perspectives on Current Events," I picked up the following: "The Jewish community in Britain …has adherents in the atheist/agnostic camp, while still claiming to hold to some aspects of Judaism. For instance, one couple gave their twin sons 'a faith-free' bar mitzvah. The two are quoted by The Jewish Chronicle as saying, 'You can be Jewish without praying to a God you don't believe in.'" Dec. 22, 2006, p.20 (I agree one hundred and ten percent! jk)

As reported in "WORLD NEWS & PROPHECY," "…Harvard Professor Niall Ferguson, the Gallup Millennium Survey of Religious Attitudes shows that barely 20 percent of Western Europeans attend church services at least once a week, compared with 47 percent of North Americans and 82 percent of West Africans. Less than half of Western Europeans say that God is a 'very important' part of their lives, as against 83 percent of Americans and virtually all West Africans. And fully 15 percent of Western Europeans deny that there is any kind of 'spirit, God or life force.'" (The Daily Telegraph, July 31, 2005) (You are free to draw your own conclusions. Mine is that Western Europeans have progressed faster on the "Evolutionary Path of Human Thinking," in other words, they are much more intelligent! Or do you think the West Africans are more intelligent? This is not meant as a snide remark. All people should be treated with kindness and respect no matter what their level of intelligence or place on the evolution of human thought may be. It is also obvious that there are individuals in any group that stand well above most others in that particular group. We are all born into the culture in which we were born and it has nothing to do with the value of the individual. All life has value. jk)

The Daily Mail Telegraph, (British) columnist and author Melanie Phillips states "Religion gives us a code to live by which helps make us better people…The value we in the West place on every individual and on the principle of equality is based on our foundation religious doctrine that we are all created equal in the image of God." (Daily Mail, Dec. 19, 2005) (Balderdash I say! Better people? Ha! This utter nonsense and self-praise has been amply answered throughout this book. Too bad that I have to say this; I would much prefer that Melanie Phillips were correct. jk)

Upon taking leave of this chapter, may I say G-d bless you all whether He exists or not! As I was writing this book, could He have laughed Himself silly after reading my mind before I composed it or did He inspire me? I do not know for sure because I have not spoken with Him in weeks! Oops, I think I saw a warning shot, a flashing bolt of lightening!

CHAPTER 2

THE NATURE OF THE MUSLIM RELIGION

Do our Democrat congressmen and women remember 911? Does our former President Bush still consider the Muslim religion as a religion of peace after the following thought is digested; where were the clerics? Why haven't Muslim clerics from around the world gathered at ground zero, held hands together and prayed to Allah for forgiveness and told the American people this is not Islam? After reading the Koran, it is obvious that Jihad, the killing of infidels is a basic part of their religion. To them the cause was just!

Why have the Muslim clerics in the Middle East, especially in Iraq, not walked hand in hand down the streets of Baghdad, Fallujah, and all other hot spots of hatred to demonstrate against violence? Tragically, here is another sign of insanity in religion. The Sunnis consider the Shiites to be infidels because they have a slightly different interpretation of the Koran and the two branches of the Muslim religion cannot agree on who should be considered the successor to the Prophet Muhammad. A real tempest in a tea pot if there ever was one! But they are slaughtering one another over the boiling tea!

It is tragic that the sensible and reasonable Muslims cannot see that this endless bloodshed is a good time for Muslim leadership to condemn the hatred and violence promoted over and over again in their Koran and bring them into the twenty-first century. If their leadership and/ or clerics do not see this, is it time for modern, sensible Muslims to leave that gang and join another religion or become Devout Orthodox Humanists? No, I am not urging Muslims to give up on their religion as long as they follow a philosophy of live and let live and accept the concept of the brotherhood of man. Notice, I used the term "Devout Orthodox Humanists rather than my "devout, orthodox atheists." I like using the latter because of its shock value and I like it because it amuses me. Actually, and in reality, and to be more exact, the former, Devout Orthodox Humanist is much more accurate, appropriate and applicable! Now, allow me to get off my soap box!

In spite of what is happening today, we need to appreciate what the Moors or Muslims of North Africa did for civilization during the Dark Ages. They kept alive the knowledge and culture achieved by the Greeks and Romans in their golden age. This was at a time when white Christian Europeans were running around killing one another – as many Muslims are doing today, on a continuing basis just as we have seen in Africa since the colonial powers were chased out or simply threw up their hands in disgust and left them to their own fate. Subsequent to the fall of Rome, the knowledge and wisdom of the ancient civilizations of Rome and Greece were lost by the barbarians migrating south to take over from them. Thanks to the Muslims – largely the Moors of Spain - some of the ancient knowledge was kept alive.

What this book will propose is a way of helping the decent, twenty-first century Muslims to take back their religion from the seventh century "Crazies." And they are crazy. Getting right down to the facts, who was the Prophet Muhammad? The last three letters of his name make it very clear. He was mad - a madman. What else can one conclude from a being who believes an angel came down from heaven and gave him the final word of G-d? He spread his malarkey (BS) by becoming a mass murderer. He slaughtered all non-believers he could lay his hands on and his Quran gives permission to go on doing the same 'til the end of time. But behold, we of the west do not have to be killed. We just need to convert to the right form of the Muslim religion. Now go figure that one out! So, George, the Muslim religion is one of peace?

Read the Koran (or Quaran). No matter how you slice it or spell it, it is still a religion of hate and violence. Throughout the Koran, there are numerous commands to kill the infidels - non-believers in Allah. What part of that four letter word "kill" does George Bush and the politically correct crowd not understand? Again, and I cannot say it too often, there are decent Muslims today who are humane enough to ignore that part of their religion just as sensible Christians ignore much of the Bible which makes no sense and is out of date and unreasonable. I refer to such things as the stoning to death of an unfaithful woman or a fornicator. If I may say so, I do not approve of such behavior, but I am not going to throw stones. I listen to that Jewish boy, Jesus, who said, "He who is without sin, must throw the first stone." I am sure you know the first part of the story, if not, read it! More will be said about this X rated stuff later; so stay tuned!

I stated elsewhere in this small tome that Christianity spread around the world only because the Roman Emperor Constantine became a Christian. After all, who would argue with the Emperor of Rome! In case Muslim readers think I am insensitive, I give equal treatment for the Christian faith. I am an equal opportunity insulter! As I said elsewhere, to believe in a man who walked on water, fed the multitude with one loaf of bread or one dead fish, raised the dead back to life, made the blind see and the cripple walk, was crucified (dead) and then rose from the dead, is as crazy as the angel writing down the word of G-d for the Prophet Muhammad. If these fantasies or beliefs were not associated with religions, the believers would be considered candidates for the nearest "loony bin." Sorry, but we need to grow up. This is the truth, not because I proclaim it, but because the logical and intelligently logical portion of your own brain confirms it.

It is my deepest hope that not only decent Muslims, but also those now imbued with hate, can understand the need to embrace the concept of the brotherhood of man and want to live in peace and harmony with the rest of the world.

* * * * * * * * *

63

I just read an article in the March / April issue of the AARP Magazine. Two honor students from the American University in Washington, D.C. went on a trip to visit several Muslim countries to better understand their culture. The title of the article is: TALKING CAN STOP HATE. Sure it can kids, just as surely as one finger in the dyke can save the town in the Netherlands! Does anyone really think that talking to Hitler would have made him love Jews or even tolerate them?

I will not call these thoughtful young students Left Leaning Liberal Lunatics because I am confident their intentions were good. The article seems to have been written or the tour guided by Akbar Ahmed, the chair of Islamic Studies at the above mentioned University. Since they were in Islamic Studies, I assume they read most, if not all, of the Koran. As you read through this book you will see quotes directly from the Koran making it a tenant of the religion to convert or kill infidels. As I said earlier, what part of that endlessly repeated four letter word "kill" do they not understand?

Their leader, Muhammad, was an expert in killing. That is how he spread his religion and this book shows how this practice continues into this modern age. I do not know which mass murderer or gang leader was the worst: Genghis Kahn or Muhammad! The former did not need to invent a religion, he just enjoyed the thrill of killing, raping, plundering and gaining power for himself! One has to admit that Muhammad, at least, had a good imagination to give himself an excuse for doing the same thing! Maybe we should excuse the both of them. After all, there were no Gold's Gyms and Bally's around, as I remember. Fighting, killing and all the rest of those good things was a way to keep in shape and a way to make life interesting considering that TV and radio were not yet invented, as far as I can remember! One might surmise that killing ones neighbor was a sport or form of exercise that the Jews tried to spoil when Moses came down with the Ten Commandments. This is likely the real reason behind the hatred against Jews. Their Ten Commandments would spoil all of their fun, damn it!

Yes, the Koran advises compassion, hospitality and good acts toward others, but only if they are Muslims. You do not believe me? Read the

Koran for yourself! One of the countries the above mentioned group of American students went to visit was India to learn more about the culture of the Muslim world. The host of these students in Delhi, India, was a young man named Aijaz. He told them, and I quote: "The actions of Osama bin Laden, Hezbollah, Hamas, and the Taliban, even if they kill women and children, are perfectly justified in Islam." So George (Bush), do you still believe it is a religion of peace? Our President should have done some more reading! Later, Aijaz declares with a straight face that "Muslims feel persecuted"! Sure they are, poor kids! Just the same as a recalcitrant student in school complains that the teacher just picks on him! And if they feel persecuted, how should the Hindus, Christians, Buddhists, Jews and others feel after so many millions of their members were attacked and killed by Muslims!

* * * * * * * * * *

Thank G-d (whether He is there or not) for the writer of the article below. It just about tells it all!

Subject: "Allah or Jesus"
This is an article by Rick Mathes I found on the internet:

… The Muslim religion is the fastest growing religion per capita in the United States, especially in the minority races!! (This is just another reason for strengthening our education by going for a voucher system. In our public schools, they would not dare tell the truth about the Muslim religion. It would be counter to their idea of multiculturalism! jk)

Last month I attended my annual training session that's required for maintaining my state prison security clearance. During the training session there was a presentation by three speakers representing the Roman Catholic, Protestant and Muslim faiths, who explained each of their belief systems. I was particularly interested in what the Islamic Imam had to say. The Imam gave a great presentation of the basics of Islam, complete with a video. After the presentations, time was provided for questions and answers.

When it was my turn, I directed my question to the Imam and asked: 'Please, correct me if I'm wrong, but I understand that most Imams and clerics of Islam have declared a holy jihad [Holy war] against the infidels of the world. And, that by killing an infidel, which is a command to all Muslims, they are assured of a place in heaven. If that's the case, can you give me the definition of an infidel?'

There was no disagreement with my statements and, without hesitation, he replied, 'Non-believers!' I responded, 'So, let me make sure I have this straight. All followers of Allah have been commanded to kill everyone who is not of your faith so they can go to Heaven. Is that correct?'

The _____ expression on his face changed from one of authority and command to that of a little boy who had just gotten caught with his hand in the cookie jar. He sheepishly replied, 'Yes.' I then stated, 'Well, sir, I have a real problem trying to imagine Pope John Paul commanding all Catholics to kill those of your faith or Dr. Billy Graham ordering Protestants to do the same in order to go to Heaven!'

The Imam was speechless. I continued, 'I also have a problem with being your friend when you and your brother clerics are telling your followers to kill me.'

Let me ask you a question? 'Would you rather have your Allah, who tells you to kill me in order to go to heaven, or my Jesus who tells me to love you because I am going to Heaven and he wants you to be with me?'

You could have heard a pin drop as the Imam hung his head in shame. Needless to say, the organizers and/or promoters of the Diversification training seminars were not happy with Rick's way of dealing with the Islamic Imam and exposing the truth about the Muslim's beliefs.

I think everyone in the US should be required to read this, but with the justice system and media, and the ACLU, there is no way this will be widely publicized.

Please pass this on to all your e-mail contacts. This is a true story and the author, Rick Mathes, is a well known leader in prison ministry.

(I approve of this message. jk)

* * * * * * * * * *

A FACT CONVENIENTLY OVERLOOKED

Dec. 1, 2006 — Newly-elected congressman Keith Ellison, who'll be the first Muslim to serve in Congress, sparked a heated debate this week after he revealed his plans to use the Quran during his swearing-in ceremony. He'll raise his right hand and solemnly swear — or affirm — to support and defend the Constitution "so help me God." God for a Muslim who knows what he is talking about means Allah. This is just another Democrat who does not know which end is up! Ellison was born a Christian but converted to Islam in college. If he ever seriously read the Quran, he should know that if he should want to return back to the Christian fold, Muslim (Sharia) law would require that he be killed!   Republicans have questioned Ellison's ability to succeed in juggling his loyalty to the Ummah - or the global Muslim community - with his loyalty to the US and its Constitution. This is not diversity; it is lunacy and ignorance! The Constitution demands rule by we the people; the Muslim religion demands rule by the Quran - Sharia law - based upon countless passages which demand that infidels be killed if they do not accept Allah as G-d.

Can his swearing in be really considered valid? How can he be sworn in over a book that demands that all infidels be slaughtered? That means that most citizens of the USA must be liquidated. I feel it is right for a Muslim citizen of our country have the right to serve in Congress, but to be sworn in over a hate book? If any reader finds it shocking for me to call the Koran (Quran) a hate book, ask yourself if anyone can really call Hitler's Mein Kempf a book about his love for humanity.

I am disgusted with the Democrats who say they support our troops and then want to withhold funds needed to support them to make their service worthwhile by enabling us to win. Worse yet, many are feeble minded enough to demand withdrawal! I do not understand how the American people can support such ideas while our sons and daughters have their lives at risk every day for us and for everything our country stands for!

If you think I am condemning the Democrat Party too much, just wait. I will later advise the dissolution of both parties – with good reasons given – and replace them with a better idea. Stick around and you will find out. Right now, I will keep it a secret!

* * * * * * * * * *

Islam does not flourish and spread without the heavy handed oversight of Islamic fundamentalism, Sharia Law, fear, intimidation and war.

In Somalia the population is statistically 100 percent Muslim. **So where did all of the other religions go? They were forced to convert or be killed just like what's happening in Sudan.** Despite being 100 percent Muslim, pro-U.S. Muslim forces were just recently forced from the capitol, Mogadishu, by Al Qaida aligned forces under the guise of restoring peace and stability.

Published; 7/31/07, 7:05 PM EDT
By MOHAMED OLAD HASSAN
MOGADISHU, Somalia (AP) - ...government troops and their Ethiopian allies are battling Islamist militants ...

...Ethiopian troops supporting Somalia's fragile government drove out a radical Islamic group that had seized control. The defeated insurgents vowed to wage an Iraq-style guerrilla war until the country becomes an Islamic state.

(If Israel were to be wiped off the face of the earth, would it matter in cases such as above which abound in the world? jk)

Other Middle East and North African nations are more subtle about the elimination of non-Muslims. They close their eyes or secretly support those who are carrying out atrocities because it is too politically sensitive to be seen supporting such things. And when it comes to supporting jihad outside their own boarders there always seems to be a will and a way to get it done.

Saudi Arabia has made minor changes to the books used by its school curriculum eliminating some of the violent overtones of the past, but claims that "it cannot do it all at once." Saudi school books teach the Wahhabi version of Islam, which is one of the most violent sects of Islam. Several years ago Saudi school books teaching jihad and hatred of Jews and Christians were being used in the US just outside of Washington DC in private Islamic schools. With some pressure being applied over the years they have moderated the language somewhat, but Islam is anti-Jewish and anti-Christian at its core, thus making the new books anti-Islam to those Muslims who hold to the more virulent strain of Islam. Even Osama bin Laden has weighed in by way of audio tape, warning against US interference with the school Curriculum. (See NOTE 15)

In North Africa the percentage of Muslims in every country is nearing 100 percent; that is, except for Sudan where it is only 73 percent. Sudan just happens to be where a government declared genocidal jihad was declared in 1989, and has been raging since. **About two million Christians have been slaughtered or made refugees for simply being Christians**. However, it was not until the Darfur region genocide, where Government backed Muslims are killing non-government sanctioned Muslims that the world sat up and took any interest.

WANT TO BE RICH? START A RELIGION

Dear reader, imagine that you lived in Arabia hundreds of years ago. You realize that you could make a lot of money if you start a religion. You could declare that you are God. After some thought, you might realize that is not the best way to go about it. If you claim to be God to people, they will want to see miracles and you can't perform miracles. Another option is to try and convince them that you are God's prophet and that God communicates through you and to you. Now the pressure to perform miracles is lessened. What kind of obstacles and problems would stand in your way if you wanted to get religious followers to believe that you are a prophet? One is that people would think you were a nut case; in fact there is evidence that some people thought that way about Muhammad. Although some people might doubt your sanity, you might be able to con some impressionable people into believing that you really do have a special line of communication with God. Inevitably you will also find some people who don't believe in you because they already believe in other religions. One approach to persuading these people to believe in you would be to tell them that everything they believe is true but that you are a prophet with an additional message. That was the approach that was taken by Muhammad.

One problem you would face is that if you persuade these people to believe in you, they might tell their friends about their new religion and their friends may convince them that you are a con-artist after their money. How can you prevent that from happening? Somehow you need to stop them from communicating with their friends. You could take the approach Muhammad took which was to command them: *O ye who believe! Take not the Jews and the Christians for friends.* [Koran, al-Ma'idah 5:51.11]

What if they start having doubts on their own? You could terrify them into staying by instructing your followers: *Whoever changes his Islamic religion, kill him.* Sahih Al-Bukhari (9:57)

You could also threaten them with burning in the eternal fires of hell.

> *Garments of fire have been prepared for the unbelievers. Scalding water shall be poured upon their heads, melting their skins and that which is in their bellies. (Koran 22:19-22:23)*

One way to increase your wealth and power and wipe out those that spread doubt about you at the same time, would be to conquer the infidels who dare not honor you as their prophet and seize their money. You might instruct your followers: *Slay the idolaters wherever you find them, and take them captives and besiege them and lie in wait for them in every ambush.* (Koran 9:5)

If you wanted revenge against those who refuse to accept your religion and you were a totally ruthless and vicious "sicko" you might tell your followers to torture the non-believer. You might say: *Take him and fetter him and expose him to hell fire. And then insert him in a chain whereof the length is seventy cubits.* **(Koran 69:30-37) and *I will instill terror into the hearts of the unbelievers, Smite ye above their necks and smite all their finger tips of them.* (Koran 8:12) and *They should be murdered or crucified or their hands and their feet should be cut off on opposite sides. (Koran 5:33)***

The problem with encouraging your followers to attack the infidel is that the non-believing infidel is likely to defend himself. That might deter your followers from attacking. You could give them the incentive of sex and booty by saying that it's fine with Allah if your followers have sex with the captured women and keep them as slaves and that your followers can keep whatever booty they seize.

> *33:50 - "Prophet, We have made lawful to you ... the slave girls whom God has given you as booty."*
>
> *4:24 - And all married women (are forbidden) unto you save those (captives) whom your right hand possesses.*
>
> *The person who participates in (Holy battles) in Allah's cause ... will be recompensed by Allah either with a reward, or booty (if he survives)* (Hadith Sahih Bukhari, Vol 1 Book 2 Number 35)

Still the risk of death might deter some of your followers. If you were a brilliant and evil man you might think of and carry out the following ingenious solution to the problem. You could tell your followers that they will go to paradise if they die fighting for the faith. You might complete the previous sentence as follows: *The person who participates in (Holy battles) in Allah's cause ... will be recompensed by Allah either with a reward, or booty (if he survives) or will be admitted to Paradise (if he is killed in the battle as a martyr).* (Hadith Sahih Bukhari, Vol 1 Book 2 Number 35) and remind your followers that: *"Know that paradise is under the shades of swords."* Sahih al-Bukhari Vol 4 p55

So tell us what it is like to be in paradise your followers might ask. You might say that those who enter paradise will enjoy: *"abundant fruits, unforbidden, never-ending."* **There will be** *"gushing fountains"* **and everyone** *"shall recline on jeweled couches face to face, and there shall wait on them immortal youths with bowls and ewers and a cup of purest wine."* Suras (or chapters) 55 and 56 of the Quran.

That might not be enough to convince your lusty male followers to risk death in battle so you might tell them some even more thrilling aspects of Paradise. You might tell them: *"Therein are bashful virgins whom neither man nor jinnee will have touched before ... virgins as fair as corals and rubies,"* **sura 55. A few lines later, you might remind them of** *"virgins chaste and fair ... they shall recline on green cushions and fine carpets."*

By now you have a rapt audience of eager male listeners. "How many virgins are there for a man who dies for Allah?" an eager follower asks?

Why the smallest reward for every believer who is admitted to Paradise is 72 wives. The proof is in the Book of Sunan (volume IV, chapters on "The Features of Paradise as described by the Messenger of Allah," Chapter 21: "About the Smallest Reward for the People of Paradise," Hadith 2687). The Tafsir of Surah Al-Rahman (55), verse 72: mentions servants as well "It was mentioned by Daraj Ibn Abi Hatim that Abu-al-Haytham Abdullah Ibn Wahb narrated from Abu Sa'id Al-Khudri, who heard the Prophet Muhammad saying: *'The smallest reward for the people of Paradise is an abode where there are 80,000 servants and 72 wives, over which stands a dome decorated with pearls, aquamarine, and ruby, as wide as the distance from Al-Jabiyyah [a Damascus suburb] to Sana'a.'"*

"Are they really virgins?" a starry eyed follower asks.

The chastity of the black-eyed was not violated by man nor jinn (verse 74 of Surah Al-Rahman (55))

What if you are surrounded by all those women but can't do it. Don't worry. TIRMZI, vol. 2 states on page 138: *A man in paradise shall be given virility equal to that of one hundred men.*

Congratulations. Now you have men eager to kill and die for you. The problem is you have to deliver on the promise of the booty and yet you want it. So tell them that since Allah granted victory the spoils belong to him and one fifth should go to his prophet (you) and let them have the rest (Al-Bukhari, Volume 4, Book 52 Number 46 8:41). What if your followers want to rape their captive women? If you want them to kill for you, it would be wise to satisfy their sexual desires and to sanction rape so you tell them that Allah decrees that they can rape their captives (Sahih Muslim, Book 8, Number 3371).

There are still individuals who are threats to you. Order them assassinated! Those people left, who are still skeptical of your sanctity will have a powerful incentive to pretend to believe when then they see how your followers get booty and women and how those who refuse to believe get killed. If they are compelled to pray 5 times a day with other Muslims they are likely to be brainwashed into becoming true believers. If they don't pray they will get in trouble with your other Muslim followers which happened to an Egyptian friend of mine in Saudi Arabia.

Congratulations, your brainwashed followers now have time and are killing the infidel right and left and you are getting wealthy off the booty. But wait a minute. You could be making more money. What good do a lot of dead non-believers do for you? Wouldn't it be better if they all paid taxes? You don't want the non-believer killed, you want them enslaved. So you would tell your followers: *Fight those who do not believe in Allah, ... until they pay the tax in acknowledgment of superiority and they are in a state of subjection. [Koran 9.29]*

Now you're making money. Oh, oh, some of your idiot followers have decided to force the infidel to convert to Islam. If they do that you won't get as much taxes. Ah, tell them: *Let there be no compulsion in religion: Truth stands out clear from Error (Koran 2:256)* and *If it had been thy Lord's Will, they would all have believed, all who are on earth! Wilt thou then compel mankind, against their will, to believe? (Koran 10:99)*

As you became rich other people might get the idea to declare that they are prophets too. They might even copy your tactics and threaten those who don't believe in them with hell. If such tactics worked for you it might work for them too. Then there'll be less money for you. Their followers might even become a threat to you. Not a problem. Just declare that you are the last prophet.

> *In My Ummah (Islamic Nation), there shall be born Thirty Grand Liars (Dajjals), each of whom will claim to be a prophet, But I am the Last Prophet; there is No Prophet after Me. (Abu Dawood Vol 2 p. 228; Tirmidhi Vol 2 p.45)"* [1]

Once you declare yourself the last prophet you can accuse anyone who declares himself a prophet after you of being a heretic and you or your followers can have him eliminated. This was the fate of a Persian, Siyyid 'Ali-Muhammad who announced in May 23, 1844, that he had a mission to herald the arrival of *"One greater than Himself"*. **This announcement was the birth of the Bahai religion. Siyyid said:** *I am one of the sustaining pillars of the Primal Word of God. Whosoever hath recognized Me, hath known all that is true and right, and hath attained all that is good and seemly; and whosoever hath failed to recognize Me, hath turned away from all that is true and right and hath succumbed to everything evil and unseemly...all those who cherish My love and follow My behest abiding within the mansions of Paradise, and the entire company of Mine adversaries consigned to the lowest depths of hell-fire.*

Although Muhammad was dead by 1844 his followers
were not. Since Muhammad had said that he was
the last prophet, Siyyid was considered a heretic by
Moslems and killed and his followers persecuted.

You've got power now. It's time for revenge. Those Jews wouldn't worship
you and they have a lot of hot women and money. Order a massacre
but only of the men and children. Your devout brainwashed followers
will now carry it out without hesitation. Now your followers have the
women and you want them. One of your soldiers has a particularly
pretty one. You could command your soldier to give her to you but he
might get very upset and soldiers tend to be dangerous. Since you are
rich you could pay him a lot of money for her and that might get him
a little less angry. You've got plenty of money since your followers give
you a cut of the loot. This is what Mohammed did after he heard that
a soldier called Dahia had obtained a Jewish woman of "incomparable
beauty" by the name of Safiya bint Huyay after participating in an
attack against her Jewish brethren. He sent for Dahiya, paid him
Safiya's price and married her. (Ibn Saad, al-Tabaqat, pp. 120-123).
Rayhana Bint Zayd was another Jewish woman, whom Mohammed
made his concubine after her family and tribe were totally butchered
by his followers. Followers of Muhammad, if four Muslim wives are
not enough to satisfy your lust, and you haven't had the opportunity
to add to your concubine recently don't be disappointed in Islam, you
have options. Just say I divorce you 3 times to a wife you have and
marry a sexy teenager. This is exactly what a lot of Viagra charged
Muslims old geezers are doing. (One Minor Girl, Many Arabs)

Now you're rich and powerful. But you still have a problem. You have
to pretend that you are good. You can't do all those deliciously immoral
acts that you want to do. Let's say you want to engage in immoral sexual
behavior. People might not approve and question your saintliness. Not
a problem. You can say that God commanded you to do it. Let's say
you saw a hot babe and want to add her to your burgeoning collection
of wives and you already have more than four wives and you told your
followers that they can just have four wives. You can say that God allows
as many infidel slave sex partners as you want. What if your infidel

wife has the bright idea to convert to Islam so that you can't have her and your four wives. Make Islamic law say that a slave who converts to Islam is still a slave! What if the girl you are lusting after is Muslim and is not a slave. Just say that you got a special dispensation from God granted through the archangel Gabriel and go for it! Lets say you want to marry into a powerful family but the only girl available is only 9 years old. That won't look good to your followers. So you explain to them that God wanted you to have sex with the child of your desires: ***"...the Prophet said to her (Aisha), 'You have been shown to me twice in my dream. I saw you pictured on a piece of silk and someone said (to me). 'This is your wife.' When I uncovered the picture, I saw that it was yours. I said, 'If this is from Allah, it will be done.'"*** ***(Hadith, Sahih Bukhari 5:58:235)***

Let's say your son Zayad has married an incredibly beautiful wife by the name of Zainab who is ravishing and you want her. Not a problem. Have Allah command him to annul the marriage.

> ***(Sura 33:37) Then when Zayad had dissolved his marriage with her (Zainab) we joined her in marriage to thee: in order that there may be no difficulty to the believers in the matter of marriage of the wives of their adopted sons....***

Some of your followers get excited and raise their voice to you. You could tell them to keep it down but it would be far more effective if Allah would do so through you. In the Koran that is exactly what Allah does in sura XLIX.

> ***Believers, do not raise your voices above the voice of the Prophet, nor shout aloud when speaking to him as you do to one another...Those who speak softly in the presence of God's apostle are the men whose hearts God has tested for piety.***

A devout Muslim named Shaikh (see Leaving Islam) was reading this passage when a question entered his mind. Why is it really for Allah to tell people to show reverence to Muhammad? Can't Muhammad tell the people these things himself? God was acting as a servant to Muhammad. Shaikh wrote:

> *I came to the conclusion, all of a sudden, that it was Muhammad himself who was telling the people how to bow before him in the name of Allah, as though it were a command from Allah.*

This was the beginning of Shaikh's realization that his dear and beloved Islam was a lie. Shaikh points out another example. He writes: *If you read sura XXXIII.56 you will see it says, "Verily, God and His Angels pray for the prophet." In every other religion, it is man who worships God, but here God appears to be worshipping man.*

Previously I wrote about a conversation one could have with one's followers about paradise in order to motivate them to kill. Such a conversation was reported by the New York Times between <u>Sheik Omar Bakri Mohammad</u> and his followers in England. The New York Times reported: (<u>Militants in Europe Openly Call For Jihad and the Rule of Islam</u> 4/24/2004)

In Slough, Sheik Omar spent much of his time Thursday night regaling his young followers with the erotic delights of paradise — sweet kisses and the pleasures of bathing with scores of women — while he also preached the virtues of death in Islamic struggle as a ticket to paradise.

Muhammad's use of religion to justify his exploitation of women to satisfy his sexual desires has led to <u>Islamic sexual exploitation of women</u> throughout history. <u>His use of sex and divine revelations into manipulating his followers into going to war against the infidel</u> has led to a history of bloody wars against the non-believers and murder of non-believers that continues to this day.

The sinister use of sex to motivate murder is a factor in suicide bombings. Death announcements of suicide bombers in the Palestinian Press, often takes the form of a wedding not funeral announcements. Serge

Trifkovic in his book <u>The Sword of the Prophet</u> gives the following examples: *With great pride, the Palestinian Islamic Jihad marries the member of its military wing ... the martyr and hero Yasser Al-Adhami, to the black-eyed." (Al Istiqlal, October 4, 2001)*

> *Sa'id Al-Hutari, who exploded himself and 23 Israeli teenagers at a Tel Aviv disco on June 1, 2001, wrote in his will: "Call out in joy, oh my mother, distribute sweets, oh my father and brothers; a wedding with 'the black-eyed' awaits your son in Paradise." (Al Risala, July 7, 2001)*

The terror guide to the hijackers who crashed planeloads of innocent people into the World Trade Center said: *It will be the day, God willing, you spend with the women of paradise...Know that the gardens of paradise are waiting for you in all their beauty, and the women of paradise are waiting, calling out, "Come hither, friend of God." (See NOTE 15 "Reprise" = "repetition," a sneaky way for me to teach a little French)*

> In 2002 Muhammed Yusuf was approached by two strangers who tried to recruit him as a suicide bomber. Yussuf said: *They promised that if I died that way I would get 70 virgins in heaven and even talked about how I would be given a place to have sex, covered in diamonds and pearls, where even angels couldn't see me.*

Al Jazeera calls these suicide murders "Paradise" operations. (<u>Al-Jazeera's New Name for 'Martyrs'</u> wnd.com 10/29/05)

Muhammed had recently lost his father. They told him that if he committed a suicide bombing he'd see his father real soon. (<u>Matt Roper, Exclusive: They Tried to Make Me a Suicide Bomber</u> mirror. co.uk, 7/14/05)

The lure of booty and sex with conquered women has motivated Muslim soldiers throughout history. The Turkish historian Seaddedin wrote about how the offer of booty motivated Muslim soldiers when he wrote about the fall of Constantinople to his fellow Muslims in 1453. He wrote: *Having received permission to loot, the soldiers thronged into the city with joyous hearts and there, seizing the possessors and their families, they made the wretched unbelievers weep.*

The Reverend Jerry Falwell said that Muhammad was a terrorist. He was condemned by the National Council of Churches among other organizations. Ali Sina wrote an article defending Falwell called <u>Is Falwell to be Blamed for Calling Muhammad a Terrorist?</u>

Here is one paragraph from that essay: *What Falwell said was not factually untrue. Muhammad did things that by today's standard would be seen as acts of terrorism. He raided towns without any previous warning, killed unarmed men who had gone to the fields and markets after their daily business, captured their wives and children and distributed the younger women among his soldiers while always keeping the prettiest ones for himself and having sex with them in the same day he murdered their fathers, husbands and loved ones. These are not fables but historic facts recorded and preserved by Muslims themselves.*

The Koran describes Muhammad's massacre of the Jews <u>http://main. faithfreedom.org/Articles/sina/jews.htm</u> which leads modern Moslems to think such behavior is a good thing. After the battle all 700 men left in the tribe were slaughtered in one day the unfortunates being forced to dig their own graves before their heads were struck off. The women were enslaved.

Muslims always prized females not only because they could be used to do domestic work, but also because they could be used to satisfy their carnal appetites of their owners and also be used as breeding stock to breed more slaves. Islamic enslavement of the non-believer continues today in the Sudan. In fact Islamic genocide against the non-believer is occurring in the Sudan.

What Muhammad did hundreds of years ago radical Muslims are doing today. Suicide bombers and holy war jihadists in search of paradise open the gates of hell on earth with the flaming explosions they create and in the process destroy the paradises that existed on earth. Islam has turned the Paradise of Kashmir into a terrorist hell. A terrorist bomb has ended tourism in the paradise of Bali for the foreseeable future. Muslims are committing genocide in the Sudan. Islam has caused endless wars in the Middle East and throughout the world. 95% of the conflicts in the world as of 2001 involved Muslims. One of the greatest threats to the world today (other than Iraq and North Korea) is that of Islamic fanatics getting hold of weapons of mass destruction. These fanatic Muslims have no fear of the consequences of setting off such weapons as they believe that Allah will grant them victory or at the worst will bring them to paradise and the much desired virgins.

Apologists for Islam have made arguments that Islam is a tolerant, peaceful religion. Their arguments are addressed on the Islam and Jihad web page of this web site. I have received some responses arguing with my thesis that Muhammad's goal was wealth and power. Those responses are addressed at http://www.primechoice.com/philosophy/shelp/noblemuhammad.htm. For a book that goes further in depth about who Muhammad was, I recommend The Sword of the Prophet: The Politically Incorrect Guide To Islam. Paul Eidelberg wrote a review of The Sword of the Prophet. I give an excerpt of the review below:

In her extraordinary work, Islam and Dhimmitude: Where Civilizations Collide, Bat Ye'or avoids discussing Islam per se. She lets Islam's thirteen-century record of plunder, rape, and genocide discredit that religion. One would hardly know of such barbarism reading the doyan of Islamic scholars, Bernard Lewis. Judging from his book What Went Wrong? (2002), nothing is intrinsically wrong with the religion that enthralls 1.2 billion people. And Lewis, unlike John Esposito, is not known as an apologist of Islam. Enter Serge Trifkovic, a man of extraordinary intellectual courage. His The Sword of the Prophet departs from the moral "neutrality" of academia and, in six lucid and well-documented chapters, provides a "Politically Incorrect Guide to Islam."

Chapter 1, "Muhammad," portrays a simple preacher who became a fanatical warlord in the process of conquering Mecca and Medina. After slaughtering Arab tribesmen and looting their camels, the prophet and his followers kidnapped their women and staged an orgy of rape. One Hadith explains:

We desired them, for we were suffering from the absence of our wives, but at the same time we also desired ransom for them. So we decided to have sexual intercourse with them but by observing 'azl [coitus interruptus]. But we said: We are doing an act whereas Allah's Messenger is amongst us; why not ask him? So we asked Allah's Messenger and he said: It does not matter if you do not do it, for every soul that is to be born up to the Day of Resurrection will be born. To the men of one Jewish tribe, Muhammad offered the choice of conversion to Islam or death. Upon their refusal, up to 900 were decapitated in front of their women and children. "Truly the judgment of Allah was pronounced on high," was Muhammad's comment. The women were subsequently raped.

Ibn Warraq in his book <u>The Quest For the Historical Muhammad</u> presents evidence that, many of the sayings attributed to Mohammad in the Koran and the Hadiths were not made by him. If Ibn Warraq is right and much of the Koran and Hadiths were the result of creative writing and not historical reality then the creators of Islam must have had the motives ascribed above to Muhammad of achieving wealth, power and beautiful women. The purpose of the above article is not to engender hostility to Muslims, but simply to portray Muhammad as accurately as possible based on readings of the Koran and the Hadiths. It's important to keep in mind when reading this that there are <u>good, even heroic Muslims</u> and that <u>scriptures of other religions have appalling statements as well</u>. For a more in depth discussion of who Muhammad was see the online book <u>Prophet of Doom: Islam's Terrorist Dogma, In Muhammad's Own Words</u>.

The X-RATED PARADISE OF ISLAM

Prophet Muhammad was a genius. He thought up the unique institution of Jihad, where men would gladly volunteer to go to wars & die in wars for no pay other than war booty & slaves. That wasn't it! If they died or were willing to sacrifice themselves in battle then Heaven/Jannat would be instantly theirs. The martyr's Heaven was laden with things rare in the desert of Arabia: beautiful virgins, young boys, water, wine, fruits and wealth. Jannat laden with virgins, boys, wealth, etc. is the lure for the Jihadi willing to do battle, let's say in Kashmir, Afghanistan. This is no secret - ask any muslim; ask Fah here at the forum. Please check out the following verses from the Koran and quotes from the Hadiths.

VIRGINS (HOURIS)

Prophet Muhammad knew that sex would sell very well among the group of his lecherous followers who were motivated to fight battles by the promise of sex slaves and booty. Once the followers go to heaven, they can conveniently ditch their wives for the fresher and more pleasurable sexual encounters with 'Houris' (beautiful virgins). Not only that, the poor wives who gave up their virginity for the pleasure of their husbands do not get even one Male Sex Bomb. But wait, Allah is all merciful! He gives the wives the rare honour of watching their husbands deflower those 72 Houris (virgins) and 28 young pre-pubescent boys. The relevant verses from the Koran are:

Koran 78:31 As for the righteous, they shall surely triumph. Theirs shall be gardens and vineyards, and high- bosomed virgins for companions: a truly overflowing cup. Koran 37:40-48 ...They will sit with bashful, dark-eyed virgins, as chaste as the sheltered eggs of ostriches. Koran 44:51-55 ...Yes and We shall wed them to dark-eyed houris. (beautiful virgins) Koran 52:17-20 ...They shall recline on couches ranged in rows. To dark-eyed houris (virgins) we shall wed them... Koran 55:56-57 In them will be bashful virgins neither man nor Jinn will have touched before. Then which of the favours of your Lord will you deny?" Koran 55:57-58 Virgins as fair as corals and rubies. Then which of the favours of your Lord will you deny?" Koran 56:7-40

...We created the houris (the beautiful women) and made them virgins, loving companions for those on the right hand…. " Koran 55:70-77 "In each there shall be virgins chaste and fair... Dark eyed virgins sheltered in their tents whom neither man nor Jin will have touched before... In the Hadiths, Prophet Muhammad goes one step further - Women and young boys are on display as if in a fruit market where you can choose the desired ripeness.   Quote from Hadiths

Al Hadis, Vol. 4, p. 172, No. 34 Ali reported that the Apostle of Allah said, "There is in Paradise a market wherein there will be no buying or selling, but will consist of men and women. When a man desires a beauty, he will have intercourse with them."

YOUNG BOYS

Homosexuality was and is widely practiced in Islamic countries. To please the homosexuals among his followers he promised them pre-pubescent boys in Paradise. So after committing plunder, loot, rape and murder in this life, the followers of Islam get "rewarded" by untouched virginal youths who are fresh like pearls.

The relevant verses from the Koran are: Koran 76:19 And round about them will serve boys of perpetual freshness: if thou seest them, thou wouldst think them scattered pearls. The following verses say about the same: Koran 52:24 Koran 56:17

Name: maka
E-Mail: kaka1232@yahoo.com
    Although Maka's interpretation may be correct regarding the Islamic promise to homosexual followers, there are verses in Islam that condemn homosexuality. For example: ***"We also sent Lut : He said to his people : "Do ye commit lewdness such as no people in creation (ever) committed before you? For ye practice your lusts on men in preference to women: ye are indeed a people transgressing beyond bounds." Qur'an 7:80-81***

According to the Hadiths, *"When a man mounts another man, the throne of God shakes." "Kill the one that is doing it and also kill the one that it is being done to."* (in reference to the active and passive partners in gay sexual intercourse)

There is at least one mention of lesbian behavior mentioned in the Hadith: "Sihaq *(lesbian sexual activity) of women is zina (illegitimate sexual intercourse) among them."*

There clearly is a stigma attached to homosexual behavior in Muslim countries. Nicholas Eberstat and Laura Kelly started an article titled The Muslim Face of Aids (frontpagemag.com 7/7/05) with the following paragraph: *On a cold December evening in the southern Iranian city of Kerman, the stars blazed overhead as a father took his son's life. Enraged, and with an ax in hand, the head of a prominent Iranian family chopped his child to pieces for bringing shame upon his relatives. The son's crime? Contracting HIV, the virus that causes AIDS. In a country where, in some parts, nearly 60 percent of HIV–positive citizens take their own lives within the first year of their diagnosis, the 23-year-old son faced little chance of acceptance, even from his family.*

Al-Fatiha, a foundation whose mission is to help Lesbian and Gay Muslims in reconciling their sexual orientation/gender identity with the religion of Islam, estimates that 4,000 homosexuals have been executed in Iran since their revolution in 1979. 10 public executions of homosexuals have been performed in Afghanistan by the Taliban army. (This should make our religious right leaders such as Jerry Fallwell jump in joy! jk)

So how do we explain the verses of the Koran quoted by Maka? Either his interpretation of the quotes is correct and they are examples of contradictions in Islamic texts or the verses are promising servants and not homosexual companions.

This book, and many others, is replete with many statements directly out of the text of the Koran that substantiate the violent nature of the

Muslim religion. Why are they demanding an apology from the Pope for quoting the WORD out of the book that is the very basis of their religion? Their displeasure is often followed by threats of death if he does not grovel at their feet and apology. They, including the Pope, are acting like spoiled children who have not yet been toilet trained! Where was the brain of the Pope to even bring up such a quote? Was it under his skirt? Why did he not point out that in the Christian Bible there are commands to stone people to death who have committed certain specific sins that modern man simply ignores? In the same way modern Muslims of intelligence and with open minds ignore the admonitions directly out of the Koran to spread their faith using the sword. These Muslims have come into the twenty-first century, I am glad to say! But who is demanding that the extremist Muslims, Jihadists, Islamists renounce violence? Other Muslims dare not for fear of being killed! How many Germans were able to stand up to Hitler? Few Muslims condemn the suicide bombers. On the contrary, most celebrate in the streets and pay the families of those who committed this outrage to humanity!

Has anyone ever heard of an apology from any Mullah, Mumscr, Mama or Papa for the innocent men, women and children killed by homicidal maniacal suicide bombers who killed at bus stops, weddings, night clubs, **and resort hotels ad infinitum? Isn't suicide bombing a result of the teachings of their prophet Muhammad – exactly as quoted by Pope Benedict from an ancient text out of the 14**[th] **century? Of course it was the height of stupidity to bring up this issue. This is further proof that religion often corrodes the minds of even intelligent people and too often borders on insanity! (jk)**

Recently one of the best known American magazines had an article in it which claimed that some Americans had desecrated the Koran by washing it down the toilet. I do not think anyone should deliberately profane any religion, but the Muslim reaction to this was just one more example of how religion often leads to insanity. Muslims went on a killing spree to avenge this action.

Here is the story:

With Carl Limbacher and NewsMax.com Staff

For the story behind the story...
Monday, May 16, 2005 11:56 a.m. EDT

Gen. Myers: Detainee Flushed Koran Pages

Newsweek magazine's decision to apologize on Sunday for reporting last week that U.S. interrogators at Guantanamo Bay had flushed a copy of the Koran down the toilet wasn't the first hint that the story that has outraged Muslims worldwide may not be true. On Thursday, Chairman of the Joint Chiefs Gen. Richard Myers told reporters that the only evidence of any Koran desecration unearthed so far was a log notation describing a Muslim prisoner tossing pages from his holy book into the toilet.

"A detainee was reported by a guard to be ripping pages out of a Koran and putting them in a toilet to stop it up as a protest," Gen. Myers said, in quotes picked up by the Washington Times. "But not where the U.S. did it."

The top military man said that a review of interrogation logs offers no evidence "that there was ever the case of the toilet incident" as reported by Newsweek. The magazine's misreport prompted anti-American riots in Afghanistan that have so far resulted in the deaths of 17 people - not to mention demands for an apology from President Bush. Muslim clerics in the Middle East have yet to comment on Gen. Myers' revelation that it was likely one of their own who treated the Koran like toilet paper.

EXCUSE ME FOR LIVING!

After endless apologies to Muslims from American politicians in the aftermath of the Abu Ghraib prison incident, one more is in order: Excuse me for living! Who has been pointing out the truth that the extremist Muslims have always been seeking a world in which only Muslims can exist? If we are Christians, Hindus, Jews or even a Muslim sect that does not follow the same beliefs, we must apologize

for living so as not to offend! Even so, we may be handed our heads!
Just consider that Hindus and Muslims lived as neighbors and friends
in India under British rule, but once independence was granted, the
Muslims wanted their own state because they felt they could not live in
peace with Hindus. Millions were killed on both sides.

The Christians, as well, had the same ideas and went through centuries
of religious wars. And do not forget the Catholic/Protestant strife in
Ireland that just recently ended! In the New World, the concept of
the separation of Church and state was a leap forward, but now we are
seeing pressure to impose religious dogma on all: prayer in schools, ban
abortion, condemn homosexuality as an abomination in the eyes of the
Lord, ban drugs that used to be readily available and have faith based
initiatives. Did anyone realize that money going to such groups could
go to Muslim "charities" that will donate money to support families
of suicide bombers, murderers?   Are you reading this, George? Dare
I say that this may be fine with Obama since it will be going to those
terrorists with whom he wishes to dialog?

To declare that the Muslim religion is one of peace is laughable in view
of the fact that it has been spread around the world by the sword and
that, for the most part, wherever Muslims are there is strife even today.
Certainly, there are decent, responsible Muslims who want to live in
peace and harmony with others, but they obviously do not have the
power and when do we hear from them? It is up to the latter to take
back their religion from the fundamentalists or extremists. Not an
easy task since the Muslim world is in a time warp. Their minds are
muddled with the mentality of the Middle Ages. This is true of many
elements or sects of the Christian religion as well. I refer to those who
now proudly announce that they can now get Bibles into Iraq to save
the heathens or non-believers, bring them to Christ so that they can get
to heaven and float around heaven all day! Of course their way is the
only way! True, most Christians are closer to the Twenty-first century:
they can no longer harangue and condemn Jews nor can they insist that
blacks sit in the back of the bus, but notice how many now found a
new group on which they can vent their hate and to fill the collection
plate – homosexuals!

The human race is being led to the edge of a steep cliff by the high priests of most established religions. We had best understand that our only chance to survive in this age of "weapons of mass extinction" is to quickly learn to live and let live, to have compassion and understanding of all others no matter how different they may be. Our minds must catch up quickly with our advances in technology or we are lost!

The human race needs to grow up – there is no Tooth Fairy or Santa Claus! I am not happy writing what follows as I know faith is good for many people. They need it. Fine, let them continue to believe, but they must not force their views upon others. A mind change in the human race is essential; it is a matter of survival of the planet!

We need to understand that religion has been the greatest curse placed upon the human race and that man created God to explain the inexplicable. It is evident that man has always longed to believe in something, anything to overcome fear of death and of the unknown. It is up to the individual, the human race, to create heaven on earth by being kind and good to others by doing unto others what we would have them do unto us. We need only live by: **DO ONLY GOOD; DO HARM TO NO ONE.**

The extremist Muslims, decades ago, declared war on western civilization. I fear that the only way to win this is to get all religions around the world to accept the above thoughts. I am convinced that the situation in Iraq arose because Saddam Hussein was clever enough to make the whole world believe, including President Clinton, that he had weapons of mass destruction. His purpose may have been to hold his own country in tow or to make us fear to attack. If, indeed, he had such weapons, it would have been suicide to allow him to continue with their development and then take the chance that he might pass them on to the lunatic fringe of the Muslim world! In any case, we are there because we could not go on allowing twelve years of U.N. orders to be ignored. The best and only reason needed to make an attack on Saddam's Iraq legitimate was that he was in clear violation of the agreement to stop the Gulf War and refused over and over again the requests of the U.N. to comply with the cease fire agreement. Nazi

Germany was in clear violation of the Versailles Treaty. Just think how different the world would be today if the League of Nations had insisted that Germany disarm and then make them do so if they had refused! Those who did not want to force Saddam Hussein to abide by the many (at least twelve) orders from the United Nations to live up to the agreement signed after the First Gulf War obviously did not learn from history. We were lucky to have George W. Bush who knew what to do and did it! Tragically he did not have any contingency plans and completely botched the entire operation.

Where do we go from here? We must be tough and hold the course. If responsible Iraqis cannot gain control of a city such as Fallujah, we must make it clear that the entire city may have to be leveled. Unfortunately, this may have to be done in any other city taken over by extremists. A war cannot be won with our hands tied behind our backs. War is hell. Win it and there will be peace. Yes, there should be humane treatment of prisoners. Mistreatment of prisoners is wrong, but our first responsibility is the safety of our troops. I fear that all of these apologies are going to make it difficult to interrogate prisoners who have valuable information that can save lives of the young men and women who are there to protect us from oblivion. Our President needs to point this out!

Keeping the above in mind, there are many things in life that should be a certain way. A mother should be caring and loving, but this is not always the case. A mother who neglects her children, uses drugs, sleeps with different men every night or walks the streets looking for horizontal recreation is obviously not the ideal of what a mother should be. To protect society, such a mother should be sterilized. The hard working people in the country should not be burdened with the care of unwanted children. Likewise, men who impregnate a woman and then refuse to take care of both should be castrated. The burden should not be forced upon hard working, responsible workers.

As I wrote above, prisoners should be treated humanely, but when they refuse to divulge information needed to protect our troops – our sons and daughters – all necessary action should be taken to get the results needed!

This is an excerpt from a friend's letter who objected to something I wrote in "EXCUSE ME FOR LIVING":

"…if the Iraqi invasion is justified by the number of times Saddam violated UN resolutions, we should have invaded Israeli* instead because Israel, I believe, violated even more UN resolutions. Finally, your final solution reminds me of an American officer in Vietnam who said that we had to destroy a town in order to save it…"

* Error, "Israel" is the correct word. (jk).

My response: That officer in Vietnam was right; we must die in order to be saved! One reason we lost in Vietnam was because of nuts like, what's his name, the one who ran on the Democratic ticket - oh yes, Kerry! (Obviously written some time ago.) If Israel defied the U.N., it is because they did not want to walk to the gas chambers again. Those days are over! Just look at who and what are in the U.N.: dictators, thugs, Arab states and those who want to keep the oil flowing in their direction! The whole world needs oil; so who is worried about Israel? In spite of everything being against them, Israel will not go the way of Czechoslovakia to appease tyrants! The following is an article written by a Spanish journalist, Sebastian Villar Rodriguez.

EUROPE DIED IN AUSCHWITZ

I was walking along Raval (Barcelona) when all of a sudden I understood that Europe died with Auschwitz. We assassinated 6 million Jews in order to end up bringing in 20 million Muslims!

We burnt in Auschwitz the culture, intelligence and power to create. We burnt the people of the world, the one who is proclaimed the chosen people of God. Because it is the people who gave to humanity the symbolic figures who were capable of changing history (Christ, Marx, Einstein, Freud…) and who is the origin of progress and wellbeing.

We must admit that Europe, by relaxing its borders and giving in under the pretext of tolerance to the values of a fallacious cultural relativism, opened it's doors to 20 million Muslims, often illiterates and fanatics that we could meet, at best, in places such as Raval, the poorest of the nations and of the ghettos, and who are preparing the worst, such as the 9/11 and the Madrid bombing and who are lodged in apartment blocs provided by the social welfare state.

We also have exchanged culture with fanaticism, the capacity to create with the will to destroy, the wisdom with the superstition. We have exchanged the transcendental instinct of the Jews, who even under the worst possible conditions have always looked for a better peaceful world, for the suicide bomber. We have exchanged the pride of life for the fanatic obsession of death. Our death and that of our children. What a grave mistake that we made!!!

Above is a good indication of how much Spain has evolved from the days of the Inquisition. Another great advance is their acceptance of homosexuality as being a natural expression of life. This will be beautifully evoked in CHAPTER 14.

* * * * * * * * * *

The Pope is Sorry. Muslim Terrorists Are Not

DEBKA Special Report

September 16, 2006, 3:08 PM (GMT+02:00) A firestorm of Muslim rage was ignited by a lecture on the theme of Faith and Reason that Pope Benedict XVI gave at Regensburg University in Germany Tuesday, Sept 12, 2006.

The fury that beset the Muslim world recalls the tempest which greeted the Muhammad cartoons in a Danish newspaper earlier this year. The government in Ankara said his safety could not be guaranteed during his visit in November, during which the pope had hoped to improve relations between Christians and Muslims. Turkey's Catholic bishops will meet next Monday to discuss the visit.

Benedict quoted Byzantine emperor Manuel II as saying in a learned debate with a Persian cleric in 1391: "'Show me just what Muhammad brought that was new (**DEBKA*file***: a hint to the proposition that the Koran was a copy of earlier Christian and Jewish writings, and there you will find things only evil and inhuman, such as his command to spread by the sword the faith he preached." (a denigration of jihad).

Oddly enough, no outrage was forthcoming when the leader of Israeli Arab Muslims, Sheikh Raad Salah promised a gathering of 50,000 Israeli Arabs, Friday night Sept. 15 that "very shortly the Israeli occupation of Jerusalem would be eclipsed and the city (Israel's historic and national capital), will become the capital of the "world Islamic caliphate."

His audience eagerly thundered: "With fire and blood we will liberate al Aqsa!" No one demanded of the sheik any apology although by a strange coincidence he parroted one of al Qaeda's central goals and injunctions and the justification for its terrorist campaign against the American, British and French "crusaders" and "the Jews," namely, the establishment of a caliphate for world rule from its center in Jerusalem.

Where are the demonstrations and effigies protesting the explicit threat to the Jewish state and its capital? This double standard for legitimate and illegitimate Islamic conduct ruled the thinking of much of the world before Pope Benedict dropped his clanger - and will be there after it is forgotten.

Angry Muslims clamor for the Pope's apology for his words on Islam. Israeli Arab Islamic leader Sheikh Raed Salah denounced the Pope's words and declared the "Israeli occupation" of Jerusalem will soon vanish and Jerusalem will become capital of the "world Islamic caliphate."

Has anyone ever heard of an apology from any Mullah, Mumser, Mama or Papa for the innocent men, women and children killed by homicidal maniacal suicide bombers who killed at bus stops, weddings, night clubs, and resort hotels ad infinitum? Isn't suicide bombing a result of the teachings of their prophet Muhammad – exactly as quoted by Pope Benedict from an ancient text out of the 14th century? Of course it was the height of stupidity to bring up this issue. This is further proof that religion often corrodes the minds of even intelligent people and too often borders on insanity! (jk)

The above thoughts came to me as I heard Prime Minister Tony Blair condemn Israel for killing leaders of Hamas. How does one kill a snake without cutting off its head? Would Britain or the U.S. have any hesitation in killing Bin Laden? I am appalled by the pandering, for so many decades, to extremist Muslims (that wonderful religion of peace)!

Five churches in West Bank towns hit by firebombs Saturday and Sunday in protest against Pope Benedict's remarks on Islam September 17, 2006, 1:20 PM (GMT+02:00)

No one was hurt. An explosion also damaged the Greek Orthodox church youth center in Gaza.

Muslims and Christians arrested over religious clashes in Egypt **January 24, 2006, 3:37 PM (GMT+02:00)**

Egyptian security forces have arrested 30 people in connection with religious clashes in Udayssat, south of Cairo, on January 19. Muslim youths reportedly set fires to prevent Christians from renovating a house and turning it into a church. Fourteen people were wounded in the violence between Coptic Christians and Muslims. Sorry George, but you may wish to keep this in mind when you are moved to declare that the Muslim religion is one of peace! Another indication of just how tolerant Muslim extremists are:

Afghan Christian Could Get Death Sentence

Published: 3/19/06 An Afghan man is being prosecuted in a Kabul court and could be sentenced to death on a charge of converting from Islam to Christianity, a crime under this country's Islamic laws, a judge said Sunday. The trial is believed to be the first of its kind in Afghanistan and highlights a struggle between religious conservatives and reformists over what shape Islam should take here four years after the ouster of the Islamic fundamentalist Taliban regime. The defendant, 41-yer-old Abdul Rahman, was arrested last month after his family accused him of becoming a Christian, Judge Ansarullah Mawlavezada told The Associated Press in an interview. Rahman was charged with rejecting Islam and his trial started Thursday. During the one-day hearing, the defendant confessed that he converted from Islam to Christianity 16 years ago while working as a medical aid worker for an international Christian group helping Afghan refugees in the Pakistani city of Peshawar, Mawlavezada said. "We are not against any particular religion in the world. But in Afghanistan, this sort of thing is against the law," the judge said. "It is an attack on Islam."

...Afghanistan's constitution is based on Shariah law, which is interpreted by many Muslims to require that any Muslim who rejects Islam be sentenced to death, said Ahmad Fahim Hakim, deputy chairman of the state-sponsored Afghanistan Independent Human Rights Commission.

...During questioning, it emerged that Rahman was a Christian and was carrying a Bible. He was immediately arrested and charged, the father said.

...Although leaders of several countries where the cartoons (of Mohammad) were published have expressed regret for the offense caused by the caricatures' publication, some hard-line Islamists in this Islamic nation of 150 million say the cartoonists should be sentenced to death.

Taliban Is Blamed for Beheading Teacher

Incident reported on 1/4/06. (Story rewritten from news items.)
Taliban militants beheaded a teacher in a central Afghan town while his wife and eight children watched, officials said Wednesday, describing the latest in a string of attacks targeting educators at schools where girls study. Four men stabbed Malim Abdul Habib eight times ... before decapitating him in the courtyard of his home in Qalat... Habib resumed a more than 20-year teaching career two years ago after the Taliban threatened him while he was working for an aid group helping the disabled. Since then, the Taliban had warned him twice to stop teaching.

A main goal of the Taliban is to establish a "pure" Islamic state. This requires that no girls attend school. ...Zabul province's education director, Nabi Khushal, blamed Taliban rebels for the killing. "Only the Taliban are against girls being educated," he said. "The Taliban often attack our teachers and beat them... Cleric Sayed Omer Munib, a member of the nation's top Islamic council, said there was no justification in Islam's holy book, the Quran, to prevent girls from studying. It is said about 90 percent of Afghan adults are believed to support educating girls. Many of those who oppose it are in conservative rural areas dominated by ethnic Pashtun where the Taliban who also are Pashtun are most powerful.

Pakistani Killed Daughters to Save 'Honor'

Published: 12/29/05 Nazir Ahmed appears calm and unrepentant as he recounts how he slit the throats of his three young daughters and their 25-year old stepsister to salvage his family's "honor" a crime that shocked Pakistan. The 40-year old laborer, speaking to The Associated Press in police detention as he was being shifted to prison, confessed to just one regret that he didn't murder the stepsister's alleged lover too. Hundreds of girls and women are murdered by male relatives each year in this conservative Islamic nation, and rights groups said Wednesday such "honor killings" will only stop when authorities get serious about punishing perpetrators. The independent Human Rights Commission of Pakistan said that in more than half of such cases that make it to court, most end with cash settlements paid by relatives to the victims' families, although under a law passed last year, the minimum penalty is 10 years, the maximum death by hanging. Ahmed's killing spree witnessed by his wife Rehmat Bibi as she cradled their 3 month-old baby son happened Friday night at their home in the cotton-growing village of Gago Mandi in eastern Punjab province. It is the latest of more than 260 such honor killings documented by the rights commission, mostly from media reports, during the first 11 months of 2005. Bibi recounted how she was woken (awakened) by a shriek as Ahmed put his hand to the mouth of his stepdaughter Muqadas and cut her throat with a machete. Bibi looked helplessly on from the corner of the room as he then killed the three girls Bano, 8, Sumaira, 7, and Humaira,

4 pausing between the slayings to brandish the bloodstained knife at his wife, warning her not to intervene or raise alarm. "I was shivering with fear. I did not know how to save my daughters," Bibi, sobbing, told AP by phone from the village. "I begged my husband to spare my daughters but he said, 'If you make a noise, I will kill you.'" "The whole night the bodies of my daughters lay in front of me," she said.

The next morning, Ahmed was arrested. Speaking to AP in the back of police pickup truck late Tuesday as he was shifted to a prison in the city of Multan, Ahmed showed no contrition. Appearing disheveled but composed, he said he killed Muqadas because she had committed adultery and his daughters because he didn't want them to do the same when they grew up. He said he bought a butcher's knife and a machete after midday prayers on Friday and hid them in the house where he carried out the killings. "I thought the younger girls would do what their eldest sister had done, so they should be eliminated," he said, his hands cuffed, his face unshaven. "We are poor people and we have nothing else to protect but our honor."

Despite Ahmed's contention that Muqadas had committed adultery a claim made by her husband the rights commission reported that according to local people, Muqadas had fled her husband because he had abused her and forced her to work in a brick-making factory. Police have said they do not know the identity or whereabouts of Muqadas' alleged lover. Muqadas was Bibi's daughter by her first marriage to Ahmed's brother, who died 14 years ago. Ahmed married his brother's widow, as is customary under Islamic tradition. "Women are treated as property and those committing crimes against them do not get punished," said the rights commission's director, Kamla Hyat. "The steps taken by our government have made no real difference." Activists accuse President Gen. Pervez Musharraf, a self-styled moderate Muslim, of reluctance to reform outdated Islamized laws that make it difficult to secure convictions in rape, acid attacks and other cases of violence against women. They say police are often reluctant to prosecute, regarding such crimes as family disputes. Statistics on honor killings are confused and imprecise, but figures from the rights commission's Web site and its officials show a marked reduction in cases this year: 267 in the first 11 months of 2005, compared with 579 during all of 2004. The Ministry of Women's Development said it had no reliable figures. Ijaz Elahi, the ministry's joint secretary, said the violence was decreasing and that increasing numbers of victims were reporting incidents to police or the media. Laws, including one passed last year to beef up penalties for honor killings, had been toughened, she said. Police in Multan said they would complete their investigation into Ahmed's case in the next two weeks and that he faces the death sentence if he is convicted for the killings and terrorizing his neighborhood. Ahmed, who did not resist arrest, was unrepentant. "I told the police that I am an honorable father and I slaughtered my dishonored daughter and the three other girls," he said. "I wish that I get a chance to eliminate the boy she ran away with and set his home on fire."

Saudi's Arresting Christians for 'Spreading Poison'

Despite Saudi Crown Prince Abdullah's assurance to President Bush during his visit to the presidential Texas ranch that "tolerance must extend to those of all faiths and practices," it was reported that just days earlier, Saudi police had stormed a clandestine church in a suburb of Riyadh and arrested 40 Christians for proselytizing. The New York Sun cited Saudi state-controlled newspapers as reporting on April 23 that two days earlier, security forces rounded up 40 men, women, and children of Pakistani citizenship who were worshipping at an abandoned villa in western Riyadh, according to translations provided by American-based Saudi monitors. The Sun added that the Saudi Al-Riyadh newspaper quoted a security official as saying that the Christians were arrested for "trying to spread their poisonous religious beliefs to others through the distribution of books and pamphlets." "What they are doing is saying one thing in English and giving another signal to their own people," Nina Shea, the director of the Center for Religious Freedom of Freedom House, a human rights organization told the Sun. "They are saying to the hard-liners at home that nothing is going to change. It's a way of speaking out of both sides of their mouth." During their meeting in Crawford, Texas, President Bush and Prince Abdullah issued a joint declaration in which the Saudis affirmed their commitment to religious tolerance. (But Christians and Jews remain unwelcome in Saudi Arabia. jk)

In its 2004 report on international religious freedom, the State Department declared that "freedom of religion does not exist" in Saudi Arabia. "It is not recognized or protected under the country's laws, and basic religious freedoms are denied to all but those who adhere to the state-sanctioned version of Sunni Islam," the report stated. And thus we see what kind of good friends we have in Saudi Arabia. Did you know this, Mr. President?

0UR SAUDI "FRIENDS" ARE PREPARING TO SUBVERT OUR COUNTRY!

Source: "Jerusalem Prayer Team" <jerusalemprayerteam@donationnet.net
Teaching Babies to Hate Jews - Stan Goodenough

Across the Middle East, untold millions of Arab children and adults are being indoctrinated with a pathological hatred of the Jews – wherever they are. Like tender shoots in an Arabian hothouse, these young lives are being infused with poison and malice every bit as vicious and unyielding as was Adolf Hitler's brainwashing of his followers against European (and ultimately universal) Jewry. The goal of their mentors is to raise a generation of Muslims who will consider it a tremendously great honor to swell the ranks of "martyrs."

Expert: Saudis Have Radicalized 80% of U.S. Mosques - Haviv Rettig

Over 80% of mosques in the U.S. "have been radicalized by Saudi money and influence," according to Yehudit Barsky, who heads the Division on Middle East and International Terrorism at the American Jewish Committee and is executive editor of Counterterrorism Watch. For each mosque they invested in, the Saudis sent along their own imam (teacher-cleric), meaning that "the people now in control of teaching religion [to American Muslims] are extremists…Some of the leaders have even condoned suicide bombings in Israel and against American armed forces." (Jerusalem Post)

EVOLUTION – THE DOWN SIDE

If you do not believe in my conviction that the world has been going through an evolution of human thought, just consider how the mind has concocted weapons of war, weapons to kill through the centuries. News of the latest was just sent to me by my friend Mr. Gielow. Just think what might happen if terrorists, willing to kill themselves, were to get hold of this new weapon!

Gielow Communiqué #270
EMP (Electromagnetic Pulse)
"According to a report issued last summer by a blue-ribbon, Congressionally-mandated commission, a single specialized nuclear weapon delivered to an altitude of a few hundred miles over the United States by a ballistic missile would be 'capable of causing catastrophe for the nation.' The source of such a cataclysm might be considered the ultimate 'weapon of mass destruction' (WMD) [. . .] It is known as electromagnetic pulse (EMP). See NOTE 9
DEBKAfile Exclusive Report
January 9, 2005, 7:44 PM (GMT 02:00)

* * * * * * * * * *

The prophet, may God 's peace and blessings be upon him, says: "Kill whoever changes his religion." This hadith is related by Al-Bukhari. Based on the above, the Shari 'ah Court of the Al Qa 'ida Organization in the Land of the Two Rivers has decided to carry out God 's ruling on the diplomatic envoys of the apostate Algerian Government, who are Chief of Mission Ali Belaroussi and diplomatic attache Azzedine Belkadi by killing them. This is the ruling that also applies to the ambassadors and envoys of the remainder of the infidel governments. There can be no destiny for them except killing. Praise be to God, backer of the mujahidin.

Saudi Arabia, "our friend," is the well-spring from which Wahabbism grows. America will not win its war against terrorism until it does something about ideological hatred pouring out of the Middle East, particularly out of Saudi Arabia and Wahhabism, says Daniel Silva, best-selling author of **The Messenger**.

Saudi Arabia's relationship to terrorism and America's deeply important relationship with Saudi Arabia are subjects that have been pulling at Mr. Silva for years, he says. His conclusion?   A large chunk of the Washington establishment is bought-and-paid-for by Saudi money. And the Saudis are not innocent. Instead, they are complicit with terrorism despite their protests to the contrary, he says. Using a litany of research findings from which he created his fictional world, Mr. Silva believes that it is only a matter of time before other Osamas and other networks of terrorists rise up.

Wahhabism

Relevant insight into this form of the Muslim religion, in question/ answer format, taken from FRONTLINE

Sheikh Muhammad ibn Abd al **Wahhab** ibn Sulaiman ibn Ali ibn Muhammad ibn Ahmad ibn Rashid al Tamimi was born in the year 1115 A.H.(1703 C.E.) in 'Ayina to the north of Riyadh, in the Kingdom of Saudi Arabia during the reign of Abdulla ibn Muhammad ibn Hamd ibn Muammar. He excelled over his contemporaries in intelligence and physique and was able to commit the Quran to memory by the time he was ten years old. His father found him capable of leading the congregational prayers and decided to get him married that year.

Vali Nasr, an authority on Islamic fundamentalism

... Saudi Arabia has its own particular interpretation of Islam which is very legalistic, is very austere, it's very black-and-white. Wahhabism is sort of an extreme orthodoxy that historically has not been shared by a majority of Muslims, particularly nobody outside of the Arabian Peninsula. For more than two centuries, Wahhabism has been Saudi Arabia's dominant faith. It is an austere form of Islam that insists on a literal interpretation of the Koran. Strict Wahhabis believe that all those who don't practice their form of Islam are heathens and enemies.

Critics say that Wahhabism's rigidity has led it to misinterpret and distort Islam, pointing to extremists such as Osama bin Laden and the Taliban. Wahhabism's explosive growth began in the 1970s when Saudi charities started funding Wahhabi schools (madrassas) and mosques from Islamabad to Culver City, California. (And Washington D.C. jk)

Can you show me an example of what the religious teaching is in the schools?

Well, here, this is a book, hadif, for ninth grade. Hadif is a statement of Prophet Mohammed. This is a book that starts for ninth graders. This is talking about the victory of Muslims over Jews. This is a hadif that I truly believe it's (is) not true, as a Muslim: "The day of judgment will not arrive until Muslims fight Jews, and Muslim will kill Jews until the Jew hides behind a tree or a stone. Then the tree and the stone will say, 'Oh Muslim, oh, servant of God, this is a Jew behind me. Come and kill him.' Except one type of a tree, which is a Jew tree. That will not say that." This is taught for (to)14-year-old boys in Saudi Arabia

So the state religion in Saudi Arabia is this pure, stricter form of Islam? Yes. ...

And we're told by people we've interviewed that it's the nature of this thought, its fundamentalist nature that can be easily manipulated, so that people would, for example, become violent or extremist.

I think that the new mood, the new trend, especially after the Gulf War, has become for all these neo-Wahhabis ... [is to use] Islam ... as a platform for political ideas and activities, using Islam to legitimize political, economic, social behavior. These people have been brought up in a country where Islam legitimizes everything. And they have used the teachings from the religious establishment, but became more political in expressing dissent and criticism of the regime.

And it's been exported. To Pakistan, through systems of madrassas and throughout the Islamic world.

And it has been exported, yes, indeed. We are told that it's this form of fundamentalist religion represented by this Wahhabi-influenced Islamic, if you will, ideology, or view, that has created, if you will, a seedbed for people to become violent, to become anti-American, and to do the kinds of things that we call "extremism" now. Is that true?

I don't think it has to do with Islam. I don't think it has to do with any form of this ... Islamic interpretation. ... Of course there is a problem with dogma. But I think the problem lies with the political systems that use religion. ...

There's been a politicization of Islam. You've said it. But bin Laden, and his, if you will, similar people, are using Islam to promote political goals.

Yes. **They base this on a dogmatic interpretation of the religion itself, black and white. Is the base of support that they are gaining a result of this proliferation of this view of Islam? ... Wahhabism is what I am talking about. ... Is there a relationship between that and this development that we see of bin Laden and his movement?**

Probably there would be a relation between an interpretation of Islam that lacks tolerance, and is a more narrow vision of the world. But particularly the problem is about the political systems that promote this type of interpretation of religion. This gives people the excuse, the platform, to go ahead and express themselves in Islamic language to suit their purpose of political ends.

Is there a connection between the fundamentalism of the Taliban and the fundamentalism of the Wahhabi?

The connection has been growing very, very strong in the past 20 years, and particularly in the past ten years. The dominant school of Islam with which the Taliban associate -- which is known as the Deobandi school -- is very prominent in Afghanistan and also in wide areas of Pakistan. Northern India has increasingly gravitated toward Wahhabi teaching, and has very, very strong organizational ties with various Wahhabi religious leaders.

When we saw the Taliban destroy the Buddhist statues and other artifacts in Afghanistan, is that similar to a Wahhabi view? Yes, yes. Because Wahhabis don't believe in tombstones, don't believe in images being acceptable, don't believe in statues. They believe all of these are forms of polytheism. A majority of Muslims don't share that degree of literal reading of religious texts or banning of these kinds of reflections....

And the Wahhabis dominate in Saudi Arabia? The Wahhabis dominate in Saudi Arabia, with also significant influence and presence in United Arab Emirates, Oman, Kuwait. ...

The nature of these Islamic beliefs, you're saying, foster fundamentalist extremism? The teachings are fundamentalist in the definition you have in mind. The question is who's going to cross the line and engage in violent acts or not. So you see, recruitment into terrorist movements is small generally.

There's a big swamp out there of people. Right, yes. And what we're confronting is not just flushing out Al Qaeda. The bigger headache for the U.S. government is dealing with the Muslim world as a whole, with the political ramifications of our counterattack. That's the bigger problem. ...

○ maher hathout

a senior adviser to the Muslim Public Affairs Council and the spokesperson for the Islamic Center of Southern California

But what is the creed of Islam that is preached in Saudi Arabia? What is it called? Well, the word "creed" is important because the creed of Islam is the same: the belief in one God, the belief in the oneness of his message, the oneness of the human family. And the devotion to God should be expressed in human rights, good manners, and mercy, peace, justice, and freedom. No two Muslims will argue about this creed. It is documented in the Koran as the highest authority, modeled by the authentic teaching of the prophet, and the authenticity has always been subject of study and debate. So the creed is crystal clear. But the interpretation or the way you approach life, which should be a dynamic thing, should change from time to time. When you freeze it at a certain period or at a certain interpretation, problems happen. I know that people called it Wahhabism; I don't subscribe to the term. [Muhammad bin Abd al-Wahhab] at his time was considered a progressive person. If you freeze things at his time -- which was the eighteenth century, or the late part of the seventeenth century, I don't remember the dates exactly -- it becomes very stagnant and very literalist. And a very straitjacketed puritan approach that does not cater to the changeables and the dynamics of life. People call this Wahhabism. Saudis, by the way, never say, "We are Wahhabis." They say, "We are just Muslims." But they follow the teachings, and the major booklets taught in all schools are the books of Muhammed bin Abd al-Wahhab. Anyone who's subscribing to someone else is not very much welcomed. So there's a quote in the [New York Times] article that we were looking at before that basically says that Saudi Arabians believe that their form of Islam ... is the real true form of Islam, and that pretty much any other kind of way of practicing Islam is wrong.

Yes. This is probably some of the Saudi scholars. ... They are playing the role of clergy; there should be no church in Islam. There should be no theological hierarchy. But they acquired that position and, of course, they and the ruling family are very close. After all, Muhammed bin Abd al-Wahhab is the one who paved the road for Abdul Aziz ibn Saud, the patriarch of the family, to conquer the rest of the [Arabian] Peninsula and to rule. So there is very great cohesiveness between the two. And so they believe that that's it, this is the truth. And not only that that is it, it does not change, which is very problematic. Because we know that even at the early history of Islam, as new issues emerged, new jurisprudence was created to suit the change of the time and age. That's early on, at probably 25 years after the death of the prophet.

So they, that group of people, believe that this is the only form and it does not change. This of course creates major problems, and it creates some kind of schizophrenic situation. ... I don't think that Wahhabism ... will condone or accept lots of things that are done by some of **the elite of Saudi Arabia who come to Las Vegas and have fun and do**

this and do that. And we don't hear a very strong voice exposing this or condemning them for that. **But if they see a woman driving a car, they consider this a major sin.** There is confusion here.

* * * * * * * * *

I know there are some apologists for Muslims who try to convince us that there are some Arab Muslim regimes that are moderate. Dubai, Egypt and Jordan are most frequently mentioned. I knew long ago that Egypt had reneged on its promise to secure the border between Gaza and Israel once Israel had voluntarily returned Gaza to the Palestinians. Egypt never upheld its responsibility to guard the border or to prevent the rearming of Hamas. I was almost convinced or hoping that Jordan was one of the moderates until I read the following: Two Arabs involved in the sale of a Hebron building to the Jewish community have been placed under arrest, one by the Palestinian Authority, the other by Jordon. The arrested Arabs now face capital punishment, as Palestinian Authority law dictates the death sentence for anyone found guilty of selling property to a Jew. As I am now writing, efforts have been underway by Bush and Rice to get peace talks going between Arabs and Israel. A *Los Angeles Times* report noted that the Arab League gathered in the Saudi capital to discuss the idea … sniped at Israel, which is so widely loathed in the Arab world that it does not even appear on maps in many countries there.

The conservative leaning *Washington Times* called the Arab position an "ultimatum" and not a peace proposal. "If the Saudis want to be taken seriously as peacemakers, they need to stop issuing ultimatums to Israel and start issuing them" … to Hamas.

Meanwhile, the Bush administration has backtracked on reservations about the plan. American Secretary of State Condoleezza Rice stated earlier this month that the "right of return" clause is not practical but avoided stating any reservations about the 2002 initiative after the Arab League's endorsement of it this week.

Jyllands-Posten Muhammad cartoons controversy.
From Wikipedia, the free encyclopedia

"…not all Muslims placed blame entirely on the West. In Iraq, the country's top Shiite cleric, Grand Ayatollah Ali al-Sistani, decried the drawings but did not call for protests. Al-Sistani suggested that militant Muslims were partly to blame for distorting Islam's image. [44] In the United Arab Emirates, the periodical Al-Ittihad published an opinion piece which argued that "the world has come to believe that Islam is what is practiced by Bin Laden, Zawahiri, Zarqawi, the Muslim Brotherhood, the Salafis, and others who have presented a distorted image of Islam. We must be honest with ourselves and admit that we are the reason for these drawings."[45] "Some Muslims, mainly in Europe, have supported the re-publication of the images so that individual Muslims can make up their own minds and welcomed the debate on the issues that cartoons have raised.[46] It has also been pointed out that cartoons in the Arab and Islamic press 'demonizing' Jews and Israelis are common."

* * * * * * * * * *

More good news about Muslims and the thought: "Thank G-d" came immediately into my mind. I was extremely happy to read on the internet (July 22, 2007) that the just reelected Erdogan, a devout Muslim, told supporters in his victory speech that he would preserve pluralistic democracy and work for national unity. "We will never make concessions over the values of people, the basic principles of our republic. This is our promise. We will embrace Turkey as a whole without discriminating," he said at a rally in the capital Ankara. The above is yet another example supporting my theory of the evolution of human thought.

So that you know there is still some hope for the human race if more people see the light, I urge with all my heart that all readers of this book go immediately to NOTE 16. ADD IT TO ANY E-MAIL YOU SEND OUT!

CHAPTER 3

UNIVERSAL WORLD PEACE
YES WE CAN!

If you are serious about reading this book, you will be delving into some very profound matters. This book really needs to have a warning label reading:

NOT TO READ THIS BOOK CAN BE
DANGEROUS TO YOUR LIFE
AND THE EXISTENCE OF OUR PLANET!"

I really wanted to start with a few laughs, but I have changed my mind. After all, a man has a right to change his mind and a woman has a right to change his mind! (You read that correctly!) Instead, let us start with the main purpose of this book: UNIVERSAL WORLD PEACE.

PEACE ON EARTH AND GOOD WILL
TOWARD ALL MEN (and WOMEN)

The Pope has declared that there should be no more wars.
Here is a plan for reaching that goal.

What did Tito's Yugoslavia and Saddam Hussein's Iraq have in common? They both ruled over countries with different ethnic and religious groups antagonistic to one another. They were both strongmen – dictators

– who, for the most part, kept them from killing one another and managed to keep the countries together. It certainly would have been better if these men had taken action to bring their populations together by encouraging them to be friendly and compassionate to all human beings in their midst and in the world, as this book is advocating, but that did not happen. Instead, once the lid was off, the pot boiled over. What does this tell us when considering ways of maintaining peace in the world? Clearly we need a lid! We tried the League of Nations and the United Nations. Tragically, we have, in spite of their efforts, continued to have wars, local and world encompassing. This can and must be stopped. Get ready for another one of my hair-brained ideas. I guess I am bald because of having so many hair-brained ideas in recent years. Here it is! Are you seated?

This little old school teacher is proposing that all nations which value individual freedom, freedom of religion, freedom from religion, the right of nations to govern themselves no matter how diverse they may be and those who wish to live in peace with all others, form an organization that may be called the World Peace Association (WPA) and set up programs and plans for assuring peace in the world. They would encourage all nations to allow freedom of religion, freedom to have no religion, freedom of speech, freedom to have a secret ballot to elect those they want to govern them and freedom from criminal elements in society. For the latter they would maintain a police constabulary or local police force. If they cannot handle it, as is now the case in much of Africa and Haiti, WPA nations would contribute troops to control matters. The WPA must assure to individuals the right to work and to live in safety and without fear. Nations which do not wish to join the WPA need not do so and should be left alone, but only if it can be proven that they have no military means or weapons that can threaten neighbors. The emphasis needs to be on cooperation for the benefit of all humans on our planet.

I am asking what would be impossible to consider in normal times that the sovereign right of each nation to build a military force to the extent of its choosing be relinquished. This is like the authority of the father to take away dangerous items from very young children. But we are living in a time when any lunatic dictator or extremist group can get hold of weapons that can push the button for UNIVERSAL extinction. We either give up this former right of each nation or we will continue allowing wild children – juvenal delinquents, if you will – to play with matches in a paper factory or in a gunpowder factory!

Unlike the United Nations, the WPA will be made up of like minded nations ready to take military action, if all else fails, against any renegade state that refuses to allow inspections of military forces of any kind that can be used to attack neighbors. Any civilized individual is against the horrors of war. But sometimes it is necessary to use military might to tamp down the fires of war. We saw this in the remnants of the former Yugoslavia as mentioned above. Thankfully, with outside pressure brought to bear, we no longer see the mass killings of neighbors against neighbors.

Upon the creation of the WPA, there would be no need for national armies. Yes, I know. Some may not want to give them up entirely. Fine, but the WPA must find a way to create a united force to assure world peace – all WPA nations contributing forces. Only the WPA should be allowed to have major weapons of offense. Would there be a language problem? No problem! There is now or soon we will be able to devise a small instant language translator about the size of a cell phone that will deliver commands in the language of the recipient, no matter what language may be coming out of Central Command! I am about 99.99% sure such devices already exist. If not, I will work on it after I finish my sky diving lessons!

I am troubled by the belligerent actions of the U.S.A., Russia and China by increasing military power and by making foolish moves such as our country did by placing missiles in counties bordering Russia. It can reasonably be argued that the build-up of forces in Russia and China are due to the irresponsible and foolish actions of my country, the U.S.A. We should admit our error and join with all countries to empower the WPA to protect all peace loving countries. We all need to work together for world peace. Together we can do it.

The West must not allow itself to go the way of Rome! As long as Rome maintained unity and used masses of troops to control the provinces, there was peace – called Pax Romana. It lasted for about 200 years, from 27 BC to 180 AD. Rome was destroyed because of divisiveness within the country, greed and the push for personal power and aggrandizement of individuals who gained too much power. (I hope the Democrats and the extremely wealthy are reading this.) After the fall of Rome, the Dark Ages descended upon the world – ignorance and chaos prevailed. If the West falls, this will be a repeat performance and a bloody mess as we saw in Europe for centuries!

In effect, I am saying that our present world of various nations, religions and tribes need a father figure to hold us together as one family with compassion and concern for the well-being of all. This father figure is, of course, the WPA.

I am by no means suggesting that the United States should be the next Rome to bring peace to the world. This should be the function of the WPA. Our country is now being besieged by divisiveness provided mostly by the left leaning liberal lunatic majority in the Democratic Party. Excessive power falling into the hands of the few is due to the Republican Party put into and kept in power by huge corporations and those with too much wealth with which they feel no shame in buying politicians. These parties need to vanish and be replaced with the Compassionate Conservative Party for transitional purposes. This will be explained in CHAPTER 12. You have my permission to dash ahead to read it now if you wish. No charge, you lucky chaps!

Why do I suggest replacing the UN with the WPA? Just consider how useless the UN has been in Somalia, Sudan and Iraq for just a few examples.

Below are some indications of how radical Muslims have caused conflicts and how ineffective the UN has been with so many Muslim and Arab countries having governments headed by dictators and thugs on the U.N.'s "Board of Directors." Never forget that these Muslim leaders, who are running the show, have made it very clear that their intent is world domination. Learn that the Koran is the Muslim equivalent of Hitler's Mein Kampf. According to the Koran, our destiny is determined by Allah! Either convert or feel the sword and fires of hell for eternity! Well, thanks for the choice, guys!

The Christian and Jewish Bibles also contain hateful ideas and calls for unacceptable behavior such as killing all men, women and children in a village being attacked, acceptance and regulation of slavery and the stoning to death for a number of crimes that no civilized people would consider acceptable today. Decent and sensible Muslims and Christians pay no attention to such insanity. The problem the world has today is that the lunatic fringe in the Muslim world - the religious extremists - have run away with the religion of Islam to satisfy their lust for power.

OBVIOUS FAILURES OF THE
UNITED NATIONS (UNITED?)

U.N. Chief Urges End to Somalia Fighting
Published: 4/20/07, 8:05 PM EDT By EDITH M. LEDERER
UNITED NATIONS (AP) - Secretary-General Ban Ki-moon called Friday for an immediate end to fighting in Somalia and talks between rival clans.

(What did he mean by "immediate? The fighting and instability have been going on for over seventeen years during which time it is anybody's guess as to how many have been killed or had to leave the country. Three days of fighting this week between Islamic insurgents and Ethiopian troops have killed at least 113 civilians, a Somali human rights group said recently. jk)

...Somalia has not had a functioning government since clan-based war lords toppled dictator Mohamed Siad Barre in 1991 and then turned on each other, sinking the poverty-stricken Horn of Africa nation of seven million into chaos. The rout in December of the Islamic fundamentalist movement that controlled most of Somalia by Somali government troops and Ethiopian soldiers allowed the country's weak U.N.-backed transitional government to enter the capital, Mogadishu, for the first time since it was established in 2004.

AND NOW THERE IS AND HAS BEEN SUDAN!

The Muslim murder machine in the Sudan is revealed in Chapter 2. Number of people, including some Muslims, killed by Muslims in Sudan between 1955 and today: 2.6 million - 3 million. SOURCE: *Email chayyeisarah at yahoo dot com.* MONDAY, SEPTEMBER 25, 2006 (SEE NOTE: 19)

And from the VOICE OF THE MARTYRS ... about two million Christians have been slaughtered or made refugees for simply being Christians. Well, on second thought, why make you run all the way to Chapter 2? To save your energy, I will quote some from "THE VOICE OF THE MARTYRS," a Christian evangelizing organization working in Africa to bring more Africans to understand and accept Jesus as Savior. In spite of me being against such proselytizing, I include mention of this organization because they are doing a great deal of good for those suffering people. I would rather they be doing it out of the goodness of their hearts rather than for the spreading of their religion, but if good is being done, I am on their team. See Note 5 to know how to get in touch with the organization mentioned above.

SOME DETAILS ON HOW PEACEFUL (?) MUSLIMS HAVE BEEN

Number of Muslims killed by the Soviets in Afghanistan in the 1980's: at least 1 million (There had been an attempt to create a Taliban type Muslim state.)

Number of Muslims killed by other Muslims in the Afghan civil war of the 1980's-90: 1 million

Number of Muslims killed by the Americans in efforts to overthrow the Taliban: less than 10,000.

Number of Muslims killed by other Muslims since 1977 in Somalia's civil war: Between 400,000- 550,000.

Number of Muslims in Bangladesh killed by other Muslims from Pakistan since 1977: 1.4 million-2 million

Number of Muslims killed by other Muslims in Indonesia since 1965: at least 400,000.

Number of Muslims in East Timor killed between 1975-1999 by Muslims from Indonesia: 100,000 - 200,000

Number of Muslims killed in Iraq by other Muslims (mostly those in the regime of Saddam Hussein): 1.54 million- 2 million

Number of Iranian Muslims killed in their war with Iraq: 450,000 - 970,000

With all these killings going on for so long, is it not evident that a lid is needed in the form of a WPA? The WPA (The World Peace Association) may not be able to stop all of this mutual murder, but it should be able to stop it from spreading and keep it within limits.

If we establish the WPA, just think that with so many countries not needing to pay for armies, think of the billions that could be used for the good of mankind – very likely trillions! Major Powers or those with democratic governments such as, but by no means not exclusively, China, Russia, Israel, France, the USA, The United Kingdom, South Korea would all be part of the WPA if in compliance with basic principles and would have nothing to fear from one another; thus they would have no need for having massive military forces. Such power would remain only with the WPA whose forces and might would be controlled by all those free nations. True, a few of the countries just mentioned may not now be run by fully-fledged, free, democratic regimes, but the creation of the WPA may encourage them to become so; especially of my country, the U.S.A. has the good sense to admit to its faults. All nations may, in time, realize the advantages of cooperation.

I know there is growing tension between the U.S.A. and Russia. There are real reasons for this which we need not go into because this can be ended with the establishment of the WPA. Both countries, along with other members, will be working together to maintain world peace or to bring it about. It is time for us to think of the future, not dwell on suspicions of the past. Russia and China have legitimate fears. We need to work with them to assure world peace.

A major motive behind war is money! All companies in the business of making instruments of war must agree to share their profits with the WPA after receiving a proper return just as in the case of electric utilities which serve the public interest. Naturally, sales should be made only to the WPA. I have come to this conclusion because it is obvious that we have a military-industrial complex and Russia, Israel, China, North Korea, including our own country and others no doubt, sell arms as a major way of bolstering their economies. How much better it would be to spend that money on building decent housing for the poor, curing disease and on research to make life better for all human beings?

All private companies making whatever is needed for the WPA military forces must allow the WPA to inspect their books and facilities to make sure all rules are followed and that they are not padding the books. These same companies or new ones would only be able to sell to the WPA. Sales to any state outside the WPA would be a crime against humanity and anyone involved would face life imprisonment, the closing down of the business and whatever the WPA deems necessary to discourage any others from trying this again.

The WPA needs to make it quite clear that no country will be allowed to threaten another with military force or to have any weapons of mass destruction. All nations must allow uninvited, unannounced inspections to see that there is no intent to do harm to another country. There is no need for any country to have an army because the WPA would act as the world police force – the burden will no longer fall upon one country or just a few. We need to do this quickly because now Saudi Arabia is about to buy nuclear weapons from North Korea and Pakistan. Saudi Arabia has already threatened that if Iraq breaks up and the Sunnis become endangered, they will be there to defend them. This is sure to ignite a war throughout the Middle East between the Sunnis and the Shiites. Too many Muslims do not care how many human beings they kill because, for them (the killers) being killed themselves is their ticket to heaven and to be forever entertained by virgins. This is what is taught in the Koran, the book on which a Democrat of Minnesota, Keith Ellison, insisted on using to be sworn in as the first Muslim member of our US Congress. (Bless his soul because he is so religious! jk)

For many obvious reasons, Saudi Arabia – as presently constituted - cannot belong to the WPA as long as they do not allow the freedoms listed above and if they continue to threaten to go to war. They will have every right to live as they wish, to live in the sixth or seventh century with their laws against women and whatever else keeps them living in the past rather than cooperate with more modern states to build a productive, more humane and prosperous future for the people of their country. If citizens of Saudi Arabia or any other suppressed country do not wish to stay in the past and prefer to be free of the dictators - religious or secular - controlling their lives, the citizens of these suppressed states may use peaceful demonstrations and methods of petition to bring about a change in their government with the help of the WPA, but only if that help is requested. If these petitioners or demonstrators are attacked by their governments, the WPA would have the right to step in to protect those citizens. We are all citizens of the world – human beings. We must not allow any state to attack its own citizens.

All nations, whether they belong to the WPA or not, must not be allowed to have standing armies or nuclear weapons since these can be construed as a threat to neighbors. The WPA would need to deal quickly with such defiance as is now shown by Iran. Once the WPA shows that it means business, I am confident that other countries with nuclear capabilities can be trusted to do no harm. I am thinking particularly of Pakistan, India, Russia, China and Israel which must agree not to attack neighbors. I am confident that these nations understand that peace is better than endless wars. And do not forget Libya; under the right pressure, they were sensible enough and good enough to give up their plans for having nuclear capabilities. The world should show respect and honor to that Muslim country for leading the way and helping the world toward peace. I hope we are doing things that can help that country advance economically and socially. Why didn't I think of all these brilliant ideas centuries ago! Oh well, I am a little retarded!

A SURE FIRE WAY TO HAVE
WORLD PEACE AND TO MAINTAIN IT

The first step is to stop draping ourselves, stomach down, over a barrel of oil with you know what part of the anatomy up in the air. There is now a company * that just brought out an electric car which would be perfect for people who typically drive short distances. One might call it a town car since it has to be recharged every 100 to 150 miles. They now have a car that is reasonably priced if it did not have the recharging problem. I would guess that there are a number of individuals who stay within the limit of 100 to 150 miles in a day. If the government were to subsidize the purchase of these cars for a given amount of time I believe the price could be low enough for them to sell like hot cakes. The company would be able to accumulate funds to further improve the battery system so that it would be able to go greater distances without recharging. It could thus be useful to more and more people. Besides I am in the process of getting them to try a process that may make it possible for the car to never have to stop for a recharge. I believe it possible, but I really do not know for sure…yet. Since we no doubt spent quit a bit of our money to go to the moon, a subsidy to remove us from being draped over the barrel would be well worth it. We have been pouring money into the treasuries of nations that want to destroy western culture and nations every time we use oil. The longer we refrain from switching to alternative energy, the more money the Muslim oil barons get to destroy us and the higher our debt level and trade deficit go! How different the world would be if we cut demand to a point at which domestic sources would suffice for our own needs!

Step two, is to convince Venezuela and Canada to supply a large part of our oil needs while offering Saudi Arabia $10 (ten dollars) a barrel so that they will not suddenly become paupers. After all, they are our friends, so it is said. It would be $10.00 or no deal. Eureka, this may be the answer! I strongly suspect that this can never be done unless we get away from our present two party system and replace it as described in CHAPTER 13. We should no longer allow ourselves to be hostage to oil interests. If this idea takes off, I will discuss the matter with the company leading in this field and convince them to accept making a few million dollars while protecting the country. By the way, they recently started producing a vehicle for the military that does not use gas. Worry not. If this book is ever published, we will be saved! Or as is said in German "Ve vill be zaved!"

During World War I we sold WAR BONDS, during World War II we sold DEFENSE BONDS; we now should be selling FREEDOM BONDS so that we can stop depending upon foreign governments, often not our friends, to bail us out. We need to keep the debt within the family. Are the left leaning liberal lunatics holding back our elected officials? I know of no one who has made this suggestion. Once we lose our freedom, it will be difficult if not impossible to get it back. Where have our overpaid leaders been? I don't know if I should tell you – they have been busy fighting each other rather than paying attention to what is best for the country.

*I am presently working on getting permission from the company to mention its name.

CHAPTER 4

ISRAELI/PALESTINIAN CONUNDRUM

The attempt by Muslims to kill off Jews is nothing new. "…On December 30, 1066, Joseph Hanagid, the Jewish vizier of Granada, Spain, was crucified by an Arab mob that proceeded to raze the Jewish quarter of the city and slaughter its 5000 inhabitants. The riot was incited by Muslim preachers who had angrily objected to what they saw as inordinate Jewish power. This pogrom was a precursor to incitements by the Muslim clerics of our day for their followers to kill Americans and Jews everywhere. This is Muslim racism, apartheid and genocide.

":...In the 8the century, mass murders of Jews in Arab lands occurred in Morocco, where whole communities were wiped out by Muslim ruler Idris I; in North Africa in the 12th century, where the Almohads either forcibly converted or decimated several communities; in Libya in 1785, where Ali Burzi Pasha murdered hundreds of Jews; in Algiers, where more than 300 Jews were murdered between 1864 and 1880.

"…Decrees ordering the destruction of synagogues were enacted in Egypt and Syria (1014, 1293-4, 1301-2), Iraq (1344) and Yemen (1676). …Jews were forced to convert to Islam or face death in Yemen (1165 and 1678), Morocco (1275, 1465 and 1790-92) and Baghdad (1333 and 1344)."

SOURCE: World Against Bias, 9/4/01 (I urge my readers to read their literature for a full understanding of what the civilized world is facing.)

Do the above events remind you of the 20th century where Jewish communities were slaughtered in Hebron in 1929; where Christians are arrested, falsely charged, and executed on a daily basis; where Hindus are murdered en masse; where Buddhist, Hindu, and Jewish Holy sites are plundered and destroyed by Muslims? Today is just a continuation of this Muslim history. Jews returning to Palestine since the late 1800's have been under attack from Arabs. That is long before a homeland for the Jewish state ever existed, as called for by the League of Nations and the Balfour Declaration. This idea was agreed to by the Arab King Faisal, but the world has forgotten. (jk)

FACTS THE UN AND ITS MUSLIM ALLIES WANT YOU TO IGNORE

In 2000, Israeli Prime Minister Ehud Barak went to Camp David and offered Yasser Arafat 95% of the West Bank, 100% of Gaza and part of the Old City of Jerusalem for a Palestinian State, along with $30 billion in compensation for Palestinian refugees. Arafat's response: launching the bloody Intifada which targeted innocent civilians in restaurants, malls, schools, and religious services with suicide terror attacks. Had Arafat accepted Israel's offer at Camp David there would have long been a Palestinian State alongside Israel.

"...According to Islam, any agreement made between a Muslim and an Infidel (non-Muslim) need not, and should not, be honored. Does this speak volumes on why Oslo failed? (Yet our president, George Bush, wants to force Israel into a "peace" agreement with the Palestinians. jk)

"...Today, Sudan's Islamic government continues to enslave women and children from Christian tribes...

"…Hindus and Muslims fight for the Kashmir. Thousands of Hindus are executed…

"…After NATO gave them the province, Albanians in Kosovo cleansed 80% of the Serb population and destroyed over 100 Orthodox churches…

"…In Indonesia, the Laskar Jihad (which includes veterans of Bosnia and Afghanistan) attacked Christian villages in September 2000. In two provinces, over 5,000 have died, and over 250,000 have been driven from their homes since January 1999…"

(But George W. Bush says the Muslim religion is one of peace! Does he really expect a Palestinian state to live in peace next to Israel? jk)

SOURCE: World Against Bias, 9/4/01 (I urge my readers to read their literature for a full understanding of what the civilized world is facing.)

* * * * * * * * * *

The Pew Research Center, a nonpartisan "fact tank," released a report that was one of the most exhaustive ever on Muslims living in America. It found that 25 percent of the under 30 group said they thought suicide bombing could be justified – under the right circumstances. U.S. officials have issued repeated warnings about "home-grown terrorists" mounting attacks in America much like those that occur with great frequency in Israel, and of late, in London. In a Pew Research Center report issued last year, Muslims in other countries were even more likely to support suicide bombing as a means to an end. In Muslim countries, that support is more than 50 percent; in France 33 percent; and the figures in Britain and Spain mirrored those in the U.S., 25 percent.

Palestinian woman blows herself up near a group of Israeli soldiers in North Gazan Beit Hanoun
November 6, 2006, 4:33 PM (GMT+02:00)
One soldier slightly hurt. The group saw the suicide killer approaching and opened fire. Another two Qassam missiles were fired

into Israel from the same Palestinian town bringing Monday's total to seven on the sixth day of IDF anti-missile operation in Beit Hanoun. Earlier, Israeli troops intercepted two Palestinians armed with anti-tank weapons.

My comment on above and so many others:
The way to end the daily onslaught of missiles aimed at Israeli citizens is to totally level Beit Hanoun so that other towns will know that if they are used as launching pads to kill Israelis they will cease to exist. This is not possible as long as Israel is forced to "cow tow" to the likes of former President George W. Bush or now succumb to Obama's pressures.

The Arabs could have had peace and their own state since 1948, but their goal is the whole pie even though the developed areas exist because the Jews built them up with their sweat, blood and money! Such a useless treaty would also be a flower in Condi Rice's cap. She keeps blindly pushing Israel to make more concessions as the Palestinians continue to ask for more and continue to promote and carry out terrorist attacks on innocent civilians in Israel. I wonder if anyone has bothered to ask the Bush/Rice (not so nice) team how Israel can make peace with the Palestinians now that Hamas, the most virulent terrorist organization which constantly reiterates their goal to totally destroy Israel, has most of the power since forcing the Palestinian Authority out of Gaza at the point of the gun? I fear that Israel cannot expect much help from any quarter. Oil is the problem. For this reason the West has been pandering to and quivering at the feet of Arab potentates for decades. This is why they were able to get away with stealing of the Suez Canal – our President Eisenhower stopped England, France and Israel from taking it back. (See NOTE 13) For the same reason Israel has been forced to withdraw, retreat, agree to cease fire arrangements every time they were on the path to stopping their incessant attacks on Israel. The tying of the hands of Israel by the Rice/Bush duo has acted as a vaccination against any possibility of peace. Vaccination is the act of injecting a small amount of a virus so that the body can build defenses against a major attack. Israel has been under attack, certainly since 1948 and even before that time, but every time Israel has its enemies on the run, we tell them to pull back. This is the vaccination that has enabled the enemies of Israel and of the West to rebuild their forces and develop greater strength for their next attack. The forcing of Israel to have restraint and avoid killing innocent civilians is hypocritical in face of the facts that we, the United States and its allies, pulverized most German cities with no regard to the innocent civilians left in the rubble. Did we exercise restraint or did we use excessive force when we vaporized not one, but two Japanese cities in order to bring about peace. I am not making a judgment here. Wherever possible, it is best to avoid violence. But once attacked and thrown into conflict, the best way to end it is with maximum and overwhelming force to end the bloodshed. War is hell; it is best to end it quickly with all necessary force. To do otherwise is irresponsible. That's right George!

WHAT WAS BEHIND ISRAEL'S PULL OUT FROM GAZA?

Portions taken from President Bush's letter to Prime Minister Sharon, dated April 14, 2004.

Dear Mr. Prime Minister:

Thank you for your letter setting out your disengagement plan. ... We welcome the disengagement plan you have prepared, under which Israel would withdraw certain military installations and all settlements from Gaza, and withdraw certain military installations and settlements in the West Bank. These steps described in the plan will mark real progress toward realizing my June 24, 2002 vision, and make a real contribution towards peace…. The United States appreciates the risks such an undertaking represents... Under the roadmap, Palestinians must undertake an immediate cessation of armed activity and all acts of violence against Israelis anywhere, and all official Palestinian institutions must end incitement against Israel. The Palestinian leadership must act decisively against terror, including sustained, targeted, and effective operations to stop terrorism and dismantle terrorist capabilities and infrastructure. Palestinians must undertake a comprehensive and fundamental political reform that includes a strong parliamentary democracy and an empowered prime minister.

* * * * * * * * *

The Palestinians have done nothing to implement the above yet Israel is continually urged to give into more Arab demands.   (jk)

To begin with, Prime Minister Ariel Sharon, in my opinion, did not take this suicidal step on his own volition; he did so to remain in the good graces of our President, George W. Bush, to get his vision of June 24, 2002 for his roadmap to peace pipe dream moving forward. This can only be a roadmap to annihilation for Israel if it is allowed to progress. To have peace, both sides must want it. Since 1948 and through the centuries before, Arabs and/or the so-called Palestinians of today have shown no indication of wanting peace. It seems that Israel is never allowed to have a definitive win. Once again, it is being tricked into pulling back just at the point at which they could really defeat those who want them dead. Israel launched this present effort at self defense on Dec. 27 to try to halt near-daily Hamas rocket attacks against southern Israel that had persisted for some eight years. Its key demand is for guarantees that Hamas halt the smuggling of rockets, explosives and other weapons through the porous Egyptian border. Not even our country can control our own borders; so how can anyone believe we, the EU, the UN or the Man in the Moon can control the borders between Gaza and Egypt and Lebanon and Israel. Now the dirty deed has been done. Israel has relented under the pressure from "Uncle Sam," the Bush/Rice team of dreamers or deceivers. France, Britain, Germany and the United States have all offered help in stopping the flow of weapons, but Egyptian President Hosni Mubarak has firmly rejected any deployment of international monitoring forces on its side of the Gaza border. That leaves a Swiss cheese opening through the tunnels from Egypt under the border and into Gaza through which they have continually allowed arms and money to flow to Hamas, a group sworn to kill ever Jew and destroy Israel. It is obvious that Condoleezza Rice and Bush have pressured Israel into accepting this impossible situation.

President Hosni Mubarak, the "moderate type Arab," stated unequivocally that no foreign troops would be allowed on Egyptian soil. All this is in complete contradiction to statements of the US Secretary of Foreign Affairs Condoleezza Rice. All through negotiations toward a ceasefire her statements were held to be true.

Israel has now accepted the ceasefire. Their Defense Minister Ehud Barak indicated they expect to achieve their goals and secure them through diplomatic agreements. He spoke during a trip to southern Israel, which has been the target of Hamas rocket fire for several years. The world had been led to believe that Egypt would shut down weapons smuggling routes with international help. This is a farce, a deception and a tragedy for the USA and for Israel. This help from the UN, "international help" and/or Egypt have been tried several times in the past. Either this "safeguard," these protectors, were warned by the Arabs to get out of the way or the rules and promises were totally ignored with the world standing by leaving Israel wide open to attack. Does no one remember that this same situation happened when Israel was forced to stop defending itself with regard to Lebanon? Does no one know that the Koran clearly states that no agreement made with infidels (non-Muslims) need ever be kept? Truces are just negotiated to build up their killing machines. The dream or lie that Egypt would protect Israel's border is akin to getting the wolf to protect the sheep. Instead, the wolf typically gathers together a larger and stronger pack of wolves to finish off the sheep! To add insult to injury, before Israel gave in to the deception, the Egyptian foreign minister declared that Israel is the main obstacle to a ceasefire. He surely knows that if Hamas were to simply stop firing missiles and rockets into Israel, there would be a ceasefire. This duplicity and blaming the other guy is typical of Arabs who would rather kill for Allah than live in peace. If the West keeps up its dangerous thinking, we may never live long enough to learn! The only real guarantee of safety for Israel is to allow them to smash Hamas completely. The same must apply to all terrorists who seek to impose their seventh century mentality on the rest of the world.

THE MYTH OF ARAB MODERATES

Mahmoud a-Zahar of Hamas, former Palestinian foreign minister, says even if Israel withdraws from 90% of "occupied territory", there will be no settlement

March 31, 2007, 12:57 PM (GMT+02:00)

Islam provides the only solution to the conflict and until it is achieved, armed resistance will continue. Engagement (negotiation) with Israel is a means not an end. There can be no compromise on the refugee question. The PLO, the Hamas leader declared, has no authority to represent the Palestinian people.

Arab summit ending in Riyadh **strengthens radical** Iran **and** Syria **and recognizes Palestinian Hamas**
March 29, 2007, 5:59 PM (GMT+02:00)

The conference ending Thursday, March 29, ended the isolation of the two Middle East governments backing anti-US fighting elements in Iraq, fomenting Hizballah's war effort against Israel and aiding Palestinian terror.

The Arab front, portrayed by American and Israeli policy-makers as an effective "moderate" barrier against Iranian expansionism and nuclear aspirations, jumped aboard the radical bandwagon.
SOURCE: Recent headlines from the DEBKA file

Do the above not prove that we are up against the entire Arab world?

So much for the fiction of "Moderate Arabs," the mental aberration of Bush and Rice (but not anything nice)! Does anyone not get it? To quote from above, "Islam provides the only solution to the conflict…" and "Engagement with Israel is a means not an end…" Through the centuries, the Islamic solution (their sought after "end") has been to kill all those who do not agree with them! And let me repeat a standard age-old Islamic formula:

"…According to Islam, any agreement made between a Muslim and an Infidel (non-Muslim) need not, and should not, be honored.
SOURCE: World Against Bias, 9/4/01

My advice to our former President was: George, get your head out of the clouds and come back to planet earth. Never mind smelling the roses, smell the skunk! Wake up! We are in a protracted war with age old Islam, the one that spread around the world at the end of a sword!

Tragically, most leaders of the West also do not want to admit reality. This advice needs to be heeded by all of them. We cannot wait for the "moderate" Arabs to save us; they are scared out of their robes! It is only overwhelming military might that can save the West and unity on the part of Western powers that want to remain free. I regret to have to express the belief that a strictly voluntary military force will not be enough --- unless most Americans come to the painful realization that we are faced with a life or death situation. Either we give in to buying a Persian prayer rug and are happy bending our knees toward Mecca or we do what we know we must to stay free. Hopefully, there will be enough volunteers so that a draft will not be needed, but our only chance for survival is massive mobilization, one way or another, such as we have never had before. Once this is seen, we may never have to use force. A roaring tiger with bared teeth is seldom attacked!

The costs of our present mismanaged efforts in Iraq have already run into the trillions of dollars and well over 4,150 dead, 30,182 wounded as of January 2009, but what would these figures be if we were to lose our freedom to megalomaniac religious lunatics?

LEBANON STORY

According to most of the western media, Israel was carrying out air strikes with disproportionate force that exacerbated civilian casualties. Opposition leader Binyamin Netanyahu spoke about this in the Knesset, saluted the army "in the name of all the MKs" - but then was forced to correct himself and say "in the name of almost all the MKs" when Arab MKs interrupted him with sharp words against the IDF.

Netanyahu said that Hezbollah represents a "strategic threat" which must be met with "a strategic victory." He called upon the government not to give up, not to stop in the middle of attaining its goals, and not to cede its objective of dismantling Hezbollah. When he spoke about Lebanon, he said: "They seem to have the Christians under control, for the time being, after a very bloody civil war that went on for several years. To make matters worse, Lebanon allows Hezbollah to do anything it wishes even in violation of UN resolutions designed to prevent a further breakout of war. Nobody, but nobody, is trying to stop them from violating any and every provision of the cease fire forced upon Israel. The Arabs and/or Muslims in Egypt, Gaza, Lebanon and to some degree in Jordan are allowed to prepare openly for the final solution to Israel: kill them all or drive them into the sea! In spite of UN resolutions and promises no one is stopping arms, bombs of all types, missiles, rockets or whatever is needed to bring about the final solution to the existence of Israel. The solution is their non-existence!" Nice world we live in!

The UN complicity in setting the stage for another deadly attack against Israel is well reported in the following excerpts from the DEBKAfile: **Hezbollah Shuts Reoccupied S. Lebanese Bases to Lebanese and UN forces**

DEBKA*file* Exclusive Military Report (Excerpts)

October 4, 2006, 2:05 PM (GMT+02:00)

On Yom Kippur, Oct. 2, 24 hours after the last Israeli soldier left South Lebanon and the day before UNIFIL published its rules of engagement, Hizballah placed roadblocks on all the approaches to the central sector of the South and the entrances to the towns and villages reoccupied by its forces and their rocket units.

These enclaves were declared "closed military zones."

DEBKA*file*'s exclusive military and Western intelligence sources report that neither the Lebanese army which moved south nor the international peacekeepers of UNIFIL venture to set foot in these enclaves. Nor did they raise a finger to block the first broad-daylight consignment of advanced Iranian weapons to be delivered in Lebanon via Syria since the August 14 ceasefire. (What ceasefire? Jk)

This coordinated Hizballah-Iranian-Syrian ploy has brought into question the point of UN Security Council Resolution 1701 which was to prevent the resumption of hostilities and Hizballah's rearmament while helping the Beirut government and army assert its sovereignty in the South. It has also made a mockery of the UN Force and its missions.

In other words, Hizballah has redeployed in the precise positions from which it blitzed Haifa, Nahariya, Carmiel, Acre and W. Galilee for more than a month. The UN commanders have stated explicitly they will only act with the permission of the Lebanese government and army (in which Hizballah holds the power of veto), there is no way that the international force can carry out its duties as mandated by the UN Security Council.

Lebanese police raid pro-Syrian group in N. Lebanese Koura province, make arrests and seize explosives, detonators and timers December 21, 2006, 3:10 PM (GMT+02:00)

Police have also encircled Beirut offices of the Syrian Social Nationalist Party in Beirut. **DEBKA*file*** reports that the SSNP, a Lebanese terrorist group linked to Syrian Military Intelligence, was one of the main recipients of fresh arms supplies entering Lebanon from Syria since the Hizballah-Israel war last summer and destined for pro-Syrian factions in Lebanon.

Interview with Harvard Law Professor Alan Dershowitz A7 Radio's "Walter's World" with Walter Bingham

Professor Dershowitz discusses the present fighting with Hizbullah, and explains the complicated role played by "civilians" who willingly harbour terrorists, provide material resources, and act as human shields. They are indistinguishable from the terrorists who are embedded among them. Under such circumstances, Israel is justified to occupy the war zones until Hizbullah is rendered impotent, says Dershowitz. Referring to the IAF bombing of Kana that killed 54 Lebanese adults and children, Netanyahu said, "I was interviewed yesterday by a British station and they asked me what I thought about Israeli pilots bombing children. I said, 'If you're asking, I'll tell you: This is as just a war as any that has ever been fought - but I can recall another just war, World War II, when Britain's Royal Air Force went to bomb the Gestapo headquarters in Copenhagen, but the bombers missed and hit a children's hospital nearby, killing 83 Danish children inside. This is a tragedy of war, but it happens. Unlike the other side, which rejoices when our children are killed, we are truly sorry when it happens, and we really and truly try to reduce casualties on the other side."

Here are my comments: Of course I regret the deaths and destruction heaped upon Lebanon by Israel in its legitimate effort to defend its own citizens. Considering the fact that the Lebanese people voted to allow Hamas into the Lebanese government, knowing that their oft stated goal was to totally destroy Israel, did they not cause this themselves? jk

Most Islamic countries, regrettably, have sworn to destroy Israel. The countries of the Free World must understand that if the people of Israel can live in peace in their Promised Land, peace will have a chance to reign in the whole world. If radical Islam succeeds in destroying Israel, there will never be peace, and Western civilization will have to start to buy prayer rugs to use five times a day – if they want to go on living, that is! (jk)

DEBKAfile Special Military Analysis

November 16, 2006, 1:58 PM (GMT+02:00)

Question No. 1: Did Israel counteract Egypt's permission to let Hamas' $4million cash infusion from Iran and Saudi through to the Gaza Strip on Thursday, Nov. 16? The answer is no, even though Israeli intelligence knows about Hamas' regularly smuggled moneys and their destination - not hospitals, schools or food, but guns, troops and, yes, missiles.

Has Israel called Egypt to account for failing to stop the extremist Palestinian groups smuggling of arms and cash past its border guards? No, again. One way would be to move Israeli forces one kilometer deep into the Philadelphi border route for every $100,000 reaching the Hamas war chest. After all, Egypt contracted to seal its border against terrorist traffic under an international accord brokered by the US secretary of state. But Prime Minister Ehud Olmert prefers to let Cairo off the hook. Thursday, Nov. 15, the day after a deadly Palestinian missile attack on Sderot, he again praised "Egypt's role in blocking smuggling to Gaza." (I would like to ask "What is he smoking?, but I will not.)

Have the seven Israeli cabinet ministers used their presence in Los Angeles for an intensive information campaign to expose to the American public the role the Europeans and Egyptians are playing in the availability of funds for Hamas hands, despite the freeze imposed by the Middle East Quartet? No again, although, like the Egyptians, the European monitors posted at the Rafah border crossing are instructed by their governments to turn a blind eye – not just to the suitcases stashed with dollars, but also to the Iranian and Syrian military instructors, the Hizballah agents and the al Qaeda operatives who make free of the Rafah crossing in and out of Sinai.

These entrants include bomb-makers and missile experts assigned to improving the precision, explosive power and range of the missiles fired day by day at Gaza's Israeli neighbors - Sderot and Ashkelon. Wednesday, a missile came close enough to the residence of Israeli defense minister Amir Peretz to seriously wound a sentinel as well as killing a mother of two and injuring five other civilians. The day before the lethal barrage, Shin Bet director Yuval Diskin issued a wake-up call. He used a single graphic word to describe the Gaza situation: "Red, red, red!" in the hope of driving the urgency of an effective military operation to cut down the burgeoning Palestinian threat into the heads of national policy-makers before it was too late. Diskin reported that 30 tons of explosives, arms and ammunition, enough to equip 10 brigades, have been smuggled into the Gaza Strip, and more is on the way. Hamas therefore commands an armed force which is one brigade larger than the 9 brigades available to the Galilee Division commander Brigadier Gal Hirsch as the backbone of the Israeli army fighting in the Lebanon War.

DEBKA*file*'s military experts assert that Israel made no serious effort to keep the 30 tons of war materiel out of Gaza. Preventing the smuggled explosives from reaching the terrorist organizations' missile workshops would have been a crucial step towards diminishing the missile threat against southwestern Israel.

Because Egypt is clearly a non-factor in this effort, **DEBKA*file*'s** experts offer a number of practical alternatives:

1. General measures:

Israel must stop fooling itself about Palestinian intentions.

Israeli spokesmen and pundits have been tracing blow by blow the bumpy progress of the Palestinian talks on a unity government, which foreign minister Tzipi Livni went so far as to proclaim in Los Angeles a step towards moderating Hamas' fundamental radicalism.

She evidently missed the Hamas spokesman's statement that a new Palestinian unity government will neither recognize Israel nor accept a two-state solution.

In any case, the entire unity government exercise is a fraud.

The unknown microbiologist Dr. Mohammed Shabir was practically anointed by the media the next Palestinian prime minister, before his candidacy was knocked over by none other than PA chairman, Mahmoud Abbas, the live wire in the Palestinian unity government initiative. Informed Palestinians sources privately agree that a Hamas-Fatah coalition, though effectively flogged by the media as a device to unfreeze blocked Palestinian funds, is pie in the sky, like the purported Cairo-brokered talks for the release of the Israeli soldier Gideon Shalit who Hamas kidnapped last June.

They confirm that behind the hype, the rival Hamas and Fatah factions are nowhere near accord on basics.

With their minds clouded by illusions, false hopes and enemy propaganda, Israel's policy-makers are hardly competent to get down to brass tacks on ways to halt the Palestinian missile offensive. They find it easier to say there is no solution - and leave it at that.

The only realistic note, aside from the Shin Bet director's alert, was sounded by the newly-appointed deputy defense minister Dr. Ephraim Sneh. He was the first senior Laborite to admit that Israel erred in pulling out of the Gaza Strip in 2005 without leaving behind a stable, responsible Palestinian government. But Olmert, in the opposite vein, promised US President George W. Bush at the White House Monday, Nov. 13, that Israel would let 1,500 Palestinian members of the Jordanian Badr Brigade enter Gaza to bolster Abbas against Hamas.

Does Gaza need another 1,500 armed Palestinian fighting-men? Will they stop the Qassam missiles exploding on the Israeli side of the border? Or more likely be assimilated by Hamas and the Popular Committees and tempted to join the missile crews by wads of smuggled Iranian petrodollars?

Jordan will be glad to get rid of any armed Palestinians - even if they end up with Hamas.

2. Military options:

DEBKA*file*'s military experts say there is no need to reoccupy the entire Gaza Strip or Beit Hanoun, or use artillery to bombard civilian locations.

There are military options that could get around the Egyptian border police, who are useless for stemming the flow of arms and funds, and Israel's reluctance to reestablish a military presence for sealing the Philadelphi route to smugglers.

One is the deployment of small commando units across the Egyptian border in northern Sinai. These units would pre-empt the smuggling by attacking the convoys of weapons and funds and blowing them up before they reach the Gaza border.

Our military experts are certain that Israeli intelligence agencies are fully apprised of the smugglers' movements. Their hands are tied by Prime Minister Olmert's instruction to do nothing except tip off the Egyptians and the Europeans, who then sit on their hands. Briefing the two foreign teams is not only pointless but counter-productive, because the Palestinian smugglers are then forewarned. This procedure needs to be stopped and Israeli commandos sent for direct action against the illicit convoys.

The same tactic is applicable to the Gaza Strip.

Swarms of Israeli commando units should fill the areas from which the Qassam missiles are fired, including orchards. Ambushes at every corner will deter the missile crews and make them afraid of being liquidated on their way to launchings. This tactic was tried only once before in a location outside Beit Lahiya, next door to Beit Hanoun. It caused heavy casualties among the Palestinian gunmen and the Qassam teams gave this location a wide berth for some time.

It is evident that large-scale, complex Israeli operations like Autumn Clouds against Beit Hanoun earlier this month is costly in life while offering no recipe for curbing the missile attacks. But it is incumbent on the IDF to grasp the initiative at this stage of the war on terror and strike hard at the Palestinians' fighting spirit. Since the Lebanon war, Palestinian terrorists have persuaded themselves that they are capable of continuing Hizballah's successful war against Israel from Gaza. If this confidence is not shattered now, Palestinian missile attacks will continue to proliferate, gain in explosive force and spread to more Israeli cities. The most effective counter-terror tactic cannot mend in a single day the damage caused by Israel's unilateral pullback from Gaza, but a beginning must be made without delay.

Egypt's 5,000-Strong Sinai Increment – Now You See It, Now You Don't

DEBKA*file* Exclusive Military Report

October 30, 2006, 10:21 PM (GMT+02:00)

During the weeks of Israel's military operations to uncover Palestinian arms smuggling tunnels from Sinai into Gaza, Washington quietly sent over a military delegation of counter-terror experts to take a look at the situation on the Egyptian-Gaza and Egyptian-Israeli borders. Their first task was to find out how vast quantities of smuggled Palestinian weapons and explosives, including anti-tank and anti-air missiles, were being slipped unnoticed into the Gaza Strip through tunnels burrowed under the feet of Egyptian border and security police.

The American delegation reported back that the Egyptian officers and personnel on the spot were not exactly straining themselves to guard the border; in fact, some were taking hefty bribes from the Palestinian terrorist organizations to shut their eyes to the traffic. Acting on this report, the Bush administration turned to Cairo with a demand for US officers and counter-terror experts of the US-led MFO, the Multinational Forces and Observer force stationed in Sinai, to be attached to the Egyptian border units.

Hamas Chief promises war even if Palestinian Authority is established. The media paints Hamas as the "Bad Cop" and Fatah as the "Good Cop." My conclusion is that the goal of both is the ultimate annihilation of Israel. Both Fatah and Hamas demand the right of more than five million Arabs to immigrate to Israel as descendants of half a million Arabs who fled Israel in 1948. Might one think that this is excessive population growth? One major difference between the two groups is that Fatah is a secular party. The Arabic meaning of its name is "conquest," and the word "Fatah" is also a reverse acronym for the Arabic term for the Palestinian Liberation Movement whose purpose is to grab all of Palestine. Another apparent difference is that Abbas outwardly accepts a two-state solution including Israel. But in practice, PA schools under his authority teach children that all of Israel is "Palestine." To sum it all up, the difference between Hamas and Fatah is the difference between six and half a dozen! Tragically, the Western dreamers call Fatah the moderates! These Western dreamers, and there are also some peaceniks in Israel, come into the category I call left leaning liberal lunatics! Syria and Iran have been the jihadist traffic controllers in and out of Iraq, so you can be sure they will have seats of honor at the appeasement party. To give the terrorist cartel an invitation to the VIP summit to help with stability and democracy in Iraq is the theater of the absurd. Why should anyone be shocked at chaos? The US gave Syria one billion dollars for showing support at the first Persian Gulf War. You can be sure the prize will be much higher to slow down the tide of body bags in Iraq. Israel was never allowed to fight a war against terror with the P.A. Every time they tried, the US ran to the rescue of the billionaire Noble Peace Prize winner and godfather of World Terror, Yasser Arafat.

...It all began when Israel was forced out of Lebanon by US liberals.

Iran and its death cults are on a fast track to wipe the Little Satan (Israel) off the map with an atomic bomb. Robert Gates and President Obama want to talk with Iran and Syria. Why not let the 22,000-plus American families who have a wounded son or daughter talk with Iran, especially since 85 percent of all IEDs in Iraq are from Iran, according to former IDF Chief of Staff General Moshe Ya'alon? Why not let the

American families of the dead Marines killed in Lebanon in 1983, or the thousands of families who have a wounded or dead loved one in Israel? Why not talk to Syria since Syria has armed Hizbullah, Hamas and the PLO for decades, and is presently turning Lebanon into the killing fields? …Now the issue is: Will we fight a world war on terror in Iraq or Iran or fight in our back- yard? You can be sure if we run, they will be coming to a theater near you.

Following extracted from newspaper, 7/28/06. Of course this was three years ago, but in our Obamanation regime, our heads are still in the sand. Rice's peace plan seeks an international agreement on a U.N.-mandated multinational force that can provide stability in the region …also proposes disarming Hezbollah and integrating the guerrilla force into the Lebanese army…, a no-go buffer zone be set up in southern Lebanon, Hezbollah returning Israeli prisoners… (All of this turned out to be a farce. They all watched as Hezbollah and Hamas continued to pile up more weapons. No effort was ever made to stop them! Can you imagine if our county's safety depended upon the U.N! jk) The UN complicity in setting the stage for another deadly attack against Israel is well reported in the following excerpts from the DEBKAfile:

UN Secretary Kofi Annan demands that Israel **allow UN personnel to enter Gaza Strip for an assessment of the population situation July 9, 2006, 7:40 AM (GMT+02:00)**

The Secretary also wants Israel to pay for the damage caused to Palestinian homes and property, to reopen the Karni goods crossing to Gaza, and permit the passage of food and medicine convoys. UNWRA and the World Health Organization report the Gaza population is heading for a humanitarian disaster and women and children are paying the price of war.

I am quite sure I am right in declaring that the entire world is crazy. I just heard a confirmation of this on NPR on which there was an interview with a Palestinian who was complaining about the Israelis because they came into her town to find terrorists. They came roaring in with tanks and big guns just to find a few terrorists; and they did find them. Every statement made was to garner sympathy for the poor Palestinians who could not go about their normal lives because of these hateful Jews!

Nothing was said about the many hundred Israeli men, women and children who were blown to bits by Palestinian homicidal (suicide) bombers while on buses, in private cars, in cafes, night clubs, their own homes, at schools, at weddings, etc., etc., etc! Once dead, they also were not able to continue with their daily normal living! And what would anyone with a brain think Israelis should do after these poor Palestinians voted in Hamas to govern them, an organization that is dedicated and sworn to wipe Israel off the face of the earth? And their views seem to be stronger now that they have political power.

Israelis Arrest Hamas Leaders
Published: 5/24/07, 7:26 AM EDT
by ALI DARAGHMEH
NABLUS, West Bank (AP) - Israeli troops in the West Bank arrested more than 30 senior Hamas members early Thursday, including a Cabinet minister, legislators and mayors - pressing forward with an offensive against the Islamic militant group.

Defense Minister Amir Peretz said that in the fight to neutralize Hamas, arrests were preferable to bloodshed.

"Arrests are better than shooting," he told Israeli Army Radio. "The arrest of these Hamas leaders sends a message to the military organizations that we demand that this firing (of rockets) stop."

Palestinian President Mahmoud Abbas said the arrests were a blow to peace efforts, and a spokesman for Palestinian Prime Minister Ismail Haniyeh, of Hamas, called for the immediate release of the detainees and called on the U.N. and European Union to impose sanctions on Israel.

"These aggressive practices show the extent of the Israeli escalation and arrogance in the Palestinian territories, and also show how dismissive the Israeli government is of all customs and international laws," spokesman Ghazi Hamad said. (Does anyone even bother to ask Ghazi Hamad if constantly firing rockets toward civilians in a neighboring country is within international laws? jk)

The following is what too often happens when there are non-Jews responding to attacks: As has been done in the former Yugoslavia, when one group threatened another, they proceeded to slaughter each other without mercy and with no regard to whether they were combatants or civilians! This has often been the sequel in such cases throughout history. And what do these sly and devious Jews do? They try to find the guilty Palestinian murderers and spare the lives of others. Would these poor Palestinians prefer that the Israelis come in and wipe out the entire town or village?

Sectarian violence left 130 dead across Iraq amid fury over the Samarra shrine destruction.
February 23, 2006, 11:49 PM (GMT+02:00)
Earlier, Iraq canceled police, army leaves and extended curfew hours in Baghdad to quell the turmoil. Three Iraqi al Arabiya journalists were found dead near Samarra. Iraqi Shiites bent on retribution rampaged against Sunni Arabs up and down the country Wednesday, Feb. 22, after bombers destroyed the gold dome of the 1,200-year old Askariya shrine in Samarra. More than 100 Sunni mosques were destroyed.

Various countries and the UN have repeatedly criticized Israel for using excessive or disproportionate force in response to endless attacks and now they deplore the building of the fence to keep out suicide bombers. Israel's temporary security fence has been an effective deterrent in thwarting unending Palestinian suicide terror attacks which have dropped over 90% since its construction. Israel has said that the fence will come down when the Palestinian terror stops. Israel is entitled to protect her citizens from outside threats in the same way as with any sovereign country. Before one criticizes Israelis for defending themselves, just remember what our American ancestors did to the

Indians. They were chased off their lands, killed indiscriminately and those who still lived placed on reservations.

The cabinet decision Wednesday ordered the IDF to stick to attacking missile crews and refrain from breaching the month-long "ceasefire," in the course of which the Palestinians fired 70 missiles from Gaza at Israeli civilian locations. An Israeli appeal went out to the (non-functioning) Palestinian Authority to halt the six-year old barrage. Result: Sderot and its neighbors will continue to live under daily missile harassment. **Mahmoud Abbas declares three days mourning in Palestinian Authority after 7 Palestinian civilians killed, 2 of them children, dozens injured – possibly by stray Israeli artillery shell**

June 10, 2006, 12:29 AM (GMT+02:00)

In mid-counter offensive for ongoing Palestinian missile barrage from Gaza, the Israeli chief of staff halted artillery fire on missile sites in order to investigate the civilian deaths. (What other country would care? jk) Among them was a family of five. Israeli naval and air strikes continued, after three missiles again hit Sderot Friday, June 9. One air raid hit a Hamas operative in his car; another struck and killed a three-man Hamas missile crew in the act of firing on Sderot.

This past month, Palestinians have fired 176 Qassam missiles from Gaza at Israeli locations causing numerous civilian injuries and damage
June 22, 2006, 9:34 AM (GMT+02:00)

Al Aqsa Martyr's Brigades, armed wing of Mahmoud Abbas' Fatah, vows terrorist attacks in all parts of Israel, calls on all fellow terrorist groups to follow suit. (Note that Mahmoud Abbas is said to be the "moderate" Palestinian leader. jk)
June 21, 2006, 9:20 AM (GMT+02:00)

Happy summer! This is the "moderate" group of Palestinians with which Israel is pressured to make peace. And suppose they do achieve a miracle, there will be no peace with Hamas as Hamas has proclaimed over and over again! What part of "no" do the Bush-Rice team not understand?

* * * * * * * * * *

Some 1,600 young British Muslims are being groomed as suicide bombers with links to al Qaeda in Pakistan
November 10, 2006, 2:29 PM (GMT+02:00)

Head of the British spy agency MI5, Eliza Manningham-Buller said at least 30 terrorist attacks are being plotted in Britain, which could involve chemical and nuclear devices. "Other countries also face a new terrorist threat," she warned, from Spain to France to Canada and Germany." **DEBKA*file*** adds: The two suicide bombers who attacked the Tel Aviv bar Mike's Place three years ago were British al Qaeda members who reached Tel Aviv through Syria and Gaza.

This is part of the "very sinister" intelligence picture described by Peter Clarke, head of the London Metropolitan police's anti-terror branch as Britain approaches the anniversary Friday of the July 7 London bombings that left 52 dead. Clarke reported ongoing attempts by al-Qaeda to penetrate the British MI5 security service. Three further attacks have since been disrupted.

* * * * * * * * * *

Will someone please remind our President, George W. Bush, that he more than once declared we will not talk to or negotiate with terrorists? To try to force Israel to do this is to make a mockery of his own words and is nothing but an exercise in futility. It is just as useless as it would have been to try to get Czechoslovakia to negotiate and make peace with Hitler.

Our policy is completely irrational. Hamas is outlawed in the U.S. as a terrorist organization. Now the U.S. has demanded that Israel accept this terrorist group as a peace partner, even though Hamas has trained suicide bombers to kill Jews, and the Hamas Charter calls for the destruction of the State of Israel. No one seems to be concerned that the Muslim madrassas use books that teach hatred and death to Jews and to the West. According to recent news stories, the White House has agreed to direct contact with members of the Hamas terrorist group, IF they lay down their arms, and IF they agree to temporarily stop killing innocent Jews. It seems that the US is caving in to Arab oil pressure, and to the liberal EU whose Muslim population numbers 120 million. In contrast to past calls for "total disarmament," unnamed "senior US officials" indicated that cracks were appearing in the hard-line stance toward Hamas...and that the administration "has acceded to the (terror group) running candidates in the Palestinian elections." (They did and Hamas won. As we reward terrorists, the disease is bound to spread. jk) Currently, the only book that exposes the problem and gives the answers is *The American Prophecies*. It is the only pro-American, pro-Israel, pro-Bible *New York Times* bestseller. See NOTE: 7

CHAPTER 5
ISRAEL IS BUT A SIDE-SHOW

Appeasement of Arabs is what is directly behind today's problems. It started decades ago and continues today. When Israel seeks to defend itself, Israel is viewed as the one at fault.

The terms "pre-emptive assault" and "disproportionate response to the kidnapping of two soldiers" are ludicrous. Israel did not attack Lebanon just to force the return of two soldiers. It was to stop the daily killings and rockets sent flying into Israel! What would happen if Spain were to be conquered tomorrow by Muslim extremists - Muslim Maniacs - and they started daily bombardment of France with missiles or rockets? Do you think France would do nothing? I think they would react as Israel has done, but use maximum force and not worry about civilian causalities.

We could have saved millions of Muslim lives and the lives of many other nations if we had stopped Nasser from nationalizing (stealing) the oil companies and the Suez Canal in July of 1956. France and England had tried to stop the takeover, but our President Eisenhower, instead of joining them, made them stop. In (1956) when England, France and Israel tried to take back the Suez Canal after Nasser stole it, the USA put an end to that justifiable effort. We gave in to Muslim thieves and murderers. This was the first major appeasement of Arabs and that is why we are where we are today. So you see, President George W. Bush is not entirely to blame!

It seems that the Europeans never learned much by their mistakes with Hitler. According to the Versailles Treaty, Germany was never allowed to rearm. When they saw this happening, they should have stopped it. Instead, they tried to appease him. Today's troubles with Muslim extremists did not just start. It began when the West did not have the backbone to stand up to Nasser when he walked away with the Suez Canal. Even without the support from most of Europe, George W. Bush had the good judgment to do what needed to be done in Iraq, but very poorly because of poor planning and the lack of contingency plans. Perhaps it was the misinformation from his advisors. They should have advised him to go in with maximum force in order to be able to bring the country back to normalcy as quickly as possible, instead we brought about chaos. I knew this as soon as rioting broke out and could not be stopped.

The Weekly Standard:

"On July 26, 1956, President Gamal Abdel Nasser of Egypt nationalized the Suez Canal, at that time the most vital international waterway in the world. The Middle East, and all of us, still live under the shadow of the fateful events his decision triggered 50 years ago. Even more than the Cold War, the Suez crisis has shaped the world we live in. And at its heart was the biggest American foreign policy blunder since the War of 1812.

"The socialist Proudhon said the origin of property was theft. The same could be said of the modern Middle East. By any objective standard, Nasser's seizing of the canal was theft. Until that July, it had been administered by a private company headquartered in Paris and owned by international shareholders. Nasser had even signed an agreement recognizing the Canal Zone's autonomy two years earlier, which allowed Great Britain to pull out the last troops from its bases in Suez.

"That withdrawal, of course, freed the Egyptian dictator to do what he pleased. Nasser decided to grab the canal to pay for his ill-conceived dam on the Nile at Aswan. He also reasoned that the resulting international outcry would only build up his reputation in the Arab world, and that the response from a declining British Empire, and the rest of the West, would be all talk and no action--even though Suez was vital to Britain and Europe for their oil from the Persian Gulf.

SOURCE: Taken from the internet. Posted by Steve

I contend that the Israeli/Palestinian situation is nothing but a side-show in the push of Islamic-Fascists to control as much of the world as possible. Most of their violence over the centuries, especially in recent decades, has had no bearing on the existence of Israel. Today, the existence of Western culture impinges upon their dream world! Israel represents our culture and is a democracy.

The Israelites began to return from all over the world to their ancient homeland in the mid-1800s. They bought land at horribly inflated prices in this region that had come to be known as Palestine. It was a land virtually without people and vegetation. Against all odds they began to reclaim the land that had become a total desolation of eroded rocky hills, arid deserts and malaria ridden swamps.

Because of the Jewish success in healing the land from centuries of neglect and their build up of a modern economy, migrant Muslim workers from surrounding countries began to come and work for the Israelis. But the more successful the Jews became, the more the Muslim clerics became alarmed. They began to sound the battle cry, "The Jews are stealing our land." With the liberation of the Middle East in World War 1, the Muslim nations began to flood more migrant workers and terrorists into Palestine in order to contest the Jewish presence. The declaration of the State of Israel in 1948 became the final insult. When all six Arab countries attacked Israel in an attempt to commit infanticide against the just born state of Israel, Egypt, Syria, Iraq, Saudi Arabia, Jordan and Libya ordered all of the migrant workers in Palestine to leave until they drove the Israelis into the sea. They were promised that it would only be a few weeks until they could return and take over all that the hated Jews had built. The Arabs themselves created the refugee problem. The Jews tried to encourage Arabs to stay in Israel to help create a modern state together, but they listened to their leaders, the hate mongers.

All during the period of the British Mandate for Palestine, the world and the League of Nations which set up the Mandate ignored its purpose which was to help facilitate a homeland for Jews in their ancestral homeland of Palestine. The world sat by and watched as Britain sliced off about two-thirds of the land to reward the Hashemite family for their help in World War I by creating the Kingdom of Jordan. Was this not already a partition? Why is this not considered the Palestinian state? The answer is easy; it belongs to the King of Jordan and he does not want to lose his throne or his head. That king slaughtered about 10,000 Palestinians when they tried to take over.

Again, against all odds, the rag-tag, poorly equipped Israelis defeated their combined armies. One of the biggest lies of history is that the Arab former migrant workers are somehow an ancient people with centuries of ties to the land of Palestine. There has never been a Palestinian race, people or nation. They are illegal immigrants from surrounding Arab countries allowed in by the British in violation of the League of Nations mandate to facilitate a Jewish homeland in the land of Palestine. The first thing the British did after World War I was to slice off 2/3 of Palestine to create Jordan as a reward for help during the war. In other words, they paid their debt by giving away a huge part of Jewish land.

Great Britain did nothing to stop the steady flow of Arabs from surrounding countries into what was to be held as a Jewish homeland. Instead of helping to facilitate the establishment of a Jewish homeland, Great Britain even took violent steps to stop Jewish immigration into Israel, sending shiploads of Jews back to Hitler's extermination camps and ovens and finally forbidding the admission of any more Jews! The world said not a word as this was happening. Is it just possible that some British officials in the Foreign Office were in full accord with Hitler's plan to solve "the Jewish Question."?

How was filling up Palestine with escapees from surrounding countries facilitating the creation of a Jewish homeland? Britain was in violation of the Mandate handed to them by the League of Nations, but who complained? When Jordan controlled the so called West Bank and Egypt controlled Gaza from 1948 to 1967, there was never any thought of giving the "Palestinians" a state. It is because these Muslim nations knew the truth—they are not an historic people to whom the land belonged. Our President George Bush should have read more! It was crazy and dead wrong for Bush to ever breathe a word about a Palestinian state next to Israel. It would be fine if they obviously wanted to live side by side in peace with Jews and Israelis, but that has never been the case. Those who do not want peace should be returned to the Arab countries from which their families came. Most of the Arabs in Palestine were there due to the fault of Britain, they were not indigenous to Palestine. They became refugees from the wars they started for the purpose of killing off all the Jews so that they could take over all of Palestine.

Surrounding Arab countries always refused to take them in as refugees because they wanted them to remain as a threat to the existence of Israel. Israel represents western culture and democracy which the Arab potentates do not want in their neighborhood. This is about the only case in world history in which refugees were deliberately not resettled. I suggest that it is time to resettle them in the Arab counties from which they came and allowed in by Britain in violation of their charge to facilitate the creation of a Jewish state. On the other hand, the "Palestinian" people have been horribly mistreated by their fellow Muslims who use them as pawns in their effort to obliterate the nation of Israel. It is long past time for them to take them in as refugees and, to be sure, many should be accepted by Britain who put them there. Israel would have been happy to have them return, but not after decades of attacks, no effort to arrive at peaceful arrangements and teaching through most of the Arab world to hate and kill Jews and non-Muslims. **<u>Who in his right mind would invite serial killers into his home?</u>**

The idea being pushed at the moment is that a solution to the Israeli situation will act as a magic wand to stop extremist Muslims from their push for world Muslim rule and domination. In my humble view, the sacrifice of Israel can only lead to the Armageddon. This seems to be the goal of both George W. Bush and of the President of Iran, Mahmoud Ahmadinejad. Why do we not learn from history? The

Europeans were willing to sacrifice Czechoslovakia for "peace in our time." This black deed only emboldened Hitler. It seems that Britain got into the habit of giving away other people's land for their own gain. I am not happy to tell these facts since I have great admiration for the British people, but there were obviously some bureaucrats in their government at that time who were not honorable men.

There can never be peace until both parties want it. The Palestinian terrorist organizations have said it over and over again that they will go on fighting Israel (Jews) until the entire area is free of Jews – "Judenrein", as Hitler so often declared.

Before the establishment of the state, Jews in Palestine tried to get the British to leave because it was obvious that they were in violation of the responsibility given to them by the League of Nations. When they saw Britain turn back to Germany ships loaded with Jewish refugees trying to escape death in the concentration camps of Europe, how can anyone blame them for trying to kick out the British? I am not happy with the idea that it finally took the blowing up of the King David Hotel in Jerusalem to get the British to leave. How much better it would have been if the United Nations had recognized the duplicity of the British and itself forcing the British out by revoking the Mandate granted by the League of Nations. I am repulsed by any violence, even that caused by the American Revolution and to be sure, the French Revolution which went to such horrendous extremes. This is why this book is proposing ways to prevent violence and wars.

THEY PUT THE BLAME ON ISRAEL!

As is so often the case, the Jews are blamed for all the problems, this time in the entire world! The situation between Israel and Palestine is nothing but a side show. It is an effort to deflect us from the truth that a fanatic lunatic fringe of the Muslim religion wants to take the world back to the seventh century and create a world caliphate, Muslim control over everyone! The Muslim religion is said to be one of peace, but events around the world presently and in past centuries seem to sing a different tune! They excuse much of their violence by blaming their anger on western powers that support Israel, but, in reality, most of it has no possibility of being connected with the Israeli/Palestinian conflict. It is my sincere hope that responsible, decent Muslims will take back their religion from the violent element that apparently now calls all the shots! Good Muslims have a need and a right to live a peaceful and fulfilling life as anyone of any other religion or non-religion. We are all children of the Creative Force of the Universe; call it G-d if you will.

The following report from DEBKAfile is a support of my contention that the struggle to destroy Israel is just a side show.

Iran's ruler Ayatollah Ali Khamenei and al Qaeda separately crow over Bush party's election defeat as their victory
November 11, 2006, 3:00 PM (GMT+02:00)

Khamenei said military maneuvers in the Gulf this week and the testing of new missile systems should make Iran ready for any threat. Al Qaeda's Iraq leader Abu Hamza al-Muhajir said his group would not rest from jihad untilit had blown up the White House in Washington and are sitting under the olive trees of Jerusalem.

ISLAMIC WORLD MOVEMENT Not the fault of Israel!

The following was a Muslim murder in the Netherlands.

In November Dutch filmmaker Theo van Gogh was murdered by a Muslim extremist. In 2000, AIVD warned that immigrant integration was failing and foreign powers were seeking to influence Netherlands' religious communities…

Head of main Dutch spy agency AIVD Sybrand van Hulst accuses politicians of ignoring intelligence warnings. (No doubt, they were afraid to offend Muslims. jk)
Source: DEBKA FILE, January 1, 2005

Uzbekistan: A Smoldering Fire of Conflicting Interests
DEBKAfile Special Report and Background

May 14, 2005, 1:35 PM (GMT+02:00)

Uzbek president Islam Karimov returned to his capital Friday night, May 13, after his troops cracked down on a violent disturbance in the eastern Uzbek town of Andijan. It was sparked by protesters storming and emptying the local prison, setting free 23 local Islamic leaders and 2000 inmates. Authorities say nine people were killed in the clashes with security forces. Protesters who filled the town square for two days say at least 200 died of indiscriminate shooting; bodies were seen to be removed by four trucks and a bus.

Despite the bloodshed of the day before, thousands streamed into Andijan's streets Saturday morning amid sounds of sporadic gunfire. Thousands more attempted flight across the border into Kyrgyzstan but were stopped there.

The town tipped over into protest over the trial of 23 local men charged with belonging to an Islamic group called Akramia, named after Akram Tahir Yuldashev, leader of the al Qaeda-linked Islamic Movement of Uzbekistan, who was sentenced in absentia to 17 years in prison in 1999. Akramia has set up small businesses that provide employment for the impoverished town and thousands more around the Ferghana Valley which is both poor and a hotbed of violent Islamic groups. One of the 23 men on trial told a reporter: "All we want is freedom from hunger. Uzbeks live like dirt."

It is not that simple. Uzbekistan's unrest is a volatile brew of conflicting interests. As ruler since 1989 of the country of 26 million – the world's third largest exporter of cotton - Karimov is one of the last Soviet-era rulers still in power. He has held on by rigged elections, questionable referenda, timely constitutional amendments and repression. He is challenged by two radical Islamic groups, Hizb-a-Tahrir and the IMU which is allied with al Qaeda, who are trying to unseat him. Karimov also stands accused of institutional torture; his methods of suppressing resistance have been denounced by Western human rights groups and the US state department.

The former Soviet republic is an important American ally in the global war on terror. It hosts American support bases for the war in Afghanistan. The White House spokesman Friday night urged restraint on both government and demonstrators.

The regime in Tashkent routinely blames the fundamentalist Hizb-ut-Tahrir for any violence in the country, although the troublemaker is more likely to be the Islamic Movement of Uzbekistan, the IMU, whose founder Yuldashev, has nailed to his mast the goal of an Islamic state in the broad Ferghana Valley which straddles Uzbekistan, Kyrgyzstan and Tajikistan. His training camps and bases are located not far from the Afghan and Chinese borders. In March and April, 2004, the IMU staged a wave of suicide terror attacks, the first seen in the republic. They were followed by street battles in which around 50 people were killed, 33 of them IMU adherents, among them 15 suicide bombers. In July, the group went on to send suicide bombers against the US and Israeli embassies and the Uzbek prosecutor-general's office in Tashkent. Three Uzbek guards were killed and 9 injured. This wave of violence was sparked by Yuldashev's return to Tashkent. After spending most of the 1990s in Afghanistan with Osama bin Laden, he had moved to South Waziristan – only to flee in early 2004 from the massive US-backed Pakistan military hunt for top al Qaeda men in that lawless region.

The Islamic Movement of Uzbekistan was founded in 1989, the same year Karimov took power, to become his most implacable enemy. Its exact membership is believed to be smaller than Hizb a-Tahrir's 4,000 to 7,000 adherents. During Taliban rule in Afghanistan, dozens and perhaps hundreds of eager Uzbek supporters crossed south for intensive guerrilla training and Islamic religious indoctrination. Since the Taliban were ousted, IMU has declared war on the American air force and special forces presence in the country. Before 2004, they killed two US soldiers and wounded several others and tried to kidnap Americans from a secret base to ransom their jailed comrades. In neighboring Tajikistan, IMU agents are fed funds and logistical support by the Iranian embassy.

The multinational Islamic Hizb a-Tahrir (The Liberation Party), forced underground in much of Central Asia as well as Russia, maintains cells in most Muslim countries. Founded in the Middle East in 1953, Hizb a-Tarir is older, larger and less virulent than Yuldashev's IMU although just as radical. Its leader Vahid Omran has stressed his movement's goals as being to disseminate the word of Islam - not spread death. Nonetheless Hizb a-Tahrir cannot be counted out of any surge of violence in Uzbekistan considering the brutal persecution its followers suffer at the hands of the Karimov regime; 500 are currently in jail. Hizb a-Tahrir supporters live mainly in Samarkand and Bukhara, two important religious centers of the golden age of Islam situated along the traditional Silk Road. It maintains an office in London. Like many other parties and organizations in Central Asia, Hizb too runs bases of operation in the southeastern Ferghana region near the border with Tajikistan. There, young Uzbeks are indoctrinated in Islamic fundamentalism and recruited into a "Muslim Education Corps". Their proximity to al Qaeda and other fundamentalist Islamic facilities gives rise to the charge in Tashkent that the party is not just dispensing "education" but building terrorist cells. Such education consists of the familiar Islamic fundamentalist fare of nostalgia for past Islamic glories, homophobia, anti-Semitism and more recently, anti-Americanism.

Numbering an estimated 5,000 to 20,000 members around the Muslim world, Hizb a- Tahrir dreams of establishing a pan-Islamic caliphate rather than an Islamic republic across Central Asia, also targeting the Ferghana Valley as its world center. While not openly committed to violence, the Liberation Party will strike hard if an opportunity presents itself to overthrow the Uzbek or any other secular regime. At some crucial point, therefore, Omran could switch tactics and make a grab for power. Karimov's troubles are far from over.

RUSSIA NOT IMMUNE FROM ISLAMIST TERRORISM

Fresh shooting erupted in three districts of the Russian Caucasian town of Nalchik Monday as police and security forces launched anti-terror operations and detentions
October 18, 2005, 9:38 AM (GMT+02:00)

Parents were advised to collect children from school and stay home. Five days ago, an estimated 139 people were killed in clashes when hundreds of Islamic extremists attacked government and police buildings in the city, capital of Kabardino-Balkaria. The attack was claimed by the Caucasian Front of al Qaeda's local cell.

ANOTHER EXAMPLE OF THE
PEACEFULLNESS OF MUSLIMS

SUDAN: The largest country in Africa has been plagued by a succession of unstable civilian and military governments since it gained independence in 1956 from an Anglo-Egyptian condominium. The long-running conflict continues between the Arab Muslim northerners of Sudan, (the base of the government), and the African Christians of the south. In the mid-90s Sudan was home to Osama bin Ladin, the international terrorist responsible for the World Trade Center attack. It is estimated that more than 1.2 million people have been killed in the Sudan war, bringing devastation to the Sudanese economy.

Damare, a small Sudanese boy was taken as a slave and forced to tend camels after his village was attacked by radical Muslims. One day Damare, who had been raised in a Christian home, snuck away from his master to attend a church service. When he returned, his Muslim master was waiting for him and accused of committing a deadly act, "meeting with infidels." The master then dragged Damare into a field where he nailed his feet and knees into a large board while the boy cried out in agony. The boy in the article above, Damare, has now received some assistance from workers with The Voice of the Martyrs. His wounds are still open and additional medical attention as well as some rehabilitation is still needed. (VOM is looking into further assistance.) Damare is not alone in the persecution he has endured. The Muslim government of Khartoum in the North has declared a jihad, or holy war, against the mostly Christian South. Omar Hassan al-Turabi, an Islamic leader, has stated that anyone who opposes Islam "has no future." Since 1985, approximately two million have perished due to the genocide. Families in the South are terrorized-fathers killed, mothers raped, and children sold into slavery. Yet in the midst of these atrocities, the Christians in Sudan remain strong, worshipping their Savior and leading others to Him. Thankfully, in recent months the onslaughts have begun to subside and peace talks are on the table.

Taken from a long story on the Net: State Department:
http://www.state.gov
Sudanese Guards Rough Up Rice Delegation

Published: 7/21/05
War-induced hunger and disease have killed more than 180,000 people and driven more than 2 million from their homes in what Rice reaffirmed Wednesday was a case of genocide. (Reference to Darfur)

Sudan formed a new reconciliation government this month, following a peace agreement to end a 21-year-year civil war between the Muslim north and the mainly Christian and animist south that killed an estimated 2 million people.

Darfur Destroyed
Ethnic Cleansing by Government and Militia Forces in Western Sudan
This 77-page report documents how Sudanese government forces have overseen and directly participated in massacres, summary executions of civilians, burnings of towns and villages, and the forcible depopulation of wide swathes of land long-inhabited by the Fur, Masalit and Zaghawa ethnic groups. The report also documents how "Janjaweed" Arab militias — whose members are Muslim — have destroyed mosques, killed Muslim religious leaders and desecrated Korans belonging to their enemies.
HRW Index No.: A1606
May 7, 2004

* * * * * * * * * *

NETROKONA, Bangladesh (AP) - A suicide bomber on a bicycle blew himself up on a crowded street Thursday, killing six people and wounding dozens in the latest attack authorities blame on extremists who want to create an Islamic state in Bangladesh....There was no claim of responsibility, but officials blamed the attack on Jumatul

Mujahideen Bangladesh, a banned Islamic group believed to be behind a wave of blasts that have killed 21 people in the past two weeks. A police officer at the scene, Ali Hossain Faquir, said a handwritten leaflet warning police to follow Islamic law and stop protecting "man- made" laws was found near the site... The second bomb, however, was packed with high explosives and iron balls that tore through the crowd and instantly killed four people, including the bomber. Three others died later from their wounds, police said. At least 45 people, including nine police officers, were wounded, many seriously, witnesses and police said....

A series of explosions this year have been blamed on militants who seek to establish Islamic rule in Bangladesh, a largely Muslim country governed by secular laws....Officials have said the banned group has up to 2,000 potential suicide bombers ready to strike....The scope of the group's network was made clear on Aug. 17 when more than 400 small explosions were detonated across the country in near-simultaneous attacks that killed two people.

Bangladeshi Police Clash With Protesters

Published: 8/21/05
At least a dozen protesters were hurt Saturday when riot police used batons to control the crowd in two neighborhoods in the capital, Dhaka. Police arrested 30 protesters, local media reports said. The protest was part of a daylong general strike called by opposition parties that blame Prime Minister Khaleda Zia's government for failing to prevent more than 100 homemade bombs from going off across the country on Wednesday. The blasts killed a rickshaw driver and a 10-year-old boy and injured 125 people. Political strikes are a common opposition tactic in the South Asian nation to press demands and embarrass the government. They often turn violent. No one has claimed responsibility for Wednesday's bombings, but leaflets from the banned Islamic group Jumatul Mujahedin were found at all of the blast locations, officials said. The group wants to establish an Islamic state in Bangladesh, a Muslim-majority nation governed by secular laws.

(At the risk of belaboring the point, what does any of the above have to do with the existence of Israel? Nothing! jk)

Police have so far interrogated more than 100 people in connection with the bombings.

The following are excerpts from an AP story about 2006 New Year's celebrations around the world:

Published: 12/31/05 A bomb thought to be the work of Islamic extremists ripped through a crowded market frequented by Christians in Palu on Indonesia's Sulawesi Island, killing eight people and wounding 45. The island has been plagued by religious violence and terrorism by radical Muslims. In Bangladesh, 5,000 security officers searched cars and patrolled the streets of the capital to thwart possible violence in the wake of a series of bombings blamed on Islamic extremists that have killed at least 26 people. (What do either of these have to do with the existence of Israel? Nothing! jk)

Islam Gaining a Foothold in Mexico - Jens Glusing

The indigenous Mayans in southern Mexico, long a bastion of Catholicism, are converting to Islam by the hundreds. Anastasio Gomez, a Tzotzil Mayan from Mexico, fondly remembers his pilgrimage to Mecca. In his home state of Chiapas, Mexico's poorest, the indigenous people are viewed as second class humans, and whites and Mestizos treat the Indian majority as if they weren't there. The Mexican government suspects the new converts of subversive activity, and Mexican President
Incente Fox has said he fears the influence of the radical fundamentalists of al-Qaeda. (Der Spiegel-Germany)

* * * * * * * * * *

There has been almost constant violence in India between Muslims and Hindus since the British withdrew in 1947 and it continues to this day! (Again, and again, and again, nothing to do with the existence of Israel! jk)

Religion, violence, and political mobilization in South Asia
By Ravinder Kaur

More than a dozen Islamic rebel groups have been fighting security forces in India's portion of Kashmir for the region's independence or its merger with mostly Muslim Pakistan. The 15-year insurgency has claimed more than 66,000 lives, mostly civilians. This had nothing to do with existence of Israel.

Militants Fire at Indian Security Forces
Published: 7/30/05

Gun battle ends raid of important Indian religious site
July 5, 2005, 1:16 PM (GMT+02:00)

Indian security forces regained control of the flashpoint religious complex at Ayodha 600 km southeast of New Delhi after killing five armed raiders. Thirteen years ago, Hindus, who believe the site is the birthplace of Lord Ram, destroyed a mosque built there, sparking Muslim-Hindu rioting that left 2,000 dead. Islamic extremists have again been threatening site.

Indian troops clash with Muslim intruders in Kashmir
July 13, 2005, 3:48 PM (GMT+02:00)
A fierce gun battle raged Wednesday, July 13, in northern Indian Kashmir between Indian troops and a large group of heavily armed Muslims who crossed the military line of control near Gurez. This is the biggest clash since Indian-Pakistan peace talks began 20 months ago.
SOURCE: DEBKAfile

Car bomb kills 6 Indian soldiers, injures 15 in Kashmir
July 20, 2005, 4:58 PM (GMT+02:00)
The explosion went off in Srinagar outside a school in a high security district where government officials live. No children were hurt. The attack was claimed by the extremist Muslim Hizbal Mujahideen.

Separatist groups have been demanding Kashmir's independence from India or its merger with neighboring Pakistan for more than five

decades. The campaign turned violent in 1989 with more than a dozen militant groups fighting Indian security forces. The insurgency has killed more than 66,000 people, most of them civilians.
SOURCE: AP

Islamic extremists assassinated the Indian Kashmiri education minister Ghulam Nabi Lone in his home at Srinagar… Three others died in the attack

October 18, 2005, 9:48 AM (GMT+02:00)
There has been no let-up in Kashmir violence since a deadly earthquake struck the disputed region despite the struggle on both sides of the divide to rescue survivors.

Indian police have detained suspected coordinator and financier of last month's bomb blasts that killed 60, injured 300 in New Delhi
November 13, 2005, 11:37 PM (GMT+02:00)
Ahmed Dar was arrested in Indian Kashmir and reported to be a member of the Lashkar e-Toiba, an Islamic terrorist group that fights for Kashmir's separation from India

MUSLIM RELIGION ONE OF PEACE?

PROOF THAT HATE MONGERS HAVE TAKEN OVER THE MUSLIM RELIGION

Eleven burned to death when mob torched Karachi KFC food outlet in revenge-attack for string of bomb blasts against Shiite mosques
Source: the Debka File

11 Killed in Pakistan Sectarian Violence, Published: 1/8/05

ISLAMABAD, Pakistan (AP) - A Shiite Muslim cleric was ambushed as he drove through the once serene Himalayan tourist destination of Gilgit, setting off a rampage of sectarian violence and arson that left at least 11 people dead, including a family of six that was burned alive in its home. Pakistan, a key ally in the U.S.-led war on terrorism, has suffered a wave of attacks blamed on Islamic militants in recent years, sometimes targeting top government officials and Westerners but more frequently hitting religious targets. In October, a suicide bombing at a Shiite mosque killed 31 people in the eastern city of Sialkot. Six days later, a car bombing at a gathering of Sunni radicals in central Multan killed 40 people. Authorities imposed an indefinite 24-hour curfew and army troops patrolled Gilgit to contain the violence, the second bout of unrest between rival Shiites and Sunnis there in six months. Residents as far as 30 miles from the town said roads into Gilgit, home to about 25,000 people, had been blocked. Police said hundreds of Shiites and Sunnis had clashed, setting fire to shops, homes and government buildings. The Associated Press of Pakistan, the state news agency, reported the immolation deaths of the six family members. Geo television network said the father was a government forestry official. Jamil Ahmed, regional chief administrator, said 11 people were killed in all. APP reported that 10 other people were injured. The trouble started when unidentified gunmen shot and wounded a prominent Shiite cleric, Agha Ziauddin, as he traveled through the city in a car. His private security guards, one of whom was killed, fired back, killing at least one attacker. The motive for the attack on Ziauddin, who was hospitalized in stable condition, was not known. Later, the local health chief, Sher Wali - a Sunni - was shot dead, Ahmed said. Gilgit, a town set amid steep mountains, about 150 miles north of the capital, Islamabad, suffered sectarian unrest in June, when Shiites staged protests, demanding changes in Islamic textbooks used in state schools. The protests spiraled into violence that claimed several lives. Authorities imposed a curfew for 13 days and had to airlift out some foreign tourists who were stranded in the city. Although tensions had since eased, some schools have yet to reopen in the Gilgit area. About 80 percent of Pakistan's 150 million people are Sunnis and 17 percent Shiites - although Shiites are in a majority in Gilgit and some other mountainous northern areas. Most of the Muslims live together peacefully, but small groups of militants on both sides stage attacks.

The schism between Sunnis and Shiites dates back to the 7th century over who was the true heir to the Prophet Mohammed. (Remember me writing that religion can be a form of insanity?)

Pakistani Information Minister Sheikh Rashid Ahmed condemned the killings in Gilgit, saying they were "the work of terrorists and such people have no religion." Fearing the unrest could spread to other parts of the country, the Interior Ministry instructed authorities in each of Pakistan's four provinces to step up security for Muslim clerics and at places of worship. How can anyone really believe that if Israel were to suddenly vanish, anything would be different in Pakistan or anyplace else in the tumultuous world of Islam?

CARTOONS OF MUHAMMAD
RAISING A WORLD-WIDE CHORUS OF PROTEST

…The cartoons of Muhammad, <u>published September (2006) by Jyllands-Posten</u> , had telling repercussions. They told us a lot about the Muslim mentality! After Flemming Rose, the paper's cultural editor, heard that Danish cartoonists "were too afraid of Muslim militants to illustrate a new children's biography of Islam's Prophet Muhammad," **The Christian Science Monitor** reported. Depictions of Muhammad are forbidden in Islam, as they are considered idolatrous.

…For his part, Mr. Rose has <u>refused to back down</u> in the face of Muslim criticism. He told **The Times** of London, "There is a lot at stake. It would be very naive to think this is only about Jyllands-Posten and 12 cartoons and apologizing or not apologizing."

"This is about standing for fundamental values that have been the (foundation) for the development of Western democracies over several hundred years, and we are now in a situation where those values are being challenged," he said.
"I think some of the Muslims who have reacted very strongly to these cartoons are being driven by totalitarian and authoritarian impulses, and the nature of these impulses is that if you give in once they will just put forward new requirements." Rose refuses to apologize. "We do not apologize for printing the cartoons. It was our right to do so."

Iran Blames U.S., Europe in Cartoon Crisis
Published: 2/11/06, 8:47 PM EDT

…Yemen announced that three chief editors of privately owned Yemeni papers will stand trial for printing the Danish cartoons and their publishing licenses suspended. The Information Ministry officials said the editors are charged with offending the prophet of Islam and violating religions. Earlier this month, two Jordanian editors were put on trial for reprinting the Danish caricatures of Muhammad. Saudi Arabia's top cleric said in a Friday sermon that those responsible for the drawings should be put on trial and punished. Nothing has been said by Muslim clerics about the threat to kill all Jews and drive the Israelis into the sea. Muslims in several European and Asian countries, meanwhile, kept up their protests, with thousands taking to the streets in London's biggest demonstration over the issue so far. Last week, demonstrators in tightly controlled Iran attacked the Danish, French and Austrian embassies with stones and firebombs and hit the British mission with rocks. Iranian President Mahmoud Ahmadinejad, who is at odds with much of the international community over Iran's disputed nuclear program, launched an anti-Israeli campaign last fall when he said the Holocaust was a "myth" and that Israel should be "wiped off the map."…

Sixteen killed and 11 churches burned Saturday in northern Nigeria **in continuing Muslim violence over Muhammad cartoons. February 19, 2006, 9:50 PM (GMT+02:00)**

All the above, and then some, are due to religious insanity; now Muslim, but in the past, it was Christian even into the twentieth century. I refer to Ireland. Thankfully, it seems to be over!

PHILIPPINES: The Philippines armed forces, with assistance of US troops, are fighting Moslem rebels - they have been linked to Osama bin Laden's el Qaeda terrorist group - on the southern islands of the country. Muslim rebel groups seek autonomy/independence from the mostly Christian Philippines. One rebel group, the Abu Sayaf Group, is believed linked to Osama bin-Laden's Al-Qaida. This connection, plus their tactic of kidnapping and beheading Americans, led the United States to send Special Forces to aid the Philippine Army.

UNITED STATES OF AMERICA: At war with terrorism.

This is only a partial list of how and where we have been under attack!

REMEMBER the MUSLIM bombing of PanAm Flight 103!

REMEMBER the MUSLIM bombing of the WorldTradeCenter in 1993!

REMEMBER the MUSLIM bombing of the Marine barracks in Lebanon!

REMEMBER the MUSLIM bombing of the military barracks in Saudi Arabia!

REMEMBER the MUSLIM bombing of the American Embassies in Africa!

REMEMBER the MUSLIM bombing of the USS COLE!

REMEMBER the MUSLIM attack on the Twin Towers on 9/11/2001!

REMEMBER all the AMERICAN lives that were lost in those vicious MUSLIM attacks!

Now the United States Postal Service REMEMBERS and HONORS the EID MUSLIM holiday season with a commemorative first class holiday postage stamp.

REMEMBER to adamantly and vocally BOYCOTT this stamp when purchasing your stamps at the post office. To use this stamp would be a slap in the face to all those AMERICANS who died at the hands of those whom this stamp honors.

REMEMBER to pass this along to every patriotic AMERICAN you know and we do have some American Muslims who would agree with this.

How can anyone aware of these facts declare that we are fighting Bush's war!

MUSLIM ON-GOING CONFLICTS IN THE WORLD COMPILED BY MICHAELSAVAGE.COM

AFGHANISTAN: The war in Afghanistan is ongoing. Since Soviet troops withdrew, various Afghan groups have tried to eliminate their rivals. Although the Taliban strengthened their position in 1998 they have not achieved their final objective. Afghanistan harbors Osama bin Ladin, a wealthy Saudi Arabia dissident responsible for terrorist acts around the world. On 11 September 2001 members from bin Ladin's el Qaeda group high jacked 4 passenger jets in the USA, crashing one into the Pentagon and 2 into the World Trade Center, killing more than 2,000 citizens. The USA and its allies declared war on terrorism and counter-attacked, removing the Taliban from power. The war on terrorism and the el Qaeda continues.

ALGERIA: Armed Islamic groups formed and since 1992 have carried out attacks on key economic points, security forces, officials and foreigners. In 1995 Algeria's first multiparty presidential elections were held and the incumbent president Liamine Zeroual won 60% of the votes in a poll with a 75% turnout. The first multiparty legislative elections were held in June 1997 which were won by the National Democratic Rally, which holds the majority of seats along with the FLN. Although the armed wing of the FIS declared a ceasefire in October 1997, an extremist splinter group, the Islamic Armed Group (GIA), continued attacks. There is also evidence that many attacks are carried out by militias backed by the Algerian security forces. After years of civil strife, Amnesty International estimates that around 80,000 people have died

The Caucasus and Russia: The Central Asian republics have a long history of conflicts. Fighting breaks out regularly between warlords and religious groups calling for the establishment of Islamic states outside the Russian Federation. Russia is trying to hold on to the federation because the Caucasus is a vital supply route for the oil riches of the Caspian and Black Sea. With the break-up of the Soviet Union various groups fought for control in the republics. Conflicts from one republic spills over to the other and they continually blame each other for attacks. Chechnya, still part of Russia, was flung in an almost full-scale war in 1994-96 and, after a disastrous campaign, Russia was forced to re-evaluate its involvement in the area. In August 1999 Russia stepped up security in the Caucasus region as rebels from within Dagestan - a small republic where more than 100 languages are spoken - went on the attack in support of Chechnyan Muslim groups who claim independence from Russia. In September 1999 Russia launched a ground invasion into the area to cut rebels off from Central Asian supply routes. By January 2000 Russia was once again involved in a full-scale conflict in Chechnya. The Caucasus issue is complicated by the more than 50 different ethnic groups each insisting to proclaim their religious convictions on the area. The situation holds serious danger for neighboring countries, Kazakhstan, Georgia and Russia itself.

EYGPT: Fundamentalist Muslim rebels seek to topple the secular Egyptian government. At least 1,200 people have perished since the beginning of the rebellion. The conflict was primarily waged as an urban guerrilla/terrorist war. The opposition Muslim Brotherhood took part in elections in 2000, indicating that they felt armed force would not work.

INDONESIA: The struggle on the Indonesia islands is complicated by leaders of pro- and anti-independence movements, and by religious conflicts. More than 500 churches have been burned down or damaged by Muslims over the past six years. Both the Christians and Muslims blame each other for the violence and attempts at reconciliation made little progress. After a bloody struggle East Timor gained independence in 1999. The hostilities on other islands continue to claim dozens of lives, to such an extent that the break-up of Indonesia seems imminent.

INDIA/PAKISTAN: Muslim separatists in the Indian section declared a holy war against the mostly-Hindu India and started attacks in 1989, mainly from Pakistan-occupied section of Kashmir, and from Pakistan and Afghanistan. The conflict continues, with Pakistan also crushing rebellions with brute force in their section.

IRAQ: Supports Islamic terrorist acts around the world. Differing culture and religious groups within Iraq continues to clash with Shiite Muslims.

ISRAEL: Within its own borders, Israel continues to battle various Muslim organizations that seek independence for a Palestine state, areas made up of the Gaza strip, West.Bank, and part of Jerusalem. There is heavy international pressure on Israel to recognize a Palestinian state. The area of what today is Palestine was settled by Semitic tribes at a very early date. It was then called Canaan, and controlled by Canaanite tribes for more than 1,000 years. In about 1500 BC Hebrew, or Jewish tribes began to enter the area. They later came into conflict with a people of Greek origin known as the Philistines. It is from them that the term Palestine is derived. (Let me add this: during the period of control by the Ottoman Empire, Palestine became a wasteland with a very low population of some Jews and Bedouin Arab tribes. Trees and plants were gone as the land had been abandoned and neglected for centuries. It was not much more than a watering hole on the camel routes between Egypt and Syria, which was part of the Ottoman (Turkish) Empire. It was not until the end of the 1800's when Jews started to return to Palestine to create a Jewish homeland that the land became alive again! As they prospered, some Arabs began to come in because there was now food, schools, hospitals, bagels and lox!)

IRAN: After the Iranian Revolution in 1979 toppled the government of the Shah, the Mujahadeen Khalq soon began a bloody guerrilla war against the new Islamic government. The Mujahadeen are currently based in Iraq and conduct cross-border raids into Iran, as well as conducting urban guerrilla operations in the cities and conducting political assassinations. Iran occasionally launches raids against Khalq bases in Iraq.

KOSOVO: The ethnic Albanian KLA (Kosovo Liberation Army) in this Serbian province fought a guerilla war against Serbia to claim the region. Beginning in February 1999, Albanians were forced out of the province, prompting NATO to attack Serbia. By July 1999 Serb troops were forced out of Kosovo, only to open an avenue for Albanian

Kosovars to attack Serb Kosovars. The Albanian Muslims have since burned down dozens of centuries-old Christian churches. In an effort to establish a Greater Albania, Albanian Muslim rebels also launched attacks in Macedonia.

NIGERIA: There are violent religious clashes in the city of Kaduna in northern Nigeria beginning February 21 2004 and have continued. Kaduna is the second largest city in the north. The clashes followed a march by tens of thousands of Christians to protest the proposal to introduce Muslim sharia law as the criminal code throughout Kaduna state. Reports speak of rival armed gangs of Christians and Muslims roving the streets. Churches and mosques have been put to the torch. Corpses were seen lying in the streets and people's bodies hanging out of cars and buses, apparently killed while attempting to flee the violence. Local human rights workers said that more than 400 had been killed as a result of the clashes. (Again, wiping out the Jewish state of Israel will have no effect upon these inbred hatreds! jk)

CHAPTER 6
WHY WAS IRAQ A WRECK?

Talking about the left leaning liberal lunatics, why is it they get all the news coverage? I am referring to Alec Baldwin, Tom Cruise, Martin Sheen, Tim Robbins, Madonna, Dixie Chicks, Sean Penn and other Hollywood types who make front page news with their anti-everything American. How is it that Denzel Washington's patriotism doesn't even make page 3 in the Metro section of any newspaper except the local newspaper in San Antonio? This is his story: Denzel Washington's act of patriotism at Brooks Army Medical Center. Wounded military personnel come to this center to be hospitalized in the United States, especially burn victims. There are some buildings there called "Fisher Houses". The Fisher House is a Hotel where soldiers' families can stay, for little or no charge, while their soldier is staying in the Hospital. BAMC has quite a few of these houses on base, but as you can imagine, they are almost filled most of the time. While Denzel Washington was visiting BAMC, they gave him a tour of one of the Fisher Houses. He asked how much one of them would cost to build. He took his check book out and wrote a check for the full amount right there on the spot. The soldiers overseas were amazed to hear this story and want to get the word out to the American public, because it warmed their hearts to hear it. (Thank you, Denzel. We need more Americans like you! jk)

* * * * * * * * * *

The growing number of deaths of Iraqis, Americans, and others trying to help to stabilize the country, is heart-rending. If only some leader would study Chapter 9 in this book, they would find out how to put an end to war in general and the daily bloodshed taking place in Iraq, mostly against Shiites.

One sample headline below is enough.

At least 55 people killed in Karbala south of Baghdad when a parked car blew up between two Shiite shrines Saturday
April 28, 2007, 10:09 PM (GMT+02:00)
    Scores more were hurt. This was the second deadly car bomb attack in the same area in two weeks. The US military reported Saturday that three marines died Thursday in combat in the restive Anbar province. So far this month, 90 American military personnel have been killed in Iraq.

THE WRONG QUESTION ON IRAQ

Politicians are piling up on one side or the other on the question of getting out of Iraq and now Afghanistan or staying to finish the task. This is not an "either or" type of question. One must consider the entire picture. President Bush did not start the war, but he was wise enough to understand that war had been declared on us by the lunatic fringe of the Muslim mullahs starting over twenty years before. Our president had the choice of sitting back and waiting for the religious extremists of Islam to hit us again or of attacking them at the source - in the Middle East. The Democrat stand against the war in Iraq is saying that they would rather do nothing but sit back and wait for the next attacks. All of the attacks over the last twenty years and two attacks on the World Trade center and the Pentagon were not enough for them. What does it take to wake them from their slumber? Or what does it take to make them stand up for our country?

A world with any sense could not go on tolerating a rogue state like Iraq from defying orders of the UN indefinitely, especially since all intelligence agencies of several countries felt certain Saddam either had or was working on WMD's which he could have used himself or sold to terrorists, of which there were and are many in the Middle East and elsewhere. The question that should be asked is "Are we going to turn tail and run or are we going to stand up to those who have already been attacking us long before Iraq or Afghanistan became an issue?" These Muslim religious fanatics, fascists and trained, brain-washed killers who want to set up a Caliphate to control our lives through the Muslim laws of Sharia are not going to be pacified by making nice to them! When faced by a rattle snake making the noise they make when they are about to attack will not be charmed by kind words. Why do the Democrats not understand that they (rattlesnakes or terrorists) do not understand human words! The answer is simple. Democrats do only what they think is best for getting into political power. They think that coming out against the war will gain votes for them because the President seems to be on the other side. Even though they were in favor of the war at the beginning, they are now against it. It is now nothing but an opportunistic ploy on their part. But no Republican or humane individual can be for any war, but we know we must stand up for the best interests of this country. We must be prepared and willing to defend ourselves which means we must be successful in creating a safe, stable and prosperous environment for the Middle East as a practical means of countering the Islamist radicals. We cannot leave behind a failed state which can only become a breeding ground for more terrorists. Is it not better to be taking the battle to their heartland rather than face them in ours? Our President George W. Bush was doing what had to be done. I write this as an American, not as a fan of our former President. On most other issues I feel he was wrong as is explained often enough in this book. This book is an equal opportunity "fixer upper." We intend to "fix up" the Demorats as well as the Revoltingrats or whatever I called them before by getting rid of both of them. We should be voting only for individuals, not parties that have turned government into a game. The individuals elected to Congress should have only one interest – WHAT IS BEST FOR OUR COUNTRY, not what is best for the party! Stay tuned to learn more. (The secret is let out of the bag in Chapter 13)

* * * * * * * * * *

Those in Congress who argue that we should pull out of Iraq with our tail between our legs should read the following – and, of course, this entire book! It would be helpful to keep in mind that during our Civil War between the Union and the Confederacy, the North (Union side) was losing the war badly until just near the end. Can you imagine what would have happened if television existed at that time and casualty lists had been read after every battle and commentators against the war were airing their views daily? Traitors like Dennis (the menace) Kucinich and Senate Majority Leader Harry Reid, a Democrat, would have told the Confederates that the North had already lost the war! We would have declared the Civil War as won, but slavery would have remained and there would be no United States of America today. After we had walked away from Vietnam, tens of thousands of Vietnamese were slaughtered. What do these "turn tail and run" Democrats think would happen to any Iraqis who supported us if we were to follow their advice and get out? Would anyone ever trust us again? These get out fast fools do not care; all they want to do is win the next election. I am furious with those who speak out about ending the war in Iraq by pulling out our troops. I sent the following out to "All Ships at Sea"

LEAVE IT TO GEORGE

I am just sick and tired of hearing the Democrats, and other weak-minded people who urge us to get out of Iraq. They are seeing only what one might see through a key hole. They are blind to the whole picture. They obviously are so dense that they do not realize we have been under attack for over twenty years by Muslim religious fanatics and did nothing about it. They have absolutely no idea of what the free world is facing. (See NOTE 14 for an "early bird special.")

Some seventeen resolutions by the UN had been passed to get Iraq to abide by the Armistice they had signed to bring the Gulf War to a halt. All resolutions were ignored over and over again. Why have a U.N. that is so easily ignored? It needed teeth; Bush had them implanted! Good for Bush! If former President Bush had not acted, the U.N. and Saddam Hussein would have been going on the merry-go-round endlessly. Inspectors would have been thrown out, inspectors would have been invited back in - after some threats were made - and the game of "In and Out the Window" would go on and on until Saddam would have had time to prepare actual WMD's or wore the U.N. down until they would give up and assume they had done all they could. Or the inspectors could have remained and given Saddam a "clean bill of health"! Would the world then be at peace? Think again. President Bush was right to go into Iraq, but he used the wrong reason. He should have made it clear that we had to make sure the U.N. needed teeth or it would remain useless. I do not fault him entirely because all the intelligence agencies around the world were misinformed or deceived by Saddam into believing the WMD argument. He assuredly was not lying. Bush's worst fault was having no contingency plans and going in with woefully insufficient troops to control the country, among other errors one of which follows. In his 2006 memoir of the occupation, Bremer wrote that senior U.S. generals wanted to recall elements of the old Iraqi army in 2003, but were rebuffed by the Bush administration. Bremer complained generally that his authority was undermined by Washington's "micromanagement."

Let us imagine we had a President Carter in office or a Bill Clinton who was too busy with more pleasurable endeavors to confront these issues and Saddam was then free to do as he wished. Seeing the weakness of the West, does anyone seriously think Saddam would not want to play "big man on the block" by developing atomic weapons and other such toys? After all, he had already taken that route until Israel had the good sense to put an abrupt halt to it. How many American lives were saved by that action we will never know, but can only guess! Saddam could have made quite an impression with his neighbors by passing his new toys on to Hamas, the Hizbollah, the Islamic Jihad or you name it to destroy Israel, take over Kuwait and then go on to steal the oil wells of Saudi Arabia which had stolen them from individual investors and western nations that had discovered the oil and had the knowledge to bring it to the surface and create great wealth from it. Who would stop Saddam if America preferred to hide its head in the sand? Just think, these men in long white robes had been wondering around across the desert on their camels for centuries, not knowing what was under their feet until western entrepreneurs discovered it for them.

Never look to the Democrats to take action! Even with our troops on the ground, in harms way, they do all they can to keep us from reaching our objective – the objective of a peaceful and prosperous Iraq. They say they support our troops and then talk about cutting funds. Is this not talking out of both sides of the mouth? This is giving support and encouragement to our enemy. It is treachery and amounts to treason. To my mind, they are traitors because they are giving support and encouragement to the world-wide Islamo-fascists that they are too dense to understand are the real enemies. The "Get Out Now Democrats" are no different than the Vichy French, the collaborators with the Nazis who had their heads shaven after the war when allied troops helped liberate France. George Bush did one thing right when he chose to battle that bunch in the heart of their territory rather than on our shores at home. He chose to attack Iraq because all intelligence of every country in the world, many democrats and even former President Clinton believed they had weapons of mass destruction. George Bush took no chances that such intelligence may not have been correct! He stood up for his responsibility to protect this country. This is why I voted for him even though I disagree with just about everything else he does or stands for. Our country's safety must come first. As I will explain later, I am hoping for a new party to replace both the Demorats and the Republicrats. A suggested name is the Compassionate Conservative Party that would pick up some or most of the brilliant ideas I have put forth in this remarkable book, written to save the world and put together by an old teacher with half a brain! You see, I love to make fun! I like to set SMALL goals!

The European Union seems to be in the same camp as our Democrat Party. They both should recall that we had to save Europe twice in the past because they did not know how to avoid war. They should have stopped Germany from rearming in the first place as it was a violation of the Versailles Treaty. When it became too late and they were faced with a militarily strong Germany and a rug-chewing leader like Hitler, they thought they could negotiate with The Great Dictator (Hitler, not Charlie Chaplin) to arrive at peace. At this time, they are thinking of negotiating with another madman, Armadinejad of Iran.

The Europeans are being very short-sighted in not helping us save Iraq from the Muslim thugs who are intent on destroying the West. Europe is in the direct line of fire of these terrorist killers. Wake up, my dear friends! You are repeating the same mistakes as you made with Hitler. You cannot be "whishy washy" in such dangerous affairs! Is "whishy" a word or is it "wishy"? What would I know! Only G-d knows and He has not spoken to me in weeks! There I go off the deep end, again! Better for me to do that than the West being destroyed by shutting their eyes or keeping them in the sands – oily sands.

The following was written by a man who speaks my mind better than I can.

PATRIOTSIM and the "AXIS OF IDIOTS"

"I would hope that the conservatives in this country take heed to what the Cmd Sgt Maj is saying as he speaks the truth. Not only are the below listed people cowards they are aiding and abetting the enemy and should be tried for treason. It is time to stand up and be counted.

"The silent majority needs to start making a noise or we can kiss our freedom goodbye.
Don Bossio, USA Ret

"SGT MAJOR SPEAKS (J.D. Pendry is a retired Army Command Sergeant Major who writes for Random House. HE IS QUITE ELOQUENT and he seldom beats around the bush!!!)

"Jimmy Carter, you're the father of the Islamic Nazi movement. You threw the Shah under the bus, welcomed the Ayatollah home, and then lacked the spine to confront the terrorists when they took our embassy and our people hostage. You're the runner-in-chief.

"Bill Clinton, you played ring around the Lewinsky while the terrorists were at war with us. You got us into a fight with them in Somalia, and then you ran from it. Your weak-willed responses to the U.S.S. Cole and the First Trade Center Bombing and Our Embassy Bombings emboldened the killers. Each time you failed to respond adequately they grew bolder, until 9/11.

"John Kerry, dishonesty is your most prominent attribute. You lied about American Soldiers in Vietnam. Your military service, like your life, is more fiction than fact. You've accused our Soldiers of terrorizing women and children in Iraq. You called Iraq the wrong war, wrong place, wrong time, the same words you used to describe Vietnam. You're a fake. You want to run from Iraq and abandon the Iraqis to murderers just as you did the Vietnamese. Iraq, like Vietnam is another war that you were for, before you were against it.

"John Murtha, you said our military was broken. You said we can't win militarily in Iraq. You accused United States Marines of cold-blooded murder without proof. And said we should redeploy to Okinawa. Okinawa John? And the Democrats call you their military expert. Are you sure you didn't suffer a traumatic brain injury while you were off building your war hero resume? You're a sad, pitiable, corrupt and washed up politician. You're not a Marine, sir. You wouldn't amount to a good pimple on a real Marine's ass. You're a phony and a disgrace, 'Run away John'.

"Dick Durbin, you accused our soldiers at Guantanamo of being Nazis, tenders of Soviet style gulags and as bad as the regime of Pol Pot, who murdered two million of his own people after your party abandoned South East Asia to the Communists. Now you want to abandon the Iraqis to the same fate. History was not a good teacher for you, was it? Lord help us!! See Dick run.

"Ted Kennedy, for days on end you held poster-sized pictures from Abu Grhaib in front of any available television camera. Al Jazeera quoted you saying that Iraqi's torture chambers were open under new management. Did you see the news this week, Teddy? The Islamic Nazis demonstrate real torture for you again. If you truly supported our troops, you'd show the world poster-sized pictures of that atrocity and demand the annihilation of it. Your legislation stripping support from the South Vietnamese led to a communist victory there. You're a bloated drunken fool bent on repeating the same historical blunder that turned freedom-seeking people over to homicidal, genocidal maniacs. To paraphrase John Murtha, all while sitting on your wide, gin-soaked rear-end in Washington

"Harry Reid, Nancy Pelosi, Carl Levine, Barbara Boxer, Diane Feinstein, Russ Feingold, Hillary Clinton , Pat Leahy , Chuck Schumer, et al ad nauseam. Every time you stand in front of television cameras and broadcast to the Islamic Nazis that we went to war because our President lied, that the war is wrong and our Soldiers are torturers, that we should leave Iraq, you give the Islamic butchers - the same ones that tortured and mutilated American Soldiers - cause to think that we'll run away again, and all they have to do is hang on a little longer.

"American news media, the New York Times particularly: Each time you publish stories about national defense secrets and our intelligence gathering methods, you become one United, with the sub-human pieces of camel dung that torture and mutilate the bodies of American Soldiers. You can't strike up the courage to publish cartoons, but you can help Al Qaeda destroy my country. Actually, you are more dangerous to us than Al Qaeda is. Think about that each time you face Mecca to admire your Pulitzer.

"You are America's "AXIS OF IDIOTS". Your Collective Stupidity will destroy us. Self-serving politics and terrorist abetting news scoops are more important to you than our national security or the lives of innocent civilians and Soldiers. It bothers you that defending ourselves gets in the way of your elitist sport of politics and your ignorant editorializing. There is as much blood on your hands as is on the hands of murdering terrorists. Don't ever doubt that. Your frolics will only serve to extend this war as they extended Vietnam. If you want our Soldiers home, as you claim, knock off the crap and try supporting your country ahead of supporting your silly political aims and aiding our enemies. Yes, I'm questioning your patriotism. Your loyalty ends with self. I'm also questioning why you're stealing air that decent Americans could be breathing. You don't deserve the protection of our men and women in uniform. You need to run away from this war, this country. Leave the war to the people who have the will to see it through and the country to people who are willing to defend it.

"No, Mr. President, you don't get off the hook, either. Our country has two enemies: Those who want to destroy us from the outside and those who attempt it from within. Your soldiers are dealing with the outside force. It's your obligation to support them by confronting the AXIS OF IDIOTS. America must hear it from you that these self-centered people are harming our country, abetting the enemy and endangering our safety. Well up a little anger, please, and channel it toward the appropriate target. You must prosecute those who leak national security secrets to the media. You must prosecute those in the media who knowingly publish those secrets. Our soldiers need you to confront the enemy that they cannot. They need you to do it now. J.D. Pendry Army Command Sergeant Major, retired"

* * * * * * * * *

Those in Congress who argue that we should throw in the towel in Iraq should read the following – and, of course, this entire book! jk)

The following is from Mike Evans' Iraq journal.

As I finish the research for this book in Iraq, my mind is spinning with memories of my time here during the Persian Gulf War. Iraq possesses the largest untapped oil reserves in the world in the Kirkuk fields. Like the diamond mines of Cambodia, the fragrance of the oil of Kirkuk has, like a snake charmer, seduced Turkey and Iran into an insane obsession. Iraq is a small country about the size of California, yet two-thirds of it is not inhabited; it is simply dessert. The majority of the population lives in Central and Northern Iraq. I can't sleep. I keep thinking about the events of the last twenty-four hours throughout Iraq, as the final minutes of Ashoura slowly sift away like the sands in an ancient, apocalyptic hourglass. This is the holiest day on the Shiite calendar and commemorates the 7th Century death of the martyr-saint Imam Hussein, the son of Ali, the Prophet Mohammad's cousin. Like dry leaves on the wind, millions of pilgrims have been blown (flown) into Iraq from Iran and Muslim countries worldwide. In Najaf to the north, hundreds of thousands of men vowing to become martyrs beat themselves with chains and cut themselves with swords in an attempt to feel the pain of Imam Hussein. Their blood flows like a river, mixing with the blood of hundreds of thousands throughout Iraq. With joy, they cry out to their fallen and martyred Imam.

Suddenly, chaos erupts as Sunni Arab gunmen and Shiite followers of Ahmed Hassani Yemeni, a vanguard of the Mahdi, attack. (The Mahdi is a messiah-like figure in Islamic mythology. He is referred to by some as "the perfect human being," and his apocalyptic appearing will usher in the perfect world in which all Christians and Jews will bow down to Islam.) The battle began as terrorists moved closer toward Najaf with plans to kill Grand Ayatollah Ali-Sistani, the most powerful cleric in Iraq. His followers believe that he speaks for Allah. Sunni terrorists wearing the headbands of martyrdom that declared them to be "Soldiers of Heaven" opened fire on the pilgrims. It was the perfect storm...a conspiracy timed to coincide with the climax of Ashoura.

High-level Iraqi intelligence leaders have told me that it was an operation by Iran and coordinated with the Mahdi Army under the leadership of Sheikh Moqtada al-Sadr in an attempt to drive the last nail in President George Bush's coffin. The plan was to kill al-Sistani, since he was a moderate, and blame it on the Sunnis. Al-Sistani is the enemy of the radical al-Sadr who believes al-Sistani to be a traitor to the Islamic revolution. Without a quick response from the U.S. and Iraqi military, it would have happened. Maniacal screams of "Bush, the infidel's greatest Satan" interspersed with cries mocking Christians and Jews as monkeys, pigs and infidels, could be heard reverberating through neighborhoods. As the day-long battle continued, I realized it could spark an Islamic revolution. U.S. troops rushed in and averted a holocaust that the murder of al-Sistani would have ignited. Red flames from U.S. Abrams tanks and Blackhawk helicopters lit up the dark sky near Najaf. Suddenly a burst of machine gun fire hit its mark and a trail of black smoke followed one of the helicopters as it crashed to the ground. The streets of Iraq were covered with more U.S. blood as ground troops and armored vehicles poured into the city. Some two hundred people were arrested and three hundred were killed during the attack. Najaf was turned over to the Iraqi army in December to provide security operations. In the first major battle, the Iraqis had to be bailed out by American ground forces. Hundreds of terrorists had set up fortified encampments, complete with tunnels, blockades, forty heavy machine guns, and at least two anti-aircraft weapons ten miles north of the city. The government sent one battalion and police to raid the armed camp. They were surrounded and pinned down, and had to call in American help.

Today, I looked into the eyes of Iraqi widows whose shy smiles are tinged with pain. The WMDs of Saddam Hussein killed every living thing in their village. These women in black mourn the deaths of their husbands, fathers, sons and brothers. The pictures of their loved ones are their only link to the past. In tears, they tell me, "We hear the American media asking, 'Where are the weapons of mass destruction?' Tell them to come here; we will show them. These weapons of mass destruction are in our blood and in our souls. We will take you to the mass graves." Tomorrow, we will go with them. Many, however, do not even have a gravesite to visit. The bodies of their loved ones were completely destroyed, preventing the widows young and old from remarrying. Entire villages were exterminated, erased from the map as if they never existed. Every living thing was destroyed...dogs, cows, but especially the men. It mattered not whether they were six months old or sixty years old. This genocidal barbaric atrocity has been erased from the minds of the people and from the newspapers of the world. It is as if it never happened. It did happen...as the world slept. Iraqi weapons of mass destruction killed more than one million Iranians and almost 200,000 Iraqi Kurds. Still, the anti-war liberals scream about an unjust war because the WMDs could not be found. Iraqi intelligence officials believe that they were shipped to Syria. They also are convinced that Saddam's top leaders smuggled billions into Syria and are now working with Iran to defeat the Great Satan (America) in Iraq. (Something I suspected ages ago! jk)

Early in the day, I met with the Speaker of the House in Kurdistan, Adnan Mufti. Northern Iraq is run by a Kurdish president. I asked him to tell me about terrorist attacks in Erbil, one of Iraq's largest cities, and the city over which he presides. With us was U.S. Colonel Harry Schute. "Terrorist attacks?" smiled Mufti. "This city has not had a terrorist attack in over one-and-one-half years. U.S. Colonel Harry Schutte spoke up, "The U.S. media will not tell you that. [The city is so safe] our airport has over 80 flights per week."   Mike Evans   See NOTE 6

To receive articles by Mike Evans, intelligence reports from Iraq, and to receive notices of scheduled showings of the television documentary, *The Final Move Beyond Iraq, go to your internet address line and type in "The Jerusalem Prayer Team." Leave out the quotation marks.*

* * * * * * * * * *

Posted: July 28, 2006   Buchanan comes out of the closet 1:00 a.m. Eastern   The following is from: Michael D. Evans, author of "The American Prophecies," He is also the founder of America's largest Christian coalition, the Jerusalem Prayer Team.   He expresses my thoughts exactly. (jk)

* * * * * * * * * *

Pat Buchanan's anti-Semitism finally came out of the closet for the entire world to see. Buchanan has been accused of anti-Semitism for years, but has played the artful dodger and managed to remain, albeit on the sidelines, in the public arena while hiding an obvious disdain for Israel and the Jewish people. But no longer. His outrageous remarks last week have permanently marked Buchanan as a nutcase. This in the face of growing world opinion that it is finally time to stop talking to terror organizations like Hezbollah and Hamas and instead eliminate their ability to wage war against civilization.   What Buchanan, and most of the left-leaning world press seem ignorant of is the fact that Israeli blood is paying for American and Western freedom, right now, on the ground, in the real world.   You see, Pat, in the real world, you cannot negotiate with terrorists.   In the real world, 45 million-plus Islamic fundamentalists want to annihilate Israel and America.   In the real world, they will not stop killing us until we kill them. This is not about some short-term geographical or political agenda; this is about a world religion gone mad in the minds of 10 percent of its adherents and their apocalyptic vision for the overthrow of all governments, religions and peoples to usher in a new world of Islamic conquest. They do not want land, freedom, political power, money or rights. What they want is simple: Your soul ... or your blood. How do you negotiate with an Islamic radical who has only one goal: ***Total world domination resulting in the conversion, or destruction, of every human being on earth.***

Do you offer to convert or murder *half* the world if they will delay their attacks? Do you suggest that they should be happy with *Eastern World domination* instead of total world domination? Do you ask them to give the Western nations a little respite from their homemade bombs while we consider the claims of Islam and see if there are reasons to consider converting? Do you give them the opportunity to build madrassas in Western nations to preach Islamic violence and conquest, if they will just allow us to continue our present way of life for a little while longer? (They are already here, even in Washington D.C. jk)

Just how do you negotiate with a terrorist who wants to kill himself, and you, rather than to let you live as a non-Muslim? How about it, Pat? I'm listening ... Since I don't hear anything but a tired anti-Semitic diatribe coming from you, let me tell you how: You allow the most courageous nation on earth, the one that was born out of the fires of the Holocaust, the one that has survived every attack against it, everyday, since its birth in the fires of war in May of 1948 to do what lazy, fat, over-comfortable and over-prosperous, opinionated but spineless Americans like you no longer have the gumption, spiritual will or moral clarity to do. You allow them to fight, destroy, annihilate and eliminate the threat of Hezbollah, Hamas, Syria – and Iran, if necessary. You *shut up* while they *gear up* to take on the greatest threat to American and Western freedom that we have experienced since World War II. (Instead, we have been holding them back and placing them in even a more precarious position, at our behest! jk) You cheer while they mount their tanks, you cry when you see the photographs of their missing and killed, you get angry when you hear the enemies of freedom speaking evil of them, and you use your platform, whatever it may be, to promote their cause and to defend their character. You do this because you know that modern-day Israel is doing what we in the West – for fear of disapproval (what would Barbra Streisand think?) – are too frightened to do: *Wage war against an intractable enemy until they either lay down their weapons and surrender unconditionally, or are laid down by the righteous retribution of honorable men who will not allow their criminal acts to continue.* Buchanan's latest insanity is to try and argue that the present conflagration is "not America's war." In a sense he is right. Because of the cowardice and murkiness of American opinion, supported by a leftist press and a liberal State Department, America seems to be incapable of seeing through the fog of deceit into the reality of the conflict that we are facing with Islamic extremism. This is not America's war – not because it does not represent American interests or American hopes, but because America is too blind and crippled by people like Pat Buchanan to wage it. Thank God there is still a democratic nation with moral courage and keenness of insight that realizes each day we stand back and negotiate is a day closer to the time when a new holocaust will come upon us all. Leave it to Pat Buchanan to stand even against moderate Arab regimes calling for condemnation of Hezbollah's attacks, rather than stand for a minute with the noble Jewish people. Shame on you, Pat

Michael D. Evans is the author of "The American Prophecies," an Amazon and Barnes and Noble No.1 best seller, and a New York Times best seller. He is also the founder of America's largest Christian coalition, the Jerusalem Prayer Team. SEE NOTE 6 for contacts.

A LEFTIST "PROFESSOR" SHOWS HIS COLORS

Here are some of my answers to a renowned college professor and his anti-war anti-American statements. By the way, I created the fictitious name Professor Babaloubuyaye so as to not cause the good professor embarrassment!

In the first sentence, Professor Babaloubuyaye seems to be saying that we have a "warmongering fixation on Iran." Iran is not warmongering? The author of this nonsense would say, "Of course not, it is just developing atomic power to set up colorful sparklers for the Fourth of

July." And he no doubt believes this even after he admits that Iran "… calls for Israel's obliteration and seeks nuclear arms." Get your head out of the wood pile or the sand or wherever in your body it may be hiding!

Centuries ago, the Muslim religion was spread far and wide adhering to the principle, directly out of the Koran, that non-believers must become Muslims or be killed. In this modern era, fanatical Muslims are apparently forcing their religion on to the same track and the so-called moderate ones are not willing or are unable to do anything about it. After all, the Koran is from the Angel Gabriel and contains the Truth for now and forever or until these nuts blow up the world! This is the same opinion held by many Christians with regard to their Bible and it is just as senseless and immature! We had all better grow up before it is too late! There is not much time left in the hour glass! If children are playing chess while sitting on a railroad track and they see the train coming down the track, is it not correct for them to be stoked by fear or should they ignore the situation and just sit there and do nothing as this Professor Babaloubuyaye seems to suggest? How about stopping the train! And what is wrong with having fear? If you are not fearful when you see a train heading in your direction and you cannot get out of the way, you should be experiencing fear in order to find a way out of the situation.

I feel I must quote from the good Professor Babaloubuyaye this one line: "I will vote for any Democrat or Republican who opposes pre-emptive wars against Iran, Syria or Korea."

Critic on this line by jk:
It is the threat of war and their obliteration that gives them the incentive to at least talk to us. Iran knows we have weak leadership and we are weak because of the Iraq debacle. Thus Iran feels it is safe to do as they damn well please and the hell with the rest of the world. Democrats and others who give the world the impression that we have no back bone are putting us in great danger since we are facing a mob of radical killers, minds warped by religion, set upon the eradication of

our entire culture so that they might impose their religious standards on the whole world!

I had to comment about our good professor's charge that the Republican Party was actually pursuing a policy to go to war. It was George W. Bush, whom the Democrats so revile, who had the good sense to admit that we had been under attack, had war declared upon us by the numerous acts of aggression against us for the past twenty some years. It is the duty of our president to protect our people and our country and to put an end to such attacks. These are listed elsewhere in this book. George W. Bush acted for that purpose, but, sadly, made too many errors in its execution.

I believe Saddam Hussein made the world believe that he had weapons of mass destruction (WMDs) and that he was working on making an atomic bomb. This is probably why all intelligence agencies around the world accepted this as fact. In view of this reality, it is very unfair to proclaim that our President Bush was lying. I believe we were intentionally deceived by Hussein, not by Bush. However, our President should have used the argument that war was necessary to discourage future despots from ignoring some twelve orders from the UN to allow inspectors to investigate his compliance with conditions that had been agreed to. If this can be done with impunity, why go to the expense of having a UN? For UN orders to be obeyed, they must have teeth. The USA provided the teeth! We should have driven this point home to the UN and sought their aid. With due respect to our president, I believe he did try, but France and Russia could not agree because of their economic ties to Iraq.

Our professor Babaloubuyaye said he was against attacking Iraq on the basis of "Just War Principles." Is he saying that it is not a just war to stop the attacks on our embassies, our troops, our ships? If these Muslim maniacs with minds set in the Middle Ages are not stopped, the forces of death will be unleashed on our own shores, on our cities, on our people. Hiding our heads in the sand will not make the problem go away! We did that for well over twenty years by not responding to any attacks! Of course, President Clinton was occupied with more exciting matters to be bothered with our defense!

I believed it was necessary to get rid of Saddam Hussein, but Bush ruined the entire venture by not using more troops and planning for every contingency. I find it hard to believe that his entire battery of advisors did not have the sense to lead him into better planning. When I was at the University of Pennsylvania, I joined the Army Reserve Corps. I was assigned to a special group trained to take over countries that had been overrun in order to allow the people in that country to go on normally with their lives. We were trained to take over the banks, utilities, transportation and do what was needed to reconstruct all that was needed. We should have had such units ready for Iraq. It seems that we no longer see that far ahead. How they could have made such stupid decisions, I cannot fathom or forgive! The first sign of woeful lack of planning for the time after the fall of Saddam was when it was clear that we were not able to stop the rampant rioting and looting that followed his downfall. The horrible excessive deaths on all sides have been due to the faulty planning of Bush and his advisors. We went in with inadequate troops. That is why we could not control the riots and looting and from that point on, it was all down hill!

Our bright Professor Babaloubuyaye bemoaned the fact that Israel attacked Lebanon simply because a couple of their soldiers had been kidnapped and border towns had been under almost daily rocket fire. Yes, of course, those poor Lebanese! Never mind the fact that they voted in Hisbollah, the avowed killers of Jews intent upon the destruction of Israel. Was Israel expected to thank the Lebanese government for allowing their country to be a launching pad for attacks upon Israel.

In response to our good professor's desire to say "Goodbye Democrats" because of their pro-abortion voting, I point out that I am not in favor of government making private decisions for free individuals that are based upon religious dogma. In other words, I am in favor of allowing a woman and her doctor to make such a decision in spite of the fact that I often vote the Republican ticket. How long did it take this professor to find out that most Democrats are in favor of a woman's right to make her own decisions in this matter? Some professor! I understand our universities are full of them with such ideas and deep thinking processes! These characters must have been the teachers of many journalists. No wonder our country is in trouble! I can only say, G-d save America even if He does not exist!

THERE IS HOPE

Tears welled up in my eyes when I read of the joy of the Iraqi people after their team's victory in the prestigious 2007 Asian Cup. Even though I am basically a Jew, I have been heartbroken over the countless, senseless killings of one Iraqi against another for reasons of religion or ethnic background. I sincerely hope Iraq will become one of the first peoples to determine that they will never again even consider lifting a hand or weapon to hurt or kill another human being. This is the primary goal of this book. There can be no better place to start than in the ancient culture centered in Iraq. I was overwhelmed with joy and hope for this as I read the statement of one woman made to CNN: "We are Shiite, Sunni, Kurd and Christian, we are all united." This should give hope to them and to the world.

CHAPTER 7

THE FRENCH CONNECTION

The French-Muslim Connection
By Thomas D. Segel
May 4, 2004

There are more than one billion Muslims in the world. The largest Muslim population, totaling 180 million, is in Indonesia. It is followed by 125 million in Pakistan, Bangladesh with 109 million and India with 84 million. The remainder is spread through 100 countries, including an estimated 5 million Muslims in France. Though the figure 5 million may not seem large when viewed next to the populations of countries such as Indonesia, it still represents almost twenty percent of the people in France. What it has done to this western nation is negatively impact it so severely that it may soon lose its European identity. In fact, if the birth rate continues as projected, France will have a Muslim majority in less than 25 years.

According to the international Limits To Growth Organization writer Brenda Walker, "France should be seen as a cautionary tale of immigration run amok, and how quickly things can get out of control. Muslim immigration to France is a post-war phenomenon for the most part. Just a few decades of high immigration of a group with high fertility has put France in the unenviable position of being the European nation thought most likely to be the first to introduce sharia (Islamic) law. The constant appeasement attitude of officials has also been seen to embolden the Muslim population into making strong demands on the country. As they grow in numbers most French Muslims feel they can impose the will of Islam on the entire country. There is also the threat of violence, which is always a concern by French leaders. They have already seen an increase in crime and violence against women among the Arab immigrants.

Starting in the year 2000, following the Intifada uprising, France started to experience an escalation of crimes against its Jewish citizens. Six synagogues were burned down in less than three weeks. The perpetrators were Muslims. By 2002 France was experiencing 12 anti-Semitic incidents daily. The Muslim population had grown 10 times larger than the country's Jewish community and by sheer numbers had placed themselves in a position where anti-Semitism seemed to no longer be a concern of those in government. Today French Muslims outnumber all non-Catholic ethnic and religious factions in the country combined, including Protestants and Jews.

Also frightening to the French government is the lack of assimilation into national identity by these immigrants. Decades of immigration have produced a large class of young men who claim Islam, not France, as their identity and consider crime as an acceptable life style. As France became more and more concerned about the attitudes of its Muslims, more forms of appeasement were offered. The Muslim Brotherhood, which is an outlaw organization in Egypt was given official status and allowed to preach its message of hate. One of the Botherhood's basic themes is "It is a duty to kill in the name of Allah." France also decided to make Muslims more mainstream by giving them a national council. What was thought would be a voice of Muslim moderation became instead the voice of radical Islam. By the time the United States was seeking United Nations resolutions on Iraq the French-Muslim connection was so strong that as a country they preferred an Iraqi victory and strongly rejected the United States position. There are many who feel that France lives in such fear of a violent uprising by its Muslim population that it can never take a strong western position on anything. There are writers such as Guy Milierre who have remarked,

"France behaves more and more as if she does not belong to the West any more and as though she is the leader of the Third World." If this fear of its own population does not seem possible to the reader, consider this:

Ten Arab men were convicted of raping a teenage girl. The Arab families left the court shouting revenge. Eight days later the court was burned to the ground and the girl along with her family had to flee for their lives. More than 23,000 French prison inmates are Muslim - this is more than six times the proportion of Muslims to the overall French population. From Marseille to Paris synagogues have been destroyed, Jewish men, women and children have been attacked, and schools and school buses of Jews have been stoned. Even with the strong anti-Semitic violence so openly displayed, few officials speak out and fewer members of the media report the incidents. With all of this as a background Al Qaeda is rapidly recruiting new members. In France the terrorist organization, according to best estimates, has created military style units of between 35 and 45 thousand men.
Above from The French-Muslim Connection, by Thomas D. Segel, May 4, 2004.

* * * * * * * * *

Beware the quislings in France who are pandering to the Muslims they allowed to pour into their country. Let us recall the quislings in France who allowed the Nazis to take over their country because they did not want to stand up and defend themselves. Our own country, the United States of America, must be aware of the quislings we have in our midst, mostly Democrats, who want us to pack up and run from stopping the Muslim extremists in Iraq. If they have their way, we will have to start buying Persian carpets to be used to pray on our knees five times a day to that biggest of all gang leaders, Allah! The latter idea came from a black American convert to Islam who wanted to belong to the biggest gang!

I cannot say I do not understand the "Get out of Iraq Free" card crowd, because I do understand their position. Their goal is the White House and they do not care what it takes to get there. Allah, challah, smallah,

Persian prayer rugs are not for me, and I firmly believe they are not for anyone in this country or any place in the world where freedom is valued. I would much prefer dumping both political parties, the Demorats and the Republicrats and start up a new one we may wish to call the Compassionate Conservative Party. (Please see Chapter 13 for full details) My hope is that this party will accept most of the ideas so brilliantly presented in this awe inspiring book! Modesty is one of my virtues, would you not agree?

CHAPTER 8
THE IRAN CONNECTION

Iran has its fingers in every pie and not only in the Middle East. If it was correct that we could not allow Saddam Hussein to have weapons of mass destruction (WMD's), it is even more dangerous to have Iran's Mahmoud Ahmadinejad to possess them. With his unabashed proclamation of how he intends to use them, and his world efforts to gain allies in our own back yard, not to act against him at some point would be suicidal.

Nevertheless, I think we should attempt to use the decent elements within Iran to try to replace him with a more cooperative government, a government open to a world in which there can be peace. Iran has a great and ancient culture and the people are well educated. I have great faith that there are enough good people in Iran to make the change so that we will be able to avoid confrontation. This is quite a task for our state department, but we must remain quite alert and be sure our intelligence is up to the job. Are we using modern means of communication to get to the Iranian people? If not, why not?

A quick start up for the World Peace Association (WPA) would provide a way for the Iranian people to demand a change in government that can lead them into the civilized world that longs for peace and is willing to live and let live.

WE WILL NEVER SUCCEED IN IRAQ UNLESS WE CAN STOP HELP FOR INSURGENTS COMING FROM IRAN and SYRIA

The following was picked up from the "Jerusalem Prayer Team" <jerusalemprayerteam@donationnet.net 2007/02/23 Fri AM 11:48:11 EST

Mike Evans' Iraq Journal, Part III Mike Evans talk with the Minister of State, Karim Sinjari

Al-Maliki says the U.S. should not use Iraq for a confrontation with Iran. This is another sick joke. Al-Qaeda has between 4000 and 5000 terrorists in Iraq. If we leave, the danger will be a thousand times greater, but in the U.S., not in Iraq. The terrorists will take the battle to the streets of America. The only restraining factor is the U.S. troops. We keep the terrorists occupied by fighting them in Iraq. I was told that if we leave Iraq, all of the Arab countries would run away from the experiment in democracy, and that the entire region would explode. According to Karim, Paul Bremer (head of the Coalition Provisional Authority in Iraq) opened the borders, forcing the removal of all security check points in Iraq. Bremer was warned that this would create terror, but he wanted to show the world he was tolerant of everyone. Iran is now running one of the biggest employment services in all of Iraq. For a few dollars, they put unemployed Iraqis on the terror payroll. It is also one of the biggest intelligence agencies operating through the Iraqi government. It makes no difference if you wear a police or military uniform; the vetting process does not work, and the fruit is that secrets are being shared with Iran which now is aware of every move. Said Karim, "Your army is in a holy war with global jihadis worldwide. Thousands of Iraqi fanatics lived in Iran and returned home as agents with the full support of Iran. Remember, the Iranian revolution was planned in Najaf by Ayatollah Khomeini. Najaf knows well how to plan Islamic revolutions. The only reason they are not attacking you in America is because you invited them to attack you in Iraq."

IRAN'S (Ahmadinejad's) FINGERS GRASPING AROUND THE WORLD!

<u>DEBKAfile Exclusive: Hugo Chavez signs secret anti-US cooperation pacts with Iran providing bases in Venezuela – and later Cuba – for Iranian intelligence-cum-terror agents</u>

September 21, 2006, 1:15 PM (GMT+02:00)

Iran is also pushing hard for similar bases in Sudan, Somalia and Yemen.

Venezuelan and Cuban rulers appear to be more wary of allowing the deployment of Iran-made 2,000-km range Shahab-3 ballistic missiles able to reach US targets, for which Iran's Mahmoud Ahmadinejad is pressing.

Iran's Terror-cum-Intelligence Networks Thrown across Three Continents

DEBKA*file* Exclusive Intelligence Report

September 20, 2006, 5:53 PM (GMT+02:00)

While the leaders of the Non-Aligned Movement nations were making speeches at the 14th conference of their movement in Havana in mid-September, three groups of intelligence experts were off in a well-guarded corner next door to talk about matters far from the conference's main theme of how to develop backward economies and societies.

Iranian, Cuban and Venezuelan teams were putting their heads together on ways of translating their leaders' hostile rhetoric and slogans into effective war action against the United States.

DEBKA*file*'s Exclusive intelligence and counter-terror sources disclose that the three teams were made up of intelligence officers and civilian officials on the staffs of the three rulers; their job is maintaining clandestine ties with underground and terrorist organizations. After the NAM conference ended, the Iranian and Venezuelan teams moved their talks to Caracas where Ahmadinejad continued his talks with

Chavez on Sept 17 and 18. Interestingly, Iran's Islamic revolutionary leaders have maintained warm ties of cooperation and mutual assistance with Castro's Cuba since they came to power in Tehran in 1979. They admired his revolutionary zeal and consistent anti-US policies. Tehran also exploited Cuba's economic straits to deepen its penetration of the country with a view to setting up an Iranian base in Cuba for its continental operations. But the relationship suffered ups and downs, especially when Castro declined to give Iranian agents a free hand for subversion and espionage against the United States. In 2003, the Cuban ruler was furious when Iranian diplomats, without asking for permission, installed in their homes in a farm on the outskirts of Havana jamming equipment against television programs bounced from the United States through satellite to Iran. They were trying to stop Iranian opposition-backed television broadcasters in Los Angeles calling on Iranians to rise up against the Islamic regime. Castro made the Iranian diplomats evacuate the farm and remove their gear.

Castro is too old a hand to be manipulated in matters of subversion and terrorism. Chavez in contrast is just as anti-American but also rated by Tehran an easier mark. Although he needs to be handled with kid gloves as head of an oil-exporting country, the Iranians have noted that the Venezuelan leader is also open to cooperation in the politics of oil. On Sept. 18, he insisted that Ahmadinejad attend a ceremony celebrating the gushing of the 7th Aya Well of the Kuchouy Oil Field developed by a Venezuelan-Iranian partnership. This was to be a landmark on the road to a merger between the two oil industries. Tehran is not too happy about this partnership but is going along with small, symbolic steps while extracting from Caracas – and eventually it hopes from Havana – forward facilities for running Iranian clandestine agents in North and South America.

DEBKA*file's* Iranian sources report that Ahmadinejad also talked persuasively to Chavez about making a show of deploying a few Iranian-made 2,000-km range Shahab-3 missiles – first in Venezuela then in Cuba – as a menace to the United States.

Chavez has not given Tehran his answer. But both he and Castro will think twice about granting this request, for fear of crossing one line too many for the Bush administration to swallow. However, Iranian ambitions to harm America know no limits. The three-cornered meeting in Havana between the Ahmadinejad, Chavez and Raoul Castro at the beginning of the week reached a number of decisions in principle although they remain to be fleshed out with operational details. Castro was reluctant to make final decisions because he said his brother would soon be back at the helm. They did agree that anything decided during the Iranian and Venezuelan presidents' Caracas talks would be put before the Cuban ruler. They also decided that their intelligence teams would meet again during the UN General Assembly session in New York later this week. After discovering this plan, Washington refused the Iranian president's "aides" – presented as journalists - entry visas to New York on Tuesday, Sept. 19.

The three-way talks have thus far yielded a solid decision for Iranian intelligence agents, some of them sabotage specialists, to be sent soon to Cuba and Venezuela. They will operate in the guise of road network and industrial development experts. Their real mission will be to conduct surveys on the practicability of using Cuba and Venezuela as bases for subversive activities against the United States and other parts of Latin America. Iran is also busy creating similar bases in E. Africa, favoring Sudan and Somalia. At the Havana NAM conference the Iranian president and Sudan's Omar Bashir were seen deep in conversation. Tehran believes that the Sudanese ruler will come round now to accepting expanded military and intelligence collaboration between the two countries, whereas in 2003, he threw Iranian agents out of Sudan together with all their development specialists. Bashir is now seeking support for his Darfur policy which aims to remove pro-Western military elements from Sudan. Iran is on the way to harnessing two more countries to its clandestine anti-US campaign: Somalia and Yemen. In Mogadishu, the Islamic Courts movement headed by Sheikh Hassan Dahir Aweys is strengthening its grip on Somalia. Like Iran's Islamic rulers, this group also preaches jihad and martyrdom (suicide attacks) for the sake of Islam. The Somali movement therefore provides fertile ground for recruiting terrorists for suicide missions on behalf of Iran and al Qaeda alike as part of their subversion and terror campaigns across the African continent. Mogadishu's new rulers, whose number includes a group of middle-ranking al Qaeda commanders, are busy training an army to support their regime. Al Qaeda and Iranian Revolutionary Guards instructors are building up a corps of "suiciders" to attack US embassies and Israeli targets across the continent. The Yemeni ruler, Abdallah Salah, and his army chiefs are opposed to giving Iranian agents free rein in their country, but in the last two years, Tehran is paying Shiite extremist groups in Yemen to bring the regime under increasing pressure by acts of murder and sabotage.

Iran's Islamic rulers believe they are in real danger of an American air attack on their nuclear installations some time in November or December this year. (It did not happen. jk) They are therefore pushing hard for new allies in Latin America, Africa and Arabia and points of vantage for hitting back at the United States and its centers of influence on three continents as an effective deterrent to an American attack.

SAUDI ARABIA COULD HELP, BUT THERE IS NO SIGN THAT THEY WANT TO!

I am really disgusted with these princes of Arabie who are dripping with excessive wealth from the oil industry they stole from the West in 1956 (Suez take over). With all this wealth and the fact that they are the decided majority sect of Muslims in the world, one would think they could find the heart to be magnanimous with their Shiite minority. Their Imams should be marching arm in arm with the Imams of the Shiites to demand an end to violence. They also need to come to grips with the concept of sharing the oil wealth with their own citizens in their own country by building their economy rather than squandering it on their palaces, outrageous living styles and yachts. They could be the means of bringing peace to the entire world.

Nothing is simple in this part of the world. In Iraq under Saddam Hussein, it was the Sunnis who suppressed and discriminated against Shiites. Now the Shiites are largely in control of Iraq and, as luck would have it, Iran is largely Shiite. If "luck" were with us, Iran should want to help us build up the Iraqi Shiite government, but they are supporting the Sunni insurrection. It is difficult to determine which branch of this diabolical religion is more intractable. They hate and kill one another, but are fast to condemn Israel which they seek to destroy completely and want to do the same to America and the West. The Sunnis, inspired and taught or led by Saudi Arabia, are the decided majority in the Muslim world. The Saudis should be sending Sunni Imams to Iraq to tell them it is time to put aside old hatreds and to learn to live in peace and harmony with all of mankind - and that includes the Shiites. These Imams should emphasize that we all must come into the twenty-first century and learn to live and let live. Tragically, this does not seem possible because Saudi Arabia is the heartland of Wahabbism, the most virulent and hateful form of the Muslim religion. See NOTE 14

If Saudi Arabia does not come to its senses, we should make a quick move toward the use of alternative energy sources and seek, as soon as possible, to stop buying oil from them. To help us get ready, how about "brainy" people thinking of ways to cut down on consumption of gas and oil in every way possible? I am sure this would have happened decades ago if it were not for efforts of the oil corporations to keep us addicted to oil. We do not need to give up on Saudi Arabia as a friend. We, they and the entire world can benefit if we can encourage them or show them how to evolve into a type of democratic royal regime (a constitutional monarchy?) such as that of the United Kingdom and try to convince them to allow freedoms that would make it possible for them to join the freedom loving nations of the world – the World Peace Association (WPA). Of course they would have to have freedom of religion – a very tall order in that part of the world, especially in Saudi Arabia! As of this moment, one dare not admit to being a Jew or a Christian.

Should Saudi Arabia prove to be totally intractable, we should start a campaign to inform the masses in the country that if they want to become free, have freedom of religion, have a chance to become prosperous and have individual rights, we would be willing to help. We should only urge non-violent civil disobedience to achieve this goal if they want to invite us (the WPA) in. Surely, the people must realize that most of the oil money has been squandered on the Princes of Arabie who enjoy big palaces, big cars, wild trips to casinos and loose women for their horizontal recreation. We should be honest about our intent to take back the oil properties that had been stolen from the West, but we would assure them that they would be run efficiently and the bulk of the profits would go toward making the life of average Saudis considerably better. This is most likely the best way to permit the masses to gain benefits from the natural resources of their own land. It is their property and does not belong solely to the royal princes! Here is a great chance for them to come into the twenty-first century!

Even though I am completely convinced by history and the Koran itself that the Muslim religion is based upon and was spread by hatred and violence, I am sure not all Muslims think that way. I have no doubt that through the ages many Muslims ignored that part of their religion and developed peace loving and humanistic beliefs. The Christian religion went through this transformation, for the most part, centuries ago. Well, in reality it was not that long ago that there were still religious wars in Europe with the final horror being that of the Protestant / Catholic tragedy in Ireland all too recently. Modern evidence that religion can lead to insanity.

No, it is not easy to know what to do. If the world did not have such weapons of mass destruction that could go so far as to destroy the planet itself, it would be a simpler matter. We could tolerate little wars here and there with just a few million people being blown to bits from time to time – the game played since our "merciful" G-d created the human race. Oh yes, here is one of my doubtless to become famous sayings: "Since the incident of the apple, nothing in this world has been perfect."! Do not try to tell me that the all-knowing G-d did not know what would happen! How is that from an atheist! O.K., humanist!

Since there are too many loose cannons in the world that are capable of destroying all of us, it is clear that we cannot just sit back and do nothing. It is true that I may come up with a solution to this whole mess that would make everyone happy in a week or two, but suppose G-d does not tell me the answer and I am too dumb to think of it myself! I can only conclude and pray or hope that enough residents of this fragile planet will read this book – so loaded with ideas that they may find worthy of consideration – that they themselves will realize how to resolve the problems ... peacefully.

CHAPTER 9
THE FINAL SOLUTION
TO TERRORISM

It is ludicrous to depend upon negotiations with a person or state sworn to kill you. Yet this seems to be the approach of our brains in Washington. We keep pressuring Israel to call a cease fire every time they have their attackers on the run and try to force Israel to negotiate with their enemies who have made it very clear that they do not want peace. Iran has stated unequivocally making it very clear that they intend to wipe Israel off the face of the earth. Would this be in compliance with the Geneva Convention? Israel is not the ultimate goal; it the USA and western culture. Israel is a democratic country, the only real one in the Middle East, and a member country of the UN. Their example is not wanted in that part of the world.

It is only unity on the part of Western powers that want to remain free and overwhelming military might that can save the West. I regret to have to express the belief that a strictly voluntary military force will not be enough --- unless most Americans come to the painful realization that we are faced with a life or death situation and enlistment soars. Either we give in to buying a Persian prayer rug and be happy bending our knees toward Mecca or we do what we know we must to stay free. Our only chance for survival is massive mobilization such as we have never had before. Once this is seen by our enemies, we may never have to use force. **A roaring tiger with bared teeth is seldom attacked!**

The main battle field is now in Iraq. If we lose it, the next will be in Israel, the U.S.A. and then the rest of the world which will fall under the law of Sharia, the goal of the Islamo-fascists. We will either become Muslims or be killed. The authority for this is repeated many times in the Koran, the book recently used to swear in Representative Keith Ellison (a Democrat, of course) as a new member of Congress. Why did that screwball not ask to be sworn in using Mein Kampf?

Our efforts in Iraq – and in the entire Middle East – are being undermined by the left leaning liberal lunatics - largely in the Democrat Party - who keep suggesting or demanding that we pull our troops out of Iraq. Were we to do this, the present civil war between Shiites and Sunnis could become a conflagration throughout the Middle East. An advisor to the Saudi government, Nawaf Obaid, wrote an op-ed published by the Washington Post wherein he cautioned that if U.S. troops pull out of Iraq, "one of the first consequences will be massive Saudi intervention to stop Iranian-backed Shiite militias from butchering Iraqi Sunnis." (Sunni community comprises 85 percent of all Muslims) If the Saudis have such power, why are they not helping us in Iraq to stop the Sunnis from killing the Shiites? Obviously, they want to keep the pot boiling! With friends like these, who needs enemies!

War is hell. It is likely the most horrible of human tragedies for those who value life. To the Islamists, life means nothing. The way to end war is to win it no matter what it takes. Please keep in mind that Muslims have suffered terribly because of the on-going terrorism. The violence between Sunni and Shiite Muslims is a tragedy and must be stopped. As a Jew, I derive no pleasure from seeing one sect of Muslims killing another even though I know they are both intent on killing Jews and wiping out Israel. It is better to work toward peace for all people than to clap our hands at the misfortune of others.

CARTOONS IN ARABIE

It was the incident of the Danish cartoons of Muhammad that made me finally realize my solution is the only one that makes sense. One cannot reason with crazy people. As you read through this book, it should become clear that the extremist or fascist Muslims are way beyond the stage in which reason can prevail. The war in Iraq is the front line of defense against the terrorism waged by "extremist Muslims" whose purpose is to establish a world Caliphate. I say "extremist Muslims," but I wonder if there is a difference since world domination is the religious goal of the Muslim religion. This must be their goal since their Koran (their bible) requires adherents to convert or kill infidels! I know there are Muslims who do not believe in this just as most Christians and Jews no longer believe we should stone to death idolaters and adulterers. Nevertheless, I feel Muslims need to make a personal decision to stay with their hi jacked religion or find another one more in line with their thinking. (See NOTE 16)

But never forget, including atheists, we infidels need to treat all with kindness no matter what their decisions may be. Let us hope that the lunacy can be stopped and that the Muslim religion may join us in an era of peace and prosperity.

We need not lose this war if we have the "balls" to win! Here is the road to end terrorism once and for all. Someone much wiser than I said, "... take arms against a sea of troubles and by opposing, end them!" That's right, William, I remember the first time I heard you recite that line! Sorry, but this is my way of maintaining a modicum of sanity in this mad, mad world!

THE ROAD MAP TO END TERRORISM

KEEP THIS IN MIND AS YOU READ THIS SECTION. You may think my solution is too extreme. I am really following the advice of Hamas. Until the Danish incident of the caricatures of the Prophet Mohammad, I was very reluctant to go full blast with my ideas to end terrorism once and for all. Now I know I am on the right track.

"We come to power with gun in hand!" Hamas political leader Khaled Mashaal declared at a rally in Qatar Friday night, Feb. 10 February 10, 2006, 11:41 PM (GMT+02:00) DEBKA*file*'s

"The Palestinian rifle proved its power to evict the Jews from the Gaza Strip when Israel carried out its evacuation," Meshaal declared. "Unless we use force, no one will talk to us. At this moment, Palestinian government belongs to the force whose platform pledges warfare."

It is quite clear to me that to stop bloodshed - war - overwhelming force must be used. We know that to put out a fire, it may be necessary to use fire to extinguish it. "Fight fire with fire," is an old expression (and, no, I do not remember who first said it!). We know this is true when two bullies are fighting in the school yard. A strong teacher comes along and demands an end to it and that is the end! Also, a bar that can experience fighting, will have a big, strong bouncer in prominent view!

Below is a solution to the terrorist threat to the free world, but I sincerely hope sensible Muslims will regain control of their religion so that matters never get to such a point. In the real world, they will not stop killing us until we kill them. This is not about some short-term geographical or political agenda; this is about a world religion gone mad in the minds of perhaps 10 percent of its adherents and their apocalyptic vision for the overthrow of all governments, religions and peoples to usher in a new world of Islamic conquest.

THE FINAL SOLUTION TO TERRORISM

The hair on some readers' backs may stand up as they read what I am suggesting as a solution to the problem of terrorism. Just keep in mind that no one in his right mind could have been happy to know of all the lives lost of Japanese civilians when Hiroshima and Nagasaki were incinerated with atomic bombs, **but they ended the war**!

I do not fault Tony Blair and George Bush for simply saying: "We shall prevail and they shall not" after the London blasts. After all, they needed some time to formulate a plan. Actually, this will not be necessary as I am laying it out here: **After reading the above accounts of extremist Muslims, is there anyone who does not agree that it is past time to fight fire with fire? Muslim terrorism can be brought** to a screeching halt if the freedom-loving countries will accept the following thinking and make up a statement to make our position very clear to the Muslim world. <u>It is up to them to stop it or suffer the consequences.</u>   The message must be broadcast throughout the Muslim world and stated as a direct warning making it clear that action would follow if necessary.   The below message should be distributed in every possible way using leaflets and all available media.

THIS IS A MESSAGE TO ALL WHO WISH TO LIVE IN PEACE, RESPECT LIFE AND ARE WILLING TO ALLOW FREEDOM TO ALL OTHER INDIVIDUALS.

THIS IS FROM THE WORLD PEACE ASSOCIATION WHICH IS DEDICATED TO CREATING A WORLD IN WHICH ALL PEOPLE CAN BE SAFE TO WORK AND LIVE IN A WORLD FREE OF FEAR.

We are sending out this message because it is not our wish to do any harm to anyone. On the contrary, we hope we can all work together to bring peace and prosperity to the entire Middle East region. It is our sincere hope that the Muslim world will want to join us in creating a world free of fear and violence so that we can all move forward to create a happy and prosperous world. We very much regret that we have to put out this warning, but we must because human technology has advanced to a point at which we can nearly or fully destroy all human life on our planet if we do not learn to live in peace and harmony with all members of the human race.

The free world will no longer tolerate suicide bombings, terror of any kind emanating from Muslim extremists (Islamists) aimed at getting the world to go back to the tenth or eleventh century. We will not be bombed into becoming Muslims or into giving them their way in any corner of the globe by this sort, or any other sort, of blackmail. It is up to the peace loving, responsible Muslims to STOP THE TERRORISTS THEMSELVES or the free world will gradually reduce to rubble any Arab or Muslim city, one after the other, until they agree to live in peace and make the bombings stop! The cities will be selected according to circumstances: one giving support to known terrorists; those in which Imams preach hatred and violence against any and all other groups. If this dreadful approach should ever become necessary, we intend to advise all citizens of that city to evacuate immediately so that all can be destroyed without killing anyone. We may only do this once. How many times such warnings should be given will depend upon circumstances. If this does not stop violence, we will then eradicate any city we determine should be laid waste without any prior warning so as to let the extremists know that free people will not just wait around as sitting ducks waiting for them to commit another suicide attack. This applies to any nation which threatens neighbors with Weapons of Mass Destruction and refuses to allow unannounced inspections.

IT IS OUR SINCERE HOPE THAT WE CAN WORK TOGETHER AS FELLOW HUMAN BEINGS TO CREATE A BETTER AND MORE PEACEFUL WORLD.

END OF MESSAGE
* * * *

WHAT TO DO ABOUT SAUDI ARABIA?

If we were to follow the above procedures in Iraq, the situation would soon be under control. The best way is to use the above approach against the seat of the problem - **Saudi Arabia - being the breeding ground of the Wahabbi (extremist) form of the Muslim religion and the financial center for setting up** madrassahs (even in the United States)where the terrorists are taught to hate and destroy the West and everything we stand for. This may very well be the best place to start stamping out these "flies." Depending upon circumstances at the time, this may be done before or after dealing with Iran. To do less than this is to try to rid a barnyard of flies with a single fly swat. As John McCain says below, we must eradicate the breeding grounds. Those breeding grounds are in the madrassahs largely financed by Saudi Arabia.

Saudi Arabia may have within its power the means of saving the world by agreeing that it is time to extend their hands in peace to the Shiites and all other peoples. The centuries old hatred and killing between Shiites and Sunnis must stop as well as against any other human beings. If they cannot grasp this, the free world must send them on their way with a one way ticket to dwell forever with Allah and all the virgins they can dream up! The above message must first be made widely known in the Arab countries and we must be ready to go ahead with the consequences of their refusal to come into the civilized world. We must make it clear to ordinary Saudi citizens that if their government docs not follow and agree to the above ideas, the WPA will take over and money from the selling of oil would go to make life better for them and not for the Saudi Sheiks and princes lounging in the lap of luxury!

What about our dependence on Saudi oil? Worry not! We are in a life and death struggle to preserve our civilization. If we are not ready to make sacrifices, we will get what we deserve! We must refuse to buy Saudi oil and prevent them from selling any to any other country by using our navy and the navy of any other member of the WPA. We must cut the need for oil by converting to alternative energy even though we are not fully ready. If we can go to the moon, this too can be done if we do not pay attention to the oil barons! Do you hear me Mr. Obama? For example, there is a company which can produce cars using only lithium powered batteries. The present problem is that it must be recharged after about 200 miles. We can get around that by improving them or by making it possible to go to a gas station and recharge or rent or purchase a new lithium battery. I am confident someone with a full brain and deck of cards can solve these problems. But do not look at me!

Isn't it strange that our country, the U.S.A., is over a barrel while Brazil has practically solved the oil problem? As early as the 1970's Brazil was the first country in the world to begin using bioethanol on a large scale, and today it is the world's largest producer of biofuel. Brazil's production is mainly based on sugar cane. Almost 40% of Brazil's gasoline consumption is now covered by bioethanol, and the country also exports a large proportion of its production. By 1983, nine out of every 10 new cars sold in Brazil ran on ethanol alone. I do not believe this is generally well known by the American public. Could our big oil companies prefer that this be kept quiet? (See NOTE 17)

The growing of biofuel materials may also be a way to help lift much of Africa out of poverty. How is this for an idea for someone with only half a brain – me? This is an area in which some Americans, especially black Americans, with real brains can go over there and help them to do this.

ANOTHER IDEA FOR TAKING US OFF THE BARREL.

I wrote to a few railroad king pins with this idea, but had no answers. In kindness, it could be because I sent it via e-mail. I pointed out that our government had given the railroad public land on which to build their railroads and that most of it lies vacant and suggested that they plant them with junk trees or any other appropriate crop that grows quickly that can be broken down into bio-fuel instead of using corn which has contributed to raising prices for food. Gathering and transportation would be simple since it is all at their fingertips. They could then construct the necessary conversion factories and add to their corporate income. Besides, junk trees represent a problem in many counties around the country. They can bring them to the railroad site and sell this junk to give additional revenue to counties.

Once the oil money stops flowing into the pockets of the Sheiks of Arabie, it will be interesting to see what a loss of a few billion here and there may do to their religious zeal to kill all non-Muslims! If the people and government of Saudi Arabia do not agree and cooperate as above, the U.S. President should go to the President of Venezuela, Hugo Chavez, and make it clear that he and his country would be well served to supply all the oil we need and urge him to join the WPA if he can first abide by its requirements. The Venezuelans must realize that if they do not do this they may have to submit to Sharia law and bow toward Mecca! If their president is not open to this idea, I am sure a direct appeal to the people would do the trick.

Not to do this and to take the strong steps just explained is to have every Western civilized nation and their cities open to continued indiscriminate killings. The worst danger to the West lies in any Muslim country having the ability to use atomic, biological or chemical weapons. The actions of Muslims over the decades and centuries past have given ample proof that they are not responsible enough to possess these weapons of horrific destruction. Do not forget, their emphasis is to die for their religion and sleep with virgins! If we wish to survive and live, we had best wake up! We have had too many examples in both past centuries and presently to make it quite clear that they care not about how many people are slaughtered on either side.

Considering that actual threats have been emanating from the President of Iran, we more likely should start with that country and hope that Saudi Arabia will clean up its act so that they will not have to get the same treatment. Of course, this must depend upon circumstances at the time. Because of the obvious truth and necessity of the above, we should give final notice to Iran to destroy all such capabilities and to remain under complete inspection by the world commission in charge of seeing to it that the world will no longer sit passively by until the next and then the next western nation will have its citizens slaughtered by terrorists. Leaflets should be dropped on Iran in an effort to get the responsible citizens of that country to prevail upon their leadership to join in peace with the free peoples of the world. The people of Iran should be encouraged to use peaceful, non-violent means of protest against their present government headed by President Mahmoud Ahmadinejad. If, within a reasonable amount of time (one month?), the leadership of Iran does not agree to the above, Iran should have one city after another pounded into dust or until their government agrees to live in peace or Iran will soon cease to exist on this earth. Period! I would hate to see this happen because Iran (Persia) is a great old civilization full of good people. I fervently hope they can set their government straight without violence of any kind. Perhaps they can use the methods of Mahatma Ghandi or Martin Luther King. Non-violence is the best way. I have no doubt that most Iranians want to live in a peace-loving civilized world and I am confident most do not like the present hateful regime. I do not like this solution, but G-d himself followed the same path when He had difficulty bringing a population around to His point of view! Considering the suffering and massive deaths He brought down upon the Egyptians to convince them to let His people go and what He did to the people of Sodom and Gomorra! Does any reader believe that man can do better than G-d?

Follow the above methods and we will succeed and attain world peace in spite of the Democrats who keep saying we can never win! They do not know our history. There were many times during our civil war when it looked as though the North would never prevail. It is good we did not have TV at that time or there would never be a United States of America today! Democratic Congressman Dennis Kucinich of Ohio and John Edwards, both wanting to be president at one time, claim that military experts say there is no military solution for Iraq. Have they spoken to all of them? They need to read this book which explains how we can win a military victory while gradually withdrawing our troops. We need to use air power, mostly from our aircraft carriers, and some special forces. As is explained above, we need to let the Arab world know that the civilized world, including those in the Arab and Muslim world who share our desire for freedom and prosperity and life rather than death, will not be intimidated into surrendering our freedoms by any amount of threats or suicide bomb attacks. Once our plan to end terrorism is well circulated throughout the Middle East, we will start to put it into effect if we must. But let us first make every effort to bring our fellow human beings, those of the Muslim faith, into the community of nations which welcomes the existence of the WPA to bring about peace and to maintain it.

BECAUSE THE DECENT, RESPONSIBLE MUSLIMS EITHER HAVE NOT HAD THE POWER OR THE WILL TO STOP THE EXTREMIST ELEMENTS OF THEIR RELIGION FROM TAKING INNOCENT LIVES ALL OVER THE WORLD AS THOUGH THOSE ATTACKED WERE NOTHING BUT ROACHES, the freedom loving countries must join together to put an end to violence by destroying those who insist upon violence to impose their seventh century religion on the rest of the world.

I do not take this position lightly; so let me elucidate further on the above theme. I feel it is productive to have a look at the source of the three major religions of the world. Let us go back to Genesis, to the beginning, to the Bible. It is incredible that the wise men who wrote it had such deep wisdom and astounding capabilities that they were able to write the "Greatest Story Ever Told" – The Bible. We just need to understand that some of its concepts are reflective of thinking of the age in which they lived. Modern man, through the evolution of the human mind, should be able to discern what is valid and what no longer makes any sense. This is nothing new; it has been interpreted and misinterpreted for ages. So what! What is essential is that we concentrate on its teachings that are positive.

One of my favorite stories, that of Joseph and his brothers, is a magnificent tale of human frailties and love that taught what we all need to grasp: that we should do no wrong, be forgiving, honest, and compassionate.

I keep this in mind as I suggest a way to finally end terrorism. **MY FERVENT HOPE IS THAT NO MUSLIM WILL EVER HAVE TO SUFFER IN ANY WAY AS THIS SOLUTION IS WORKED OUT. THE BALL IS IN THEIR COURT.**

I urge all Muslims to thoroughly read the Koran and notice how much emphasis is given to killing of anyone who does not want to accept the Muslim faith. This is pure insanity! Modern, intelligent, peace loving Muslims will surely see this. Why would anyone in his right mind wish to belong to such a group - a gang - intent upon killing as this one surely is. Of course there are good Muslims who abhor violence, but this in itself sets them apart from that faith. I thus urge all reasonable, decent Muslims renounce their membership in this gang or bring their religion into line with the Age of Reason or join any other religion or no religion. May I suggest that they just form humanist groups devoted to doing good in this world and practice living in peace and harmony with all other human beings even if they stay with the Islam? May they just come to realize that we are all children of G-d (to those with a religious point of view) or members of the human race who must never resort to violence?

After saying this, I am sorry to admit that the only way I see to end violence is to completely annihilate those who are intent upon killing. I was already coming around, regretfully, to this conclusion as I became aware of the daily butchering of one Muslim sect against another. It is evident that they are a danger not only to the world, but to themselves. Now, as a result of the latest news of oil trucks filled with explosives blown up in peaceful villages of Iraqi Yazidi Kurds I can see no other path to take!   (This was reported by the DEBKAfile on August 17, 2007.)   There were at least 500 killed and 1000 injured, those still living fled to the Syrian border. This massacre was the work of Al Qaeda, one of the extremist hate groups bred by the Muslim religion, the extremist element that breeds in Saudi Arabia. The killers were following the example and teachings of Muhammad!

We must find a way to separate the wheat from the sheaf, a way to make it possible for decent Muslims to exit that gang. One problem: The Koran declares that any Muslim who converts to another religion must be killed. How about making it possible for Muslims in cities to separate themselves out? Every city with a big Muslim population should have the chance to declare that their city is a peaceful enclave with all extremists removed. By doing this and by throwing out the extremists or turning them over to the defenders of liberty (likely the WPA), these cities would be giving themselves a chance to survive. Allow a reasonable amount of time for this. The next terrorist attack should be followed by the complete obliteration of any city that did not go through this transformation.

I consider this to be more merciful than the forces of nature which make no effort to separate the good from the bad when massive earthquakes or category five hurricanes kill thousands of people. When deadly disease strikes, young and old, even children, no one is spared because of how good they were. How can humans be more merciful than nature or G-d? Well, we can be! The method is explained above.

My deepest hope is that all Muslims will declare themselves to be part of the human race that wishes only peace, prosperity and brotherhood with all of humanity. It seems to be a non-sequitur to want to remain a Muslim, but that should remain a personal decision and they should never be attacked unless in self-defense. Let there be no hatred against anyone as long as they do no harm. Long live any Muslim determined to live in peace and harmony with any other human beings of any faith or of no faith.

END OF STORY and G-d bless the good people of this earth of all religions and non-religions as well!

Here is another sound idea. Excerpts from Mike Evans of the Jerusalem Prayer Team (See NOTE 6)

January 30, 2007, Northern Iraq (He was interviewing Adnan Mufti, Speaker of the House of Kurdistan.)

"I read the Iraq Study Group report that criticized your region for not flying the Iraq flag," I said. Adnan responded, "Yes, they did. This was the same flag planted in over 5000 villages that were gassed. We have a constitution, and our region is democratic… we want the new flag approved by our Constitution." Adnan also rejected the Iraq Study Group's proposal that two terror states, Iran and Syria, "meddle in our affairs." "Why," he asked, "did no one from the Iraq Study Group come here? They ask where the proof is that the Bush policy is succeeding in Iraq. We are the proof. Your nation saved us from extermination. We are a stable region that is a model of everything the U.S. wants for Iraq. Why is it being kept hidden?" I found the Kurds to be very tolerant of other religions. They enjoyed telling me their history, which traces back to the Medes. From the story of Daniel in the lion's den and the conversion of the Mede king, Darius, to the appeal of a Jewish orphan, Esther. They told me of the Magi, the wise men who followed the star and presented gifts to the Christ child, and of the Medes who were converted on the day of Pentecost.

They told me about Christians by the tens of thousands that had fled north out of Sunni and Shiite strongholds toward the Valley of Nineveh, a few miles from Erbil. The horrible story of a fourteen-year-old being crucified for sharing his faith broke my heart as I thought of the innocence of my own precious grandchildren. I heard of a pastor who was beheaded for sharing the Gospel, and of women having had acid thrown in their faces for going to church. The church in Iraq is under siege, yet the world remains silent. I found it strange that the U.S. has no base in Erbil to fight the war on terror. The greatest success story in all of Iraq, a model to inspire true democracy, is being completely ignored. Kurdistan is where America needs to invest its money rather than bleed money from Kurdistan into the coffers of the regimes that consider America the enemy. I also found it odd that 400 billion dollars has been spent in Iraq, and the Kurds have no U.S. military equipment with which to fight the war on terror… As an example, I believe the U.S. needs to move a major military base into Erbil and allow the Kurds to have 100 percent of the money they were promised. This is not happening. The U.S. needs to reward stable regimes economically. To do it, the U.S. must stand up to Turkey and Iran, both of which hate the Kurds. The Kirkuk oilfields should be turned over to the Kurds that have, in the past, controlled the Kirkuk region. Saddam killed them to get them out and moved pro-Saddam regimes in to protect his investment.

The word in the U.S. is to redefine the war goals in Iraq. Yet, it is clear that the U.S .has been 100 percent successful in the Kurdish region which represents millions of people. I have proposed to the Iraqi Kurdish leaders that I would work with them to host an Iraq Study Group in the U.S. based on moral clarity, as opposed to an "appeasement study group." The war in Iraq can be won; one only needs to go to Kurdistan to see one of the greatest success stories. Military moms and dads need to go to Kurdistan. When they do, they will be treated as heroes and will know that the sacrifice was not in vain. The Kurdish people run to kiss them and honor them in ways beyond America's ability to imagine. They love the families because they, too, have lost loved ones. They are filled with amazing compassion and gratitude. The U.S. National Intelligence Agency declassified a report suggesting that President Bush's new strategy for controlling violence must show progress within twelve to eighteen months or risk further deterioration. Show progress? What a sick joke. You have one-fourth of Iraq living in stability; not one U.S. soldier has been killed there…ever. There has not been a terror attack in 18 months. If that is not progress, what is?

Robert Gates, U.S. Secretary of Defense, says that the U.S. is planning to stop Iran from contributing to the violence in Iraq. If so, the border with Iran must be closed, the Embassy and consulates closed, and the Iraqis that have proven their allegiance, i.e., the Kurds, must be given the tools to do the job. It is not securing Baghdad; it is about isolating Iran. That will not happen unless the push is from the north to the south, with the Iraqi Kurds doing the pushing. The Turkish army has already pushed its way into Southern Kurdistan. If the U.S. does not move into the area quickly, the Turks and the Iranians will. The war must be fought north to south with allies, not south to north with enemies. Over and over I have been told that Iraqi ministries in Baghdad are helping the terrorists. The Shiites and Sunnis will not end their conflict; it is being fueled and fed by Arab countries. The only hope to save Iraq is by enlisting the Iraqi Kurds. Winning the war in Iraq will not happen by fighting in Central or Southern Iraq. America is not going to win over corrupt theocracies by distorting their reality. Getting in bed with the enemy is not the solution; it is the problem. It is so obvious to me that Iraq is headed over the cliff of an Islamic revolution that is being birthed between the Shiites and Sunnis. (See SOURCE in NOTE 6)

HOPE LIES ETERNALLY IN THE HUMAN BREAST

I could see hope for the world as I listened to Wien Jiabao, the Chinese Premier, as he spoke in front of the Japanese Diet. He must be brilliant considering the fact that he came up with an idea I had for peace many years ago. Of course, I kid, it was not exactly my light bulb that lit up, it was reading about how Germany and France sought to bring about friendship between those two historic enemies. They agreed upon setting up a "Youth Exchange Program," which helped families to send their children for a summer vacation to a family in the other country – German children to France and French children to Germany. I view this as a great way to bridge the gap and the fear between Muslim countries and non-Muslim societies once decent Muslims take back their religion.

I consider myself to be a Devout Orthodox Capitalist (DOC) as well as a DOA (not Dead On Arrival) and you know what that means. In case you forget to remember as I do from time to time, it means Devout Orthodox Atheist. I was pleased, in fact, thrilled to hear how Premier Jiabao explained how his society changed from a strict communist regime to one based upon a market based economy and an awareness of social justice. In effect, one might say they are creating a blend between capitalism and socialism. I have always had concern for the well being of China ever since I read when still a child of the severe famines they had many years ago and the attacks from Japan which were so brutal. But this is the sad past. Now, with the present regime, I see great hope for reasonable and measured change for the better. It is wonderful to see all the good they have done for the country in recent years and their efforts to bring about peace and friendship among all the countries in the region. One example is their take over of Tibet. I hope China will free that country and try to make it a friend rather than a vassal state. So far, I do not see this happening, but if China can be brought into the WPA, China would have good reason to grant greater freedom or independence to Tibet. I was greatly moved by China's Premier Jiabao's convictions and, in spite of me being a devout orthodox atheist (DOA), in my mind I said, "May G-d bless him." This makes sense to me because it makes me feel better even though I know G-d does not really exist. I warned you, irrationality reigns in religion as well as in non-religion! So, G-d bless you and keep religious salespersons away from preaching nonsense to non-believers. So let it be written, so let it be done!

One more point, if I may. Too often I hear of or see books and movies or hear people express the feeling that there must one day be war between America and China. May I suggest that we follow the wisdom of the Bible and remember that "The thought is father to the deed"? Thinking wrong thoughts is very counter productive. It is crucial, in all aspects of life, that we ban negative thoughts and think only positively. I have great confidence that there are enough good people on both sides of the Pacific to avoid tragic occurrences. And, hold on to your seats, my usual joke must come in here. I often express the fact that I always think positively. Yes, everything is positively awful!

Please do not let me throw you off base. I do not mean to make light of what I just wrote here. I very sincerely do believe that there is great hope for peace between all peoples on this fragile planet. It is not only a hope that we need, but the realization that we must all work toward that end.

CHAPTER 10
CAPITALISTS
IN DEFENSE OF CAPITALISM

Unbridled free enterprise in the economic arena when carried to an extreme is a license to steal. Unfettered, lawless capitalism, having no regard for the lives or welfare of other human beings has led us to an international financial crisis of undreamed of proportions. Yet it is capitalism that has proven to be the goose that can lay the golden egg. It has created the greatest wealth and well-being ever known to man. It is up to us to use our brains to keep it alive and well for the sake of all humanity. It is my hope that some of such concepts can be found in this book.

I believe most of us can agree - I know I do - that it is an exercise in free enterprise to smuggle in illegal immigrants or illicit drugs. If there is a demand, an entrepreneur will try to satisfy it. Price gouging, firing workers to increase corporate earnings and the value of stock options for corporate executives, forgetting about social responsibilities of employers to employees are other examples of capitalism gone berserk. I do not mind writing that "this is not the Christian thing to do." In other words, this is not the decent thing to do! This is what I mean, in a certain way, by unbridled free enterprise.

I heard a conservative commentator on the radio criticize a certain political party for wanting to take profits away from oil companies.

I feel he needs to reexamine this issue. I consider myself to be a conservative because I know it is important to keep our companies strong and viable, but there are times when government must correct imbalances. That is the situation with massive profits being racked in by the oil companies today not only because they have run their companies more efficiently or created new procedures or technologies to improve profits, but most profits today are due to unusual world conditions. They are making excess profits – much in excess of what they would make under more normal circumstances. These excesses should be shared by the people who have created them by continuing to buy no matter what the price because the product is needed. In effect, we are all "over the barrel." This sharing can be brought about by oil companies voluntarily reducing prices or by government taxing it away and returning it to the people. If it is reasonable to control profit margins in the utility industry, why should it not be the same for oil companies? It is true that prices are made in free oil markets, but that should not create abnormal profits for the producing companies, in my humble opinion. To put it another way, I do not like to see government set prices, but, on the other hand, I do not like to see the public whipsawed by world events out of anyone's control.

No doubt the pressure is there for us to cow tow to oil interests and to Arabs. Is it conceivable that if George's feet were not planted in Texas and oil, he would have put into motion a massive move toward alternative energy and have supplied the needed funding instead of just talking about it!

DEMAND EXCESS PROFITS TAX

I know that some of the ideas I suggest may seem to go a bit too far to the left. We must value moderation in all that we do. I just caution that we do not go so far as to kill the goose that lays the golden egg. Men of vision and entrepreneurial spirit must be allowed to make plenty of money, but within reason. I hope what I write here will be of some help.

Much of this chapter offers viable solutions. Please put on your thinking caps as you, the voters, will determine what ideas are reasonable! Governments may run on hot air, but they cannot run on thin air. They need to tax the citizens they serve; but they should be serving the public not special interests. Our federal income tax is a farce. Not even all members of the IRS know the code themselves or would come up with the same answer to many questions. It is an oppressive, repressive, intrusive and likely an illegal act of government against its citizens. It surely is an invasion of privacy! We are considered guilty until proven innocent which is decidedly against our legal tradition and stated public policy! It is also no secret that wealthy individuals often avoid taxes by taking advantage of provisions written into the code for their benefit. The rich can hire sharp accountants and tax planners so that they wind up paying only a fraction of what they really should. Why even discuss it? We all know it is a governmental boondoggle if ever there was one.

O.K., sit down. Here is the resolution of this inequity (or iniquity or both?). I propose a "Graduated Consumption Tax." Others have mentioned the Flat Tax. The latter is not going to do the job because it does not get rid of the biggest burden; that of having to pay the cost of the IRS and to go through the expense and trouble of reporting and proving our income. This is an unnecessary burden on American business and a huge waste of time and money that could be used for much more productive purposes. Please do not fall for the flat tax. It is a favorite of many politicians because it means preserving bureaucracy (the IRS) and keeping government employees who are usually beholden to the party in power! Government loves to create problems so as to give them reason to control the lives of citizens and to milk the masses! I extend my apologies to most government employees who do honest work and are needed. (And please do not be one of those groups that will want to assassinate me once this book gets around!)

Just consider the multi-billion dollar drug trade or any other illegal enterprises – and there probably are more than meet the eye! Do you really think they declare their income from their illegal businesses? If you do, I will not sell you the Brooklyn Bridge because I have already sold it, many times over! Using the "Graduated Consumption Tax," they would be paying a tax on most everything they might buy and the amount would hardly be noticed. In one way, we would be turning them into honest citizens! Bravo! The result would be that we would be collecting taxes from the entire population, but this would broadly spread out the burden and the actual tax paid by each individual would be much less than honest citizens are now obliged to "fork over." Very likely overall taxes could be less because of the number of people who would be paying every time they make a purchase and those who did not pay because they had expensive advisors who showed them how to escape paying most taxes would now be paying at the check-out counter! Everyone will be happy and that is the purpose of this book! And now on to some of the mechanics and what is meant by a "graduated" tax.

The above is an old idea of mine, but I was recently struck by this following advertisement:

Gucci Handbags 2006 Positano Tote

(MPN: 153033)

Price Range: **$569.00** from 1 Seller   10/12/09 found one for $5700.00

The above price is a bit out in "left field," but we know that many items on the market are marked up considerably to appeal to the luxury market. I just saw sun glasses advertised for $280.00. To me that is insanity, but if it makes the buyer happy they have my permission to go right ahead. True, they may be of fine quality and exceptional appeal. Fine, but the frugal among us and those with modest income will be happy with what is serviceable, practical and of good value. Do not tell anyone, but I shop at the flea markets or thrift shops! Our poor government would go bankrupt if it depended upon me! Let's face it. Some people like to be extravagant, the more they pay, the happier they become. It is a matter of prestige and, with this tax system, it can also be a matter of pride since everyone will know that they are contributing toward the support of needed government functions. I believe in the essential good of happiness. Remember, this book believes in happiness and aims to please!

This is why I propose that items of absolute necessity, if at a low price, should not be taxed at all. Obviously this is intended to make life easier for the poor among us – just in case this book does not entirely end poverty right away! For an example, let us consider a man's shirt. If the average price is $7.00, we should apply a low tax rate of, say 2%. A shirt under $7.00 would carry no tax at all. Once the price rises to $14.00, the rate can be increased to 4%, above $25 the rate may go to 6, 8, or any percent the Tax Commission determines is justifiable. Obviously, this entails a great deal of study and should be done by a Tax Commission set up for this purpose. I cannot do this now because I am ready to go to the beach to work on my skin cancer so that my dermatologist can make a living! I need say no more about this as it is now up to "we the people" (that's you) to set up and determine the boundaries or guidelines for the Tax Commission. And G-d bless you wherever He is and if He is!

CAPITALISM GONE BERSERK

From many parts of this book, one would think that it is primarily about religion. Well it is! My non-religion religion, called atheism (humanism is probably a better term), seeks to get people to be good to one another and to make life better for all. Keep this in mind when you read what follows which seems to be an essay on economics which was my major at the Wharton School of Finance and Commerce at the University of Pennsylvania. I do not mean to imply that I am therefore an expert, but I try. For all readers enraptured by their religions, I believe you may agree with this Devout Orthodox atheist that any decent civil society must be concerned with and take steps to help the poor and the vulnerable.

What happened to President Bush's compassionate conservatism?" To be sure, it was a hum dinger of a political slogan! Does anyone think he may have sold out to big business or to oil interests? Tragically, it all went astray and became brazen hypocrisy, I am sorry to say! I wish to preface what follows by pointing out that I have most often been a supporter of Republicans and even voted for George W. Bush – twice - for reasons explained elsewhere in this book. However, if you have any doubts about George Bush's Republican Party being in the pockets of big business, read the following:

Valid Point

"Think about this one, it's short but very interesting!

"A car company can move its factories to Mexico and claim it's a free market.

"A toy company can out source to a Chinese subcontractor and claim it's a free market.

"A shoe company can produce its shoes in Southeast Asia and claim it's a free market.

"A major bank can incorporate in Bermuda to avoid taxes and claim it's a free market.

"We can buy HP Printers made in Mexico.

"We can buy shirts made in Bangladesh.

"We can purchase almost anything we want from 20 different countries BUT, heaven help the elderly who dare to buy their prescription drugs from a Canadian pharmacy. That's called un-American! And you think the pharmaceutical companies don't have a powerful lobby? Think again!

SOURCE: Sent to me by Richard Frazer.

PUT THE ABOVE INTO YOUR SMOKE AND PIPE IT, no, I mean: Put this into your pipe and smoke it! In other words, give it some real thought.

All men are created equal? Not really. We are not created equal by our so-called merciful G-d; some were given less intelligence or with handicaps which make it difficult to keep gainful employment. Yes, we should be treated equally before the law, but we are not! If we continue to elect judges, the judges will continue to favor the rich over the poor. I know this from personal experience. I sued Bell South over loss of my First Amendment rights. My attorneys told me the judge (Judge Leroy H. Moe, dated Feb. 10 1999) did not look with favor upon my position even though I was 100% in the right. I wonder why. Could it be because in the back of his mind was the fact that to get more money for his next election campaign he might get more from a multi-billion dollar corporation than from a poor old schoolteacher? Besides, my position put the politically correct crowd in an embarrassing position. (Would that bunch vote for him considering that I advocate doing away with public schools and replacing them by using the voucher system to set up private schools, owned by the teachers if practical?) Electing judges is democracy gone berserk! The answer is in the Bible. Remember, I stated that there is great wisdom in the Bible? Just be careful when reading it to children! The Bible suggests the drawing of lots. This D.O atheist advises selecting a group of top attorneys, by seniority and their record or reputation, to create a list from all of those well qualified to become judges. Just as an example, if five judges are needed, create a list of some thirty lawyers or whatever the Attorney General of the State may deem appropriate. From that number, let them be selected by lot so that nothing would be owed to anyone or to any group.

I guess it is time for me to go to confession even though I am not Catholic. The Gospel truth is that I do not know all the answers to all of the world's problems, even though I try to address as many as possible in this book. I can only make suggestions. It is up to readers to consider them and to wiser heads to throw them out, to accept them or to modify them so that they can be workable. I am not conveying the divine word of G-d. It is up to us, we the people, to do the thinking and to decide. In the knowledge that anything carried to its extreme brings its own antithesis (brings about its own end), we intend to reign in the growing extremes in the world of capitalist endeavor. GREED MUST BE KEPT IN BOUNDS AND DISHONESTY IRADICATED or we will destroy capitalism!

Problem Number One: The rich get richer and the poor get poorer! This is no joke, especially for those getting poorer or losing their jobs. We must not sit by and watch top executive officers get paid more as they fire or reduce income of workers by cutting overtime and other benefits, such as medical benefits, and continue to move factories and jobs to low wage countries!

Solution: Roll back the compensation of top executive officers to what they were five years earlier if they have been cutting employment and benefits of remaining employees while their incomes from salaries, options and other perks have been going up. Corporate officers should not be getting rich through the losses of the working man.

Problem Number Two: Dishonesty on the part of top executive officers for the purpose of raising the value of stock and options in the company, or for any other reason, if it has caused loss for stockholders and/or employees should have the following consequences:

Solution: Retroactively, from the time this dishonesty started, no top executive officer should be allowed to keep any income received in any form from the company over and above the average salary of the ordinary workers in the company during that period of time. These culprits should be required to pay the difference between this figure and the total compensation paid in any form to them into a fund to be disbursed first to laid off employees - fired without cause other than to lower costs of production - and then to stockholders who have lost money as a result of their lies. If necessary, these officers should be required to sell any and all assets such as houses, yachts, expensive cars, etc. to make up for the losses their dishonesty has caused. No more golden parachutes should be allowed! FORBID HIDING OF ASSETS! Any effort to hide assets by transferring them to members of the family or into trusts or by any other means should be disallowed and taken away to pay for their culpability. Money illegally gained is not theirs to keep or to dispose of no matter how they try to hide their ill-gotten gains! Pull the rug out from under devious lawyers.

Problem Number Three: Rising cost of medical care, even with or in spite of HMO's.
Solution

1. The entire Congress - members of both houses - should have the same level of insurance coverage as is available to the general public through HMO's. This problem will soon correct itself, you can be sure! This may be a sure fire way to get rid of the HMO bureaucracy. Do not worry one minute. I have a perfect solution to the high costs of health care, but I will keep it a secret until later. You WILL find it or you will not get an A+.

2. A study should be made to find ways and means of cutting the length of time, cost and complexity of getting approval of new drugs through the FDA (Food and Drug Administration).

3. Consideration should be given to allow a longer period of time for patent protection before generic forms can be placed on the market. This would allow pharmaceutical companies owning the patent to lower the cost of the drug to the public and make up their research costs over a longer period of time.

4. It is said that research costs must be recovered, but how many times over? A study should be made of this. Perhaps ten times the cost, but if it is running twenty, thirty and some above, we need to place a reasonable cap on it!

Problem Number Four: Companies seeking to leave this country because of lower labor costs elsewhere or to escape the above new regulations. Solution: Such firms should never be allowed to sell their products, even if under a different name, in this country.

Problem Number Five: Manufacturing companies that have already left the U.S. because of lower labor costs overseas.

Solution: A government commission should be established to determine the advisability of subsidizing the return of these companies by agreeing to pay the wage differential. The cost may be largely made up by creating or bringing back more jobs and, therefore, increase tax receipts. If they do not return to the U.S., they, too, should not be allowed to market anything in this country.

Problem Number Six: Excessive salaries of CEO's.

Solution: Congress needs to pass a law requiring that all corporations (of a certain size, perhaps) should be obliged to pay out in dividends all but 15% of earnings and CEO's should receive no more than $1,000,000 (advice should be accepted from wealthy Americans to help set this limit) as a yearly salary. If this is too paltry a sum, they may buy more of the company's stock and collect the dividends. This would benefit everyone because it would be incumbent upon the CEO to run the company efficiently and honestly so that earnings can be as high as possible and enable the company to continue with a good dividend and possibly raise it! This is done to a degree in Canada using the concept of a Trust. Such a program would tend to spread out the wealth, increase spending for individual households or allow them to pay down debt and take a bite out of poverty. It likely could increase the savings rate for households or individuals. Many have decried our low savings rate; here is the solution. It would also make the stock markets function more like a place for savings and income rather than appear as a casino.

I prefer having no government interference in business, but it does happen and in some cases it may be necessary. The best avenue for corporations to take is to announce their policy of paying a certain percent of yearly earnings out as dividends. Some already do this, but I am hoping more will do so. If you do not agree with me that many CEO's are walking away with money that should have gone toward dividend payments or to avoid laying off workers, consider these cases!

Commerce Bancorp Inc. will give its ousted founder, Vernon W. Hill II, an $11 million going-away present -- if regulators allow the cash payment. How is anyone to know what the regulators may be paid?

A federal investigation of insider dealings, which included $12.74 million in lease and other payments to real estate firms affiliated with Hill or family members and $59.23 million to his wife's Mount Laurel design firm, led the bank's board to oust the brash and innovative Hill.

... regulators found it increasingly difficult to ignore Hill's tendency to run the bank as if it were his own private company. The board of directors decided Hill had to go when it seemed that regulators were going to cut off the bank's growth by approving no more new branches until he changed his ways or left.

The $11 million payment was disclosed ... in a regulatory filing. It is a pittance compared with the recent $200-million-plus packages for Pfizer Inc.'s Henry McKinnell and Home Depot Inc.'s Robert Nardelli. (Just read some shocking details below! jk)

Of course, Hill is no pauper, with earnings at Commerce from 2002 through last year totaling $54.16 million in salary, bonus, and profit from stock options.

He also owned 6.17 million shares of Commerce stock, according the company's most recent proxy statement, worth $224 million...

The severance for Hill, who built a 46,000-square-foot house in Moorestown called Villa Collina, includes other benefits not disclosed in yesterday's filing with the Securities and Exchange Commission. Commerce spokesman David Flaherty did not respond to a request for further information. The federal Office of the Comptroller of the Currency must approve the severance payment. (It seems that there may be enough money to go around should someone wish to influence that decision! jk)

SOURCE: Excerpts taken from (The Philadelphia Inquirer - McClatchy-Tribune Information Services via COMTEX) – Aug. 09, 2007

☞?🗐 Pfizer's McKinnell to get $180M package
The story is from December 2006

McKinnell vacated the CEO spot in July, 19 months before he was scheduled to step down, under pressure from investors angered about his retirement package and a drop of as much as 40 percent in the company's stock price during his five years in charge. ... McKinnell's package... totals more than $180 million. It includes an estimated $82.3 million in pension benefits, $77.9 million in deferred compensation, and cash and stock totaling more than $20.7 million. The total value could grow to almost $200 million if McKinnell gets an $18.3 million stock award, but that is contingent on the future performance of the stock of the world's largest drug maker. ...The deferred pension sum includes $67 million of his own money from prior compensation he chose to set aside, the company said in the filing. Beyond that, Pfizer will pay a lump sum severance of $11.9 million and will fully vest stock grants worth $5.8 million, according to the filing. He also will receive $2.2 million for 2005 bonus payments... his total compensation for the year was valued at $15.88 million...The package also provides him with an annual pension of $6.6 million until he dies. Pfizer estimated the pension's lump-sum value to be $82.3 million. Poor guy!

To see more of The Philadelphia Inquirer, or to subscribe to the newspaper, go to http://www.philly.com. Copyright (c) 2007, The Philadelphia Inquirer Distributed by McClatchy-Tribune Information Services. For reprints (of original), email tmsreprints@permissionsgroup.com, call 800-374-7985 or 847-635-6550, send a fax to 847-635-6968, or write to The Permissions Group Inc., 1247 Milwaukee Ave., Suite 303, Glenview, IL 60025, USA.

And here is the tale of another poor soul.

The CEO of <u>Home Depot</u> Inc., Nardelli abruptly resigned as chairman and Chief executive of the world's largest home improvement store chain after six years at the helm because of poor stock performance. He would receive a mere severance package worth roughly $210 million... The total package is seven times the $30 million Home Depot set aside last June for stores and employees that provide good customer service. SOURCE: Re-written from an AP story, Jan 3, 2007

Considering all the homeless people we have and those trying to live below the poverty level, how about considering my above solution to Problem Number Six? Where were all our religious right zealots as they watched this inequity unfold?

I know that some of the ideas I have suggested may seem to go a bit too far to the left. We must value moderation in all that we do. I just caution that we do not go so far as to kill the goose that lays the golden egg. Men of vision and entrepreneurial spirit must be allowed to make plenty of money, but within reason. I hope what I write here will be of some help.

Problem Number Seven: Capitalism cannot prosper where there is chaos and extreme poverty! The latter are brought about by unbridled population growth and uncontrolled immigration. Countries like Haiti, Mexico and countless others have been producing children at such a rate that it is impossible to provide gainful employment to all citizens. Thus we have them flowing into this country, helter-skelter, one way or another to escape the consequences of their own ... what should we call it? I will allow you to finish the thought! (How about: "Indulging in horizontal recreation"?) If the present trend continues, their propensity to have more and more children will continue unabated and this country will become just the same as the ones from which they sought to escape!

   Solution: Keep in mind, the solutions proposed below may sound harsh, but the alternative is poverty and chaos, a high murder rate in minority or poverty stricken areas and babies dumped into trash bins or flushed down the toilet by despondent mothers.

A. Any employer hiring an illegal immigrant should be sent to jail for five years and fined heavily. It is not a question of knowing or not knowing. I have a way for employers to know for sure if a worker is legal or illegal. Keep reading!

B. Any illegal immigrant found in this country should be put into jail for five years, required to work at hard labor, building roads or clearing underbrush in our forests, and then returned from whence he came. Once word gets out, we will be able to save money on border guards…there will soon be no need for them! Illegal immigrants will soon find their way out as easily as they found their way in! This is my answer to politicians who wonder how in the world we are going to expel ten, fifteen or twenty million illegal immigrants! We really do not know how many are here.

C. Anyone dealing in the smuggling of illegal immigrants should be jailed for ten years, sent to hard labor as above, and have all his ill-gotten wealth confiscated.

D. Any family or woman, if a citizen, seeking government assistance should receive help for the care of the first child if voluntary sterilization is accepted. If they agree to the latter, that child should be entitled to a free college (or vocational) education as long as he or she passes the examinations required of any others to gain admittance. The mother should be given all possible help to develop her own skills so that she may have a better life and be a better mother to the child. This would work toward quality of population rather than quantity! If sterilization is not agreed to, the woman can have as many children as she wishes, but no help should be available from public funds. It will be up to her to get support from the father or fathers! The courts should be available to assist her in finding the "impregnator". If this thought upsets you, keep in mind that no one is holding a gun to the head of anyone to accept sterilization. On the other hand, the gun in the hand of the government tax collector is forcing hard working workers to pay for one illegitimate child after another! Also, if the mother is illegal, the birth of her child in the U.S should not make the child a citizen – mother illegal, child illegal!

If a man causes the birth of a child and refuses to take care of the child and mother, he should be castrated as his actions create a burden on the responsible workers of our society. Any politician not agreeing to the above should be recalled or thrown out of office at the ballot box! Not the bullet box, just kidding!

THOUGHT FOR THE DAY RELATING TO ABOVE:

An illegal immigrant is very much like a street person forcing his way into your home and then insisting that you feed, clothe, house and educate him and his entire family and PAY FOR THEIR MEDICAL CARE! It is known that hospitals have been forced into bankruptcy or nearly so because of this growing burden.

There is also a problem with legal immigrants who have become citizens. Senator Clinton of New York, a city likely overloaded with immigrants of one sort or another, suddenly shows an interest in family values! She wants us to allow legal immigrants to bring over their entire families so that the unity of the family can be preserved. The train goes both ways. The family can be kept together if the immigrant returns to his native country. Once this immigrant left his country, he knew he was leaving his family behind; so why should the American taxpayers now be forced to pay the bills for his entire family? They should not come here unless they are unmarried and have no dependant children, period! Parents can still be admitted on temporary visas, but no ID card can be issued for them. I see no reason why the legal immigrant should not be able to go visit relatives and then be allowed back into his adopted country.

HOW TO KNOW IF AN INDIVIDUAL IS LEGAL OR NOT

Even though I am strongly against excessive government, there are times when it is only government that can help. In times of a national emergency, riots, fires, spread of infectious diseases, etc., government rules and help are needed. When Mother Nature plays destructive games with us over wide areas, we are glad to have government help. When we have social unrest (riots) or fires, we need and welcome help from police and fire departments. These are agents of government. To prevent spread of infectious diseases we need a health department to advise us in advance and to protect us once there is an infection spreading. Here is another constructive use of government. Immigration out of control - illegal immigration - is like an infectious disease. If people from countries with low wages, bad working conditions, social problems or for any other reason come to this country without going through legal procedures can get in and stay with no consequences, word gets back and the flow continues and grows. We cannot take in a world of impoverished people. It is up to international bodies to help find ways to get underdeveloped or poor counties to rise out of poverty. China and many nations in that part of the world have been able to pull themselves up by using their brains!

It is good that I have a secret emissary in Las Vegas Nevada who explained that if all illegal immigrants were forced to leave the country, Las Vegas would no longer be able to function. I have no doubt that this may be true in many agricultural areas and in some industries; so I feel I must slightly adjust my thinking on this matter. Behind much of this problem is the irresponsibility of our government in not enforcing immigration laws on the books. In other words, this is a case of contributory negligence. It is partially our fault that so many illegal immigrants have been able to stay here without proper authorization for so many years. Thus, for humanitarian reasons, we may want to provide a means for certain "illegals" to remain and be made legal if they comply with practical requirements.

1. A signed statement by the employer made before an immigration official that the work of the individual is necessary and that he or she will be paid at the prevailing wage plus benefits paid American employees in the same field of endeavor. This will undermine the concept of cheap labor. Also, this employee must appear before an immigration official to prove at the end of three years that he can speak and write standard English. This will help him become a part of America. If this is not accomplished, out they go!

2. One that has been working in this country and has created his own business employing others which has operated for at least three years and speaks English can apply for citizenship. If item one is met, legal status can be granted if back taxes are paid and there is no criminal record. This may be reviewed every three years three times. Any failure to pay taxes or commission of a crime would entail loss of citizenship during that nine year period and they would be required to leave.

No future illegal immigration will be tolerated, no foolish walls will be necessary and border guards can be a thing of the ugly past if ideas stated here are followed. Those found without ID Cards will go to jail as indicated above in "Problem Seven, Solution B," they will not collect $200.00, they will not get a "get out of jail free" card!

I just learned that in the short area of the fence that has been built, "illegals" have been tunneling under it to get into "Seventh Heaven." A congressperson suggested that a law be written against this! That smarty aleck! Any law not written with an immediate and severe penalty provided for breaking that law will be laughed at! This is why immigration is out of control and everyone – including employers – gets away with it!

One of the best and easiest ways to control illegal immigration is to be able to identify legal immigrants and actual citizens – that leaves us with the illegals! This is a valid and necessary reason for requiring the use of National Identity Cards. It should only have to be produced or shown when seeking employment, upon leaving or entering the country, to get a bank account, car license, to buy a gun, to be granted a social security number, to vote, or to get any social benefits (welfare, etc.), to be admitted to college or university or have children admitted to schools and should be shown when arrested or thereafter in order to be released. If this cannot be produced by detainee, the judge should determine if he must serve the prison sentence for crime committed or if the immigration authorities should be called before or after sentence is served to expel him or have him spend the required time in jail before being expelled. We have the technology to make this simple. We now swipe our credit cards to make sure they are valid. Anyone in need of checking ID Cards could use the same machine to check them. If a person does not have an ID Card or produces an invalid one, the police should be called and then the trespasser should be turned over to immigration authorities. Last but not least, if their primary language is not English, they must prove they entered the country legally in order to be given an NI Card.

In conjunction with some of the above ideas, or alone, the following may be another way to solve the illegal immigration problem. We may grant them an ID Card which will expire in two years. This will allow them a hiatus of two years during which time they will be able to adjust their lives, continue to be employed and earn money during those two years or return immediately to their native country. This will give them breathing time and choice. It will also give present employers of illegals time to replace them with citizens. As far as the National Identification Card is concerned, I know those with a religious bent will throw the following into your face, but only the lunatic fringe that believes in Satan, "beasts," devils, angels and similar nonsense. Here it is out of the usual fairy tale:

Is the coming National ID the prophesied "mark of the beast"?
There is a prophecy in the Bible that foretells a time when every person will be required to have a mark or a number, without which he or she will not be able to participate in the economy. The prophecy is 2,000 years old, but it has been impossible for it to come to pass until now. With the invention of the computer and the Internet, this prophecy of buying and selling, using a number, can now be implemented at any time. Has the time for the fulfillment of this prophecy arrived? I do not think the computer was around 2000 years ago.

Item below is related to problems 4 and 5 above:
Sen. Baucus Says Outsourcing Fact of Life
Published: 1/13/06, 5:06 PM EDT

Sen. Max Baucus, the top Democrat on the U.S. Senate Finance Committee, said Friday that outsourcing white-collar jobs to low-wage countries such as India has become a global fact of life and that America must learn to live with it. …Baucus said a majority of fellow Senate Democrats agreed with him, despite the party's longtime opposition to American companies moving jobs overseas. (I guess the big corporation lobbyists got to them too! jk)

"Everybody is concerned about job losses and so am I," he told The Associated Press in an interview in Bangalore, his first stop on a five-day tour of India. "But the world is flat and we must work harder to better retrain our people," rather than resist outsourcing, he said. "Off shoring is a fact of globalization. Opportunities for U.S. companies come from everywhere including India." (Retraining our people is meaningless if there are no jobs left in America. How much training is needed for working in a fast food restaurant? Such employment is good, needed and honorable, but we need all kinds of jobs. jk)

> (Notice Sen. Baucus says the "world is flat." He must be a fervent believer that the Bible is the source of all wisdom and cannot be wrong! Since the Bible declares: "…to the four corners of the earth," it certainly is logical to any Bible thumper that it is saying the world is flat! Will someone please enlighten Sen. Baucus to the fact that the concept of a flat earth went out centuries ago and that a globe does not have four corners! Thank you one and all. jk)

(Miracle of miracles, I agree with him that "we must work harder to better retrain our people." That can only be done if we get the government out and free enterprise into education via a voucher system as explained in my book, DISASTER ZONE – U.S.A., and in the book percolating in my mind. But more important than the difference in training is the extremely low wages outside the country. Are we going to continue to force American workers to descend to the low wages of the Third World? Feeling social responsibility toward one's workers sounds like idealism or pie in the sky, but one day the chickens will come home to roost when few Americans will be able to afford to buy what we produce, when health problems become rampant because inferior or no health care is provided by corporations only interested in the bottom line rather than their workers' well being. Much time will be lost from work and the snowball will tumble down the slippery slope until we become a country with only the very rich and the very poor! Will we be saying "If they do not have bread, let them eat sushi"?

You may help solve the out sourcing epidemic by sending a letter to all of your political representatives or use the internet as advised in Chapter 13. This is up to you. If you do not do so, I will not keep you after school, but do it!

* * * * * * * * * *

As my good Christian friend says: THIS IS A MUST READ!

The Immigration Bill
"The Senate [immigration] bill would make 25% of our population foreign born within 20 years (most of them high school dropouts), and the United States as we know it would no longer exist. It is impossible in so short a time to assimilate 66 million people whose native culture does not respect the Rule of Law, self-government, private property, or the sanctity of contracts, and where they are accustomed to an economy based on bribery and controlled by corrupt police and a small, rich ruling class that keeps most of the people in dire poverty. [. . .]

"After the U.S. Senate passed the Kennedy-McCain (a.k.a. Hagel-Martinez) immigration bill in May, the White House website advertised, in both English and Spanish, Bush's congratulations (*applaudo*) for passing what he called bipartisan (*bipartidista*) and comprehensive (*integral*) immigration reform. In fact, this may be the worst and the most expensive bill ever passed by the Senate. It is an embarrassment to the few Republicans who voted for it.

"The Senate bill grants amnesty (a.k.a. legalization or earned citizenship) to the 12 to 20 million illegal aliens currently living in the United States, who will then become recipients of our generous entitlements. The cost to the taxpayers of this monumental expansion of the welfare state will be at least $50 billion a year. [. . .]

"The bill gives the so-called temporary guest workers preferential rights that American citizens do not have. The temporaries can't be fired from their jobs except for cause, they must be paid the prevailing wage, and they can't be arrested for other civil offenses if they are stopped for traffic violations.

"The bill assures the illegals they can have the preference of in-state college tuition (something that is denied to U.S. citizens in 49 [. . .] states), plus certain types of college financial assistance. As minorities, they may even get affirmative action preferences in jobs, government contracts, and college admissions. [. . .]

"We currently have 37,000 troops guarding the 151-mile border between North and South Korea, but we have fewer than 12,000 agents to monitor 2,000 miles of our southern border. [. . .]

"The illegal alien who drove 100 miles an hour on Interstate 485 on the wrong side of the highway, killing a University of North Carolina coed in November 2005, had been returned to Mexico 17 times. [. . .] (Do you see why I would require a jail sentence on hard labor? jk)

"Bush was correct when he said this is the 'time of decision.' Republicans who want to be elected this November should pass the Sensenbrenner House border-security-only bill (H.R. 4437) without any Bush-Kennerly-McCain plans to import more foreigners to take jobs from Americans."

-- **Excerpts from** "Guest Workers Aren't Cheap; They're Expensive," by Phyllis Schlafly, *The Phyllis Schlafly Report,* July 2006, pages 1, 2, 4. Address: PO Box 618, Alton, Illinois 62002.

* * * * *

The following taken from "Open Borders Will Destroy Society," by Ira Mehlman
"NAFTA has worked remarkably well for the elite in the U.S. and Mexico, but has been a resounding dud for the vast majority of workers in both countries. [. . .] While productivity in Mexico surged by 50

percent between 1994 and 2001, manufacturing wages in that country fell by 11 percent (and, in real terms, earnings were lower than they were in 1981). According to the World Bank, 51 percent of Mexicans lived in poverty in 1994 when NAFTA went into effect. Four years later 58 percent of Mexicans lived below the poverty line, while 82 percent of those in rural areas could be classified as poor.

"Under NAFTA, wages for workers in the maquiladoras have fallen, and jobs that left the U.S. to take advantage of lower wage Mexican labor are now leaving Mexico in pursuit of still lower wage labor in China and other countries. Meanwhile American agricultural exports to Mexico (often harvested by illegal Mexican migrants in the U.S.) have wrought havoc on small subsistence farmers in Mexico. Many of these displaced farmers have migrated to the cities, or have found their way across the border to the U.S.

"On our side of the border the results have not been any better. NAFTA was sold to American workers as a treaty that would allow millions of U.S. workers who were willing to retrain themselves to move into higher value added jobs, while the migration of labor intensive jobs to Mexico would provide economic sustenance and reduce the flow of Mexican workers headed north. Neither promise has been fulfilled. [. . .]

"Illegal immigration to the United States from Mexico has exploded since NAFTA went into effect. The Pew Hispanic Center estimates that since the implementation of NAFTA, more than 7 million illegal aliens have settled in the U.S. Mexico accounts for 57 percent of those in the U.S. illegally, while all of Latin America combined accounts for 81 percent of the illegal immigrant population of the U.S. Moreover, the numbers of illegal aliens from Mexico are increasing, not decreasing, after more than a decade of free trade."

SOURCE OF above:
-- **Excerpts from** "Global Delusions: Open Borders Will Destroy Society," by Ira Mehlman, *FAIR Immigration Report,* December 2005/ January 2006, page 7. Address: 1666 Connecticut Avenue, NW, Suite 400, Washington, DC 20009. Phone: 202-328-7004.

* * * * * * * * *

I believe most of us can agree, I know I do, that it is an exercise in free enterprise to smuggle in illegal immigrants or illicit drugs. This is what I mean, in a certain way, by unbridled free enterprise. Price gouging, firing workers to increase corporate earnings and the value of stock options for corporate executives, forgetting about social responsibilities of employers to employees are other examples of capitalism gone berserk. Even though I am a devout orthodox Jewish atheist, I do not mind writing that "this is not the Christian thing to do."

Employers need to accept a sense of responsibility for their workers. If they do not, is this not the same as the attitude of nobility in France that brought on the French revolution? Will we be saying "If they do not have bread, let them eat sushi"? I know. I repeated myself. So what! So we will remember it! Sew buttons!

GOVERNMENT BAILOUT OF BANKS IS A "NO-NO."

WARNING: There is now talk that the federal government should guarantee mortgages on property about to go into bankruptcy. This is a game of musical chairs. Instead of the banks winding up owning property now worth much less than the original mortgage, the government, the taxpayers, you and I will wind up holding worthless paper. Why would any individual continue to pay for a mortgage that is much higher than the actual present value of the property? There is no stopping these properties from being dumped onto the market at lower and lower prices keeping the real estate market in a long term decline in value which, of itself, will bring about more bankruptcies.

I am not happy to be the bearer of bad news, but we have another time bomb waiting on the side-lines, for now, that will in due time hit the banks yet another blow because of unscrupulous practices within the financial sector as regulators sat by and took no action. As house values became unrealistically and unreasonably higher, money hungry mortgage dealers convinced home owners to not only increase their mortgage on their homes, but enticed the elderly to take out a REVERSE MORTGAGE. This is good in that they were enabled to live in the house, collect a monthly income or take the full value out and still live in the house until death or sale for any reason. This was not so bad as prices continued to rise, but now we are faced with rapidly declining values. This represents no danger to the elderly still living in the property and intending to remain, but should they need to sell for any reason or after death, the family member to whom it may be left may get nothing if the amount of the mortgage plus accrued interest is more than the value of the property at that time. This is very likely the case with most reverse mortgages today. So go right ahead and tell your mother-law you are leaving her your house. She will not learn that the amount owed against the property is much greater than the value until after you go knocking on Saint Peter's door, or wherever you may be dispatched. One good thing, however; she only gives up the house and does not have to repay the bank's loss. This is the next blow the financial sector will be facing as long as property values remain low or continue to slide as is likely. The banks may be stuck with houses worth much less than the amount owed.

The proximate cause of this horror story is the criminal neglect of government regulators who took no steps to stop banks from committing "hari-kari" by making such poorly considered loans. We can only prevent this in the future by requiring that they act in advance. Congress needs to set realistic laws requiring banks to adhere to rules of prudent lending and not allow them to give in to greed.

I admit again, I do not know the answers to all problems. I can only see that we must allow the free enterprise system to take its course. It will weed out the imprudent. After all, if one does something that is dangerous one can only expect to suffer the consequences. The only hope I can see is if we follow ideas in this book that will help us drastically reduce overall taxes. That in itself may help the real estate market.

CHAPTER 11
MORALS

Morals, they are not just for people who profess a religion. I believe the knowledge of what is right and what is wrong is innate in a human being just as it is for a homing bird to return to its place of birth or for salmon to swim upstream at the right time of year. I know there are many other such examples, but I am just too old to make a study of all of them and report them to you. After all, I have to leave something for you to do other than to transform the world into a living paradise. I have faith in you. I know you can do it! So, what are you waiting for!

The invention of television, which I believe is here to stay, can do a lot of harm as well as good. Programs such as: In the Heat of the Night, Matlock, Dr. Phil, Judge Joe Brown, Judge Mablean Ephriam, Judge Glenda Hatchett, and Judge Judy can be very instructive about decent and indecent human behavior, but best of all they often can improve racial feelings. I am sure there are other good TV programs with constructive messages and that do not depend on sex and violence to become popular, but I cannot watch them all. I have to go to the beach once in awhile to provide business for my dermatologist! (This is comic relief – for me!)

Perhaps I am wrong in this matter but, what bothers me most is the over exposure of women's breasts bouncing in the breeze as a result of wearing low cut gowns that leave little if anything to one's imagination.

The TV producers seem to be playing the game "How low can we go?" I can understand why religious Muslims and others are upset with Western culture. I am not saying all this should be censored, but viewers need to let the TV producers know their feelings about this. How about a little moderation, modesty and self regulation? Things that should be relegated to cable TV should not be on channels seen in the living room with children present. I believe that people should be free to do as they wish, but others should not have things thrust into their faces that they would prefer to be private. I happen to be very much in accord with this statement from a religious publication: Getting used to something bad can happen little by little. For years the networks and our culture as a whole have been moving the line of what's viewed as appropriate or decent for young people and family audiences. Slowly we have become **desensitized** in no longer feeling shocked or surprised in hearing and seeing images that show a lack of respect for women, and promote sexuality as a vehicle for self-pleasure.

I agree with it except for the idea that we should not have sex as a vehicle for self-pleasure. This comes from the idea that sex is for procreation only. That to me is nonsense. A man and a woman in love, preferably married, and any male or female couples should feel relaxed and free to enjoy one another completely. Decades ago with the invention and availability of condoms I could see what was coming. If a couple can enjoy the pleasures of intimate contact, why not as long as they take precautions against disease and the chance of having a child they are not ready for. Well, there may be a reason for not being so open to making yourself available for such horizontal recreation. If I should ever live to be normal – which I am sure will never happen – I would not want to marry a girl who was sexually available to any hunk of a man who came along! This is a matter for individuals to determine, not a religion, not the government. You have every right to consider my opinion to be wrong. I give you permission to do so, but consider such lack of constraint - doing away with all the religious taboos - is bad for the business of psychiatrists. If I am not making myself clear, I am saying that religion often creates a need for psychiatry with their "forbidden fruit syndrome." This is my personal view, but in a free country it is the market place that should control such things, not government suppression. The only thing proper to do is to shut it off in our homes and/or write to the stations expressing our feelings. Good luck! You see, this book cannot solve all world problems; it is up to the individual – you! (See how you can gain control in CHAPTER 13)

The religious fundamentalists among us are missing the boat. Instead of proposing a constitutional amendment that would condemn homosexuals into being looked upon as second class citizens, vile and outside the norm of life, they should propose a clarification of the First Amendment that would make it illegal to use hateful or demeaning speech or would encourage violence against any member of the human race. In my mind that is the "Christian thing to do." Then again, I do not consider these charlatans to be real Christians as they are far from being Christ-like. The filth on TV is nothing compared to the hateful teachings of the religious right. This is immoral!

I have been watching the Terry "Stinger" Show and others of like ilk to see how bad they can really be. It seems that money makes the world go 'round and both this filth and religion bring in piles of dough, loot or lettuce. This does not speak well of the intelligence of the general public. It seems mean to mention religion in this context because the latter can do a lot of good in this world and has been the inspiration of some of the most wonderful art, architecture and music ever created. But there is no saving grace in these shows that parade before us the ignorance and depravity of so many poor souls.

I believe very much in the importance of morals even though I call myself a Devout, Orthodox, homosexual Jewish atheist. However, I believe these shows to be harmful to society. If I had children, I would not allow them to be exposed to them – the shows, I mean. Religion, yes, because this can be instructive and teach necessary values if explained by an intelligent adult. It is much like studying history. On the other hand, these shows are harmful because they validate, glamorize and give public exposure to the most vile, despicable, dishonest and ignorant element of the human race! I have no children, but I am concerned for those who see this garbage and are led to believe that their language and behavior are acceptable. These shows are perfect examples of just how far the First Amendment has gone to a ridiculous extreme. The Founding Fathers – and I remember them well, of course – did not even dream of a world with radio, TV and the internet when they wrote the First Amendment! Little did they dream of the filth that would be flowing into our homes! Somehow, we need to encourage people to be more moderate and discreet. Perhaps the media needs to concentrate on this rather than on those who flaunt their sexuality. I may be totally wrong in this area. As I have admitted before, I really do not know the answer to everything. That is an amazing thing to admit, but it is the truth, and you know what kind of truth…the gospel of course…! Please understand that I am just thinking out loud, hoping my readers will start to consider these things on their own and decide what should be and what should not be. We may decide for ourselves, but we must not try to dictate to others.

The religious right needs to enter the twenty-first century before it is too late. They need to understand that their mentality and level of thinking are on a par with the former Nazis of Germany and the present Nazi groups all over the world who preach hate. These hate-mongers seek to demean and harm those they do not understand, are different in any way and not living up to what these bigots consider to be their ideal. Furthermore, G-d needs to speak to them, as He did to me when He explained that He created homosexuality to better control world population rather than to depend upon war, famine, disease and violence. They need to come down off their clouds to see the endless variety of all kinds of life, objects and beauty nature has created. Yes, we have much to be thankful for! To condemn and belittle an entire group is immoral. Why do they not understand this?

There is no doubt in my mind that many cultures, religions, have grappled with the concerns mentioned above. Below are some thoughts from the Muslim past that still prevail today.

> In 1928, four years after the abolishment of the caliphate, the Egyptian schoolteacher Hasan al-Banna founded the first Islamic fundamentalist movement in

the Sunni world, the Muslim Brotherhood (al-Ikhwan al-Muslimun). Al-Banna was appalled by "the wave of atheism and lewdness [that] engulfed Egypt" following World War I. The victorious Europeans had "imported their half-naked women into these regions, together with their liquors, their theatres, their dance halls, their amusements, their stories, their newspapers, their novels, their whims, their silly games, and their vices." Suddenly the very heart of the Islamic world was penetrated by European "schools and scientific and cultural institutes" that "cast doubt and heresy into the souls of its sons and taught them how to demean themselves, disparage their religion and their fatherland, divest themselves of their traditions and beliefs, and to regard as sacred anything Western.

Most distressing to al-Banna and his followers was what they saw as the rapid moral decline of the religious establishment, including the leading sheikhs, or religious scholars, at Al-Azhar, the grand mosque and center of Islamic learning in Cairo. The clerical leaders had become compromised and corrupted by their alliance with the indigenous ruling elites who had succeeded the European colonial masters.

Al-Banna was not really totally "bananas." I tend to agree with him, somewhat, and many other Muslims that our western culture has gone too far in many areas. Particularly, I find it disturbing that women so often flaunt their sexual assets publicly. Too many actresses, models and women wear such low cut dresses I would not be surprised to see a part of their anatomy flip out at their very next step! They seem to be advertising that they are ready and willing to please any three-legged men coming their way! Too many young girls and grown women, who should know better, try to emulate them. They are telling our youth that it is O.K. to be a slut, a woman of the night, afternoon; your time is my time!

I wonder if they have an inferiority complex, feeling that they have no other talent. Am I too old fashioned? I feel they have a right to do as they please since our greatest strength is maintaining our tradition of individual freedom. I just wish the media would not give them the attention they seem to be crying out for! Women can be just as beautiful and desirable wearing dresses below the knee or even long dresses. Modesty shows greater self-respect. Hopefully someone will find a way of putting this idea across without taking away our freedom.

CHAPTER 12
END FAKE WAR ON DRUGS

How many people out there, in the wild blue yonder, understand that there is a very strong resemblance of the American Christian extremist right with the extremist right of the Muslim world? I think President Bush is right in trying to bring democracy to the Middle East, Iraq at this time, but we had best clean up our own act by stopping Komeiniacs from gaining support in Washington! They have led us up a dark alley which is doing the greatest harm to the most vulnerable in our population. Our fundamentalist Christian preachers have been trying for decades to impose their religious dogmas upon the rest of us. The first idiotic idea foisted upon the sleeping public was Prohibition (making it illegal to have or to consume alcoholic beverages). We know what happened. There were more innocent citizens killed by the turf wars of gangsters to control territory than any harm alcohol ever could have caused! Once the public sobered up, we passed the Twenty – first Amendment to the Constitution, repealing the Eighteenth Amendment and returning life, liberty and the pursuit of happiness to the public! Let us drink to that! Hallaluyah! By the way, I almost never take a drink. The next insane idea from the Religious Right was to bring us the War on Drugs.

It is well known that we tried prohibition and now the drug war because of the urgings of people of religion. Remember the Christian ladies standing in front of bars, beating their tambourines and carrying signs reading, DRINK IS SIN AND LEADS TO HELL? Religion is about control and power. Religion and government represent a peach of a pear (more like the forbidden apple) because they both aim for greater control and power for themselves! These so-called do-gooders ostensibly want to stop people from hurting themselves! In the ensuing process, more people have been killed, corrupted or had their lives destroyed than if the government had just allowed us to use our G-d given right to choose for ourselves, to exercise "free will"! When crime and corruption became so rampant, we finally repealed the Prohibition Amendment. Eventually we will have to come to our senses and do likewise with the failed drug war. It will be tough because so many individuals, the religionists, the drug lords and government use it for gaining power and great wealth. They all prosper from the trade because of the weakness of others and the foolishness and corruption of government. Of course, it is "We the People," the general electorate, which allows the government to continue with this foolish waste of public funds to try to stop what is unstoppable! It is like trying to empty the Pacific into the Atlantic. Did you ever try it? Remember, where there is pleasure to be had and a profit to be made, no law can stop it! Oh yes, it can be stopped, but only if we are willing to kill all the participants. Not a very Christian solution!

Make War On The War on Drugs
Posted by FoM on July 26, 2000 at 09:19:54 PT
By Judy Mann Source: Washington Post

The Justice Department has just issued another indicator of the damage being done by the war on drugs: An all-time high of 6.3 million people were under correctional supervision in 1999--1.86 million men and women behind bars and 4.5 million on parole or probation, 24 percent of them for drug offenses. The criminal justice system reached 1 percent of the adult population in 1980. Its reach now exceeds 3 percent--about one of every 32 people. Our $40 billion-a-year war on drugs has created more prisons, more criminals, more drug abuse and more disease. An estimated 60 percent of AIDS cases in women are attributed to dirty needles and syringes. A recent U.S. Supreme Court decision probably will spur more litigation in the drug war, as prisoners use the ruling to appeal unusually harsh sentences. The court ruled that any factual determination used to increase a sentence will have to be made by a jury, not a judge. While a judge can use a standard of the preponderance of the evidence in sentencing, a jury must decide beyond a reasonable doubt, says Graham Boyd, director of the Drug Policy Litigation Project of the American Civil Liberties Union. "If the government wants to impose draconian sentences for drug crimes, they should have at the very least to prove their case to a jury by a criminal standard, and that hasn't happened in the past--amazingly." That's just one example of the civil rights casualties of a war in which paramilitary police raid people's homes and authorities seize their assets without due process, flying in the face of the Fourth and Fifth amendments. Presidents have all sworn to uphold the Constitution. They should come out of their church pews and uphold their oaths.

A few politicians are brave enough to declare the obvious: The war on drugs hasn't worked. New Mexico's Gary E. Johnson (R) was the first governor to call for marijuana legalization and other major drug policy reforms. Rep. Tom Campbell (R-Calif.), a candidate for the U.S. Senate, is the first major-party politician to run statewide with a platform that includes prescription access to heroin. They will speak at the "shadow conventions" to be held at the same time as the Republican and Democratic conventions to address three issues of critical importance that organizers say are being given short shrift by the two major parties: the drug war, campaign finance reform and the growing gulf between rich and poor. **THIS BOOK HAS ALL THE ANSWERS FOR THE TAKING!**

Drug policies affect millions of people who have family members behind bars. Some of them will be at the shadow conventions. They will put names and faces on this whole failed drug war effort. Many of them are likely to be black. While African Americans constitute 13 percent of the illegal drug users, they account for 74 percent of those sentenced for drug offenses. Convicted felons lose their right to vote, a backdoor way of reinstituting Jim Crow laws. That may not be the intent, but that is the "collateral damage." Pressure to change drug laws is mounting, and it is coming from unlikely places, including farmers, who are forbidden to grow hemp, the plant from which marijuana comes but which has other, non-drug uses. The Lindesmith Center, which advocates drug policy reform, did a survey several years ago that found more than 50 percent of farmers in five Midwestern and western states favored legalizing hemp. Only 35 percent were opposed. "This was the first indication we had that the public, in fairly conservative agricultural states, were supporting this," says Ethan Nadelmann, executive director of the center. More recently, Hawaii and North Dakota passed legislation legalizing hemp's cultivation, and similar measures are "in play" in more than 10 other states, Nadelmann says. From 30 to 40 countries, including Canada, have made it legal. "This is quite galling for farmers on the northern border who can look across the border and see people growing this stuff," he says. Nadelmann believes that both Texas Gov. George W. Bush and Vice President Gore, the Republican and Democratic presidential candidates, would be well served if they did some research on hemp. "It may be an issue that a number of people care about, and it would be sending a message they are willing to think rationally about the economic and agricultural interests of farmers even when the product has a relationship to marijuana." The Lindesmith Center is one of more than 35 public policy, health, religious and racial advocacy organizations that sent a list of 10 tough questions to the presidential candidates during the primaries, pointing out where the drug policies have failed and asking what they would do to change them.

None of the candidates have answered, according to Kevin B. Zeese, co-chair of the National Coalition for Effective Drug Policies, although the groups will try to pursue the issue during the general election campaign. "Unless the drug issue is forced on them, they prefer to avoid it rather than confront it," Zeese says. "Our basic point is the drug war is bankrupt and our policymakers aren't facing up to it. We tried to construct those questions in a way that showed the drug war methods are causing more problems than they solve, and we got a range of groups to show a breadth of concern about this."

Highly visible people, including former Minnesota Gov. Jesse Ventura (I), have called for a genuine debate on how to deal with drugs. Approaches gaining support include legalizing marijuana (except for sale to minors), prescription access to heroine, needle exchanges, taxing drugs and redirecting most of the drug war funding into public health and education. We are a nation of intelligent and thoughtful people who deserve better than overheated rhetoric and a drug policy dictated by crazy hard-liners and pandering politicians. At the very least, in the face of the well-documented harm the war on drugs has caused, we deserve a debate on how to control the drug market in a way that works.

Source: Judy Mann can be reached at (202) 334-6109 or by e-mail at: mannj@washpost.com

E-mail: letterstoed@washpost.com

* * * * * * * * * *

…With over 2 million people now locked up, the U.S. prison population is now the largest in the world, much of it the result of the war on drugs. At over 700 per 100,000 residents, for example, the U.S. incarceration rate is more than seven times higher than the rates of incarceration in Germany or France. On top of the price of inequitable enforcement and the $33 billion that the U.S. government is spending annually to enforce drug prohibition, Miron contends that the war on drugs has been more effective in fostering corruption among public officials than in reducing drug consumption.

SOURCE: Prison, race, HIV linked?
Wed 14 Dec 2005 01:01 PM CST
CONNECTICUT (myDNA News)

WORLD VIOLENCE OFTEN TIED INTO DRUG TRAFFICKING

500 Rebels Attack Village in Colombia
Published: 12/18/05

"The 12,000-strong FARC and 3,500-member ELN have been fighting for more than four decades to overthrow the government in the name of redistributing wealth in this country of 44 million people. The groups, both on a U.S. list of terrorist organizations, are also involved in drug trafficking and kidnapping for ransom."

Chaos on the U.S.-Mexican Border: Opportunity for Al Qaeda?
Tuesday, August 02, 2005

U.S. authorities closed the U.S. Consulate in Nuevo Laredo, Mexico, on Aug. 1 -- four days after intense firefights rocked the town of more than half a million people across the Rio Grande from Laredo, Texas. U.S. Ambassador to Mexico Tony Garza said the consulate would remain closed for a week, allowing U.S. authorities to assess the security situation and giving the Mexican government a chance to deal with the problem. Two days earlier, at Garza's request, the U.S. State Department renewed its warning for U.S. citizens traveling to Mexico. The U.S. moves highlight the increasing chaos in Nuevo Laredo, despite efforts by the Mexican government to intervene. On June 13, Mexican President Vicente Fox sent the Mexican army to Nuevo Laredo to take over police functions from the city's police department, which is battling internal corruption as well as warring drug cartels -- most notably from border cities Juarez, Tijuana and Matamoros, and from western Sinaloa state. The breakdown in law and order that prompted Fox's move led to the June 8 killing of police chief Alejandro Dominguez -- just nine hours after he was sworn in. In response to Fox's order, the federal government broke up the police force, detaining its officers and transferring 40 of them to Mexico City for further questioning. Since then, local police authority has been reinstated, but with fewer police officers and with federal assistance. Despite government efforts, however, the situation in Nuevo Laredo continues to deteriorate. Sources in Laredo, Texas, say Nuevo Laredo had 64 homicides in 2004, but that more than 100 homicides occurred in the first seven months of 2005. Before now, the highest homicide rate ever recorded in the city was 71. In another indication of border insecurity, a Chihuahua state police officer shot a U.S. tourist in the back of the head with an AR-15 rifle July 31. Mexican authorities said the officer's weapon accidentally discharged, but the officer and his companions reportedly left the scene without trying to help the victim, who was taken to a U.S. hospital in Columbus, New Mexico, and then to El Paso, Texas.

Illustrating the Mexican government's failed efforts in Nuevo Laredo, a group armed with heavy machine guns, AK-47 assault rifles and at least one rocket launcher attacked a house on Mexicali Street on July 28. The occupants of the house, supposedly a rival drug gang, returned fire with their own weapons. Part of the house collapsed in the ensuing battle, while grenades were left strewn around the residential street. Police investigating the scene afterward reportedly found a hit list complete with names and photographs of more than a dozen local officials who had been "sentenced to death" by the gang. Hours later, another firefight broke out in the affluent Madero neighborhood, with assailants attacking a house with automatic weapons. So far, the problems in Nuevo Laredo have not spilled over the border into Texas, possibly because the criminal gangs that control Nuevo Laredo use Laredo and its surrounding area as a trans-shipment point -- and want to keep it from becoming another battleground. Complicating the situation is Los Zetas, a group of elite anti-drug paratroopers and intelligence soldiers who deserted their federal Special Air Mobile Force Group in 1991 and began hiring their services out to the cartels. Zetas members reportedly have crossed the border and engaged U.S. law enforcement personnel. The chaos on the border is increasing concerns within the U.S. intelligence community that al Qaeda-linked groups or other terrorists could exploit the situation and cross operatives into the United States. Al Qaeda, investigators fear, could use well-established smuggling routes to bypass the enhanced scrutiny of passengers on air traffic "no-fly" lists. From an operational security perspective, terrorists could be wondering why they should run the risk of having their documents scrutinized by outbound immigration and inbound inspectors when they can bypass all of that at the U.S.-Mexican border.

One source in the intelligence community says a great number of illegal immigrants are using a pipeline that originates in Russia, crosses through the tri-border area of Argentina, Brazil and Paraguay, and passes through Mexico into the United States. In some cases, Mexico is used as a staging point while the illegal immigrant gets acclimated and money arrives from relatives inside the United States for the transit fee. Most of the illegal immigrants apprehended recently were heading for Houston; Newark, N.J.; New York or California. Despite law enforcement success in keeping the Nuevo Laredo violence from spreading into Texas, the situation on the border remains volatile -- and is unlikely to improve. Continued violence will affect U.S. business in Nuevo Laredo and other parts of Mexico, as the cost of providing adequate security soars out of reach.

Mexican Soldiers Patrol City Amid Violence
Published: 3/6/05

More than 700 soldiers and federal and state agents took to the streets of this city on the Mexico-U.S. border Sunday to help local authorities control a wave of apparently drug-related violent crime. The influx of law enforcement came after four more killings over the weekend, bringing the total number of people killed in ambush-style shootings in Nuevo Laredo to 20 for this year. Arturo Jimenez, a commander of the Federal Preventative Police, said in addition to the mobilization of forces, investigators would begin interviewing local police and state prosecutors in search of those who may be taking bribes from drug smuggling gangs. "It's difficult to combat crime when there are a lot of allies of organized crime who block our efforts," said Jimenez, who was sent to oversee the Nuevo Laredo crackdown by Mexico's Public Safety Secretary Ramon Huerta.

Jimenez said the first priority will be re-establishing law and order, but that soldiers and agents would also eventually help go after key drug smugglers. The border region in Mexico's northeast has seen an increase in drug violence after the area's alleged kingpin, Osiel Cardenas, was arrested in 2003. Authorities say the violence has intensified in recent months because another reputed drug lord, Joaquin "El Chapo" Guzman, has been fighting smugglers loyal to Cardenas to gain access to smuggling routes in Nuevo Laredo, which is across the border from Laredo, Texas. More than 40 vehicles loaded down with federal agents rolled into the city Sunday morning, while soldiers arrived to patrol poorer, violent neighborhoods. Dispatching federal and state authorities and soldiers to problem spots along the U.S.-Mexico border is not new. In recent years, special forces have descended on Tijuana and soldiers and federal agents were deployed to Nuevo Laredo amid growing violence. In the past, reinforcements usually have calmed violence-ridden areas for a few days, but have had little long-term effect. In January, the U.S. State Department warned Americans that violent crime, including murder and kidnapping, have increased along the Mexican side of the border.

Chaos in Columbia, a direct result of the war on drugs!

Rebels Kill 5 Police Officers in Colombia
Published: 12/17/05

BOGOTA, Colombia (AP) - Rebels from the Revolutionary Armed Forces of Colombia attacked a tiny village in western Colombia on Saturday, killing five police officers and kidnapping six others, top government officials said. Just before dawn, dozens of FARC fighters encircled the village of San Marino, 170 miles west of Bogota, and then began shooting at police officers, National Police chief Gen. Jorge Daniel Castro said. The attorney general's office reported five officers were killed and six kidnapped. Victor Mosquera, the government's human rights representative in the region, said witnesses reported that four other police officers and four civilians were injured in the fighting. Castro said army troops were headed to the area to track down the guerrillas. The 12,000-strong FARC, Colombia's main rebel group, has been fighting for more than four decades to overthrow the government. The group also is involved in drug trafficking and kidnapping for ransom, and has been placed on a U.S. list of terrorist organizations. President Alvaro Uribe launched a military offensive against the FARC three years ago, but the rebels remain a potent force by using surprise attacks in remote parts of the country. More than 30 police officers in far-off towns such as San Marino have been killed by the FARC in the past three months. In Afghanistan the main incendiary force keeping the insurgents going is the poppy trade. (If we finally have sense enough to legalize all drugs, making the price so low that there would be no profit in the trade for the gangsters, all of above would come to an end. Those so weak that they must use drugs or those who do not care if they destroy their own lives should be free to do so or seek medical help. As matters stand today, it is the innocent people who are having their lives destroyed. jk)

FRIDAY, MARCH 02, 2007 *Washington Times* article

The United States said today that top anti-terror allies Afghanistan, Pakistan and Colombia had fallen short in the war on drugs despite enhanced counter-narcotics efforts, and it criticized perennial foes Iran, North Korea and Venezuela for not cooperating. Yeah guys, it's *your* fault we can't control the demand for these drugs in our own country. In its annual global survey of the drug war, the department said massive opium poppy production in Afghanistan, long the world's top producer of the main ingredient for heroin, continued to pose a major threat due to its links with groups such as the Taliban. "Afghanistan's huge drug trade undercuts efforts to rebuild the economy and develop a strong democratic government based on the rule of law… the department said in the 2007 International Narcotic Control Strategy Report. …There is strong evidence that narcotics trafficking is linked to the Taliban insurgency. These links between drug traffickers and anti-government forces threaten regional stability."

DEBKA*file* Exclusive Analysis
June 20, 2006, 5:45 PM (GMT+02:00)

"…opium farmers and marketers. Taliban provides protection for the poppy fields and the drug's smuggling routes to Pakistan and Iran. In Pakistan, al Qaeda's smuggling networks take over part of the produce from the Taliban and handle its consignment to the Middle East, Europe and the Far East."

* * * * * * * * *

Isn't it evident that much of the violence in the world would be ended or cut drastically if we stopped the foolishness of declaring certain drugs to be illegal? By continuing as we are, we are just assuring financial support to the Taliban and other extremist groups. And our sons and daughters are dying to keep this law on the books that should not be there just as the alcohol prohibition laws should never have been on the books. It is true that some countries need to grow plants that produce illegal drugs for economic reasons. Why not replace this by having them grow anything that can be used for bio-fuel or to feed people? Cut the profit out of growing illegal crops and they will find another way to survive with the help of the U.N., perhaps, or the ideas of scientists. And do not forget the need for population control. With fewer mouths to feed, there is greater chance for peace and survival. (jk)

CHAPTER 13

GOVERNMENT OF THE PEOPLE, BY THE PEOPLE, FOR THE PEOPLE... VIA ELECTRONIC TOWN MEETINGS

I am writing this short introduction to CHAPTER 13 because of the disgraceful event when our Democrat controlled House violated their trust to uphold the Constitution and to protect the welfare of the people of this country. They forgot that the President is the commander of our armed forces and not power hungry members of Congress. He is the one to make military judgments with help from his military commanders. Considering the decision by the Democrat-controlled House to issue a symbolic rejection of President Bush's decision to deploy more troops to Iraq, I am now convinced we must call for the dissolution of the Democrat Party. In view of the fact that they were members of the Congress which gave power to the president to go to war in Iraq, their action today was traitorous and a brazen attempt to use this struggle to gain political advantage for the coming elections in 2008. For decades, these clowns have done only what they thought was good for their party, not what is in the best interests of the country. Their present action is asinine and dangerous. The only result was to give comfort and support to the enemy. Democracy is not perfect, but it is the best system we seem to have at the moment. This is about to change for the better if my observations bring about some needed adjustments. I am asking for the dissolution of the Democrat Party for the above reasons, but it may just die anyway because of its selfish motives. The Federalist Party vanished from the scene as a result of its anti-war stance in the War of 1812. Detroit had fallen to the British and Washington had burned. Obviously things looked bleak as it does to some defeatists today in our Iraq struggle, but we prevailed then and we will now. Once we are at war, we must stand united or we are asking for defeat! Supporters of the nonbinding resolution included 229 Democrats and 17 Republicans -- fewer GOP defections than Democrats had hoped to get and the White House and its allies had feared. Two Democrats joined 180 Republicans in opposition. Thanks to heaven we have two Democrats with brains! In my humble opinion, I am asking that the Republican Party be relegated to the trash bin as well because they represent the Oligarchy explained below.

* * * * * * * * * *

THE TECHNOLOGICAL ADVANCES OF OUR AGE MAKE IT POSSIBLE TO CREATE A MORE DEMOCRATIC FORM OF GOVERNMENT. Let us take advantage of it and not live with the imperfect past. To my limited knowledge, there is no requirement in our Constitution that requires us to have two or more political parties. In fact, in George Washington's Farewell Address, he strongly advised against having political parties. Obviously, I am not George Washington and I assuredly never would have done the dastardly things he did like sleeping around in most cities of the colonies and crossing the Delaware to kill all those nice Hessians while they were half asleep after celebrating Christmas Eve by drinking bear or was it chamomile tea? It was so long ago, I am not sure I remember all the details. I am certainly too fat, old and ugly to run for any office myself; so do not come knocking on my door.

At the time I started to write this book, I did not know that George Washington, founder of our country, and I had the same thoughts on two salient points: the evils of political parties and religions. The wisdom of Washington and many of our founders was reflected in many of their writings and speeches. Washington and others also believed that organized religion would be a terrible threat to our form of government for the same reasons that he believed that organized political parties would be a threat to the country. And the reason primarily is based upon what Lord Acton said in 1887: "Power tends to corrupt, and absolute power corrupts absolutely." Both political parties and religions both decide what is best for them, leaving no room for the ideas or opinions of others. Both organized religion and political parties base their support upon groups of people who expect others to have a belief system that coincides almost 100% with their beliefs. This "one size fits all" concept cannot work anymore in the age of the Internet and mass communication. That is why organized religion and political parties are less popular today than ever before. The country and the rest of the world are now demanding more independence. It is my opinion that both organized religion and political parties have become corrupt in the sense that they now represent the powerful elite rather than the public at large. That is what Washington suggested to us in his farewell address." (For the rest of the story see NOTE 18)

The idea of having political parties has developed because we like to be competitive as in sports where one must come out on top. From what is happening now, it should be obvious that this is not good. If one party is for Proposition X, the other automatically feels they must be against it. This is what we call "deadlock." What is good for the party is the main concern with little regard to what is best for all citizens. Their main incentive is to top the other party so that they can once again become the majority in Congress or Parliament or any other name given to what is supposed to be the governing body. And do not forget, the politicians get into or gain power by giving away our tax money to pet groups for the sake of getting votes. This is one reason government keeps getting bigger and more expensive. The whole thing has been turned into a game – a sport! I suggest that we disband all parties and form a new political party with the name, perhaps, of "The Compassionate Conservative Party," having the goal of reforming capitalism and our political system so that we might survive and prosper. In this instance, the word "Party" is not to be understood in the regular sense. It should be a <u>temporary administrative organization</u> to enable us to facilitate the transition toward <u>creating government run by the People</u> through extensive use of the internet and other media. By getting rid of the multi-party system, each individual elected to

Congress will have only one concern – WHAT IS BEST FOR THE COUNTRY, not what is best for the Party! It is essential that we have citizens directly involved with the making of laws, get rid of lobbyists and have public financing of political campaigns. The air waves should or do belong to the people; so why not have the media contribute time for the airing of all political views. These programs would attract viewers and listeners just as any other programs. If their profits do not prove to be up to par, why not allow them tax write-offs for the time donated toward democracy and or the inclusion of ads at the top or bottom of the screen?

As matters are moving now, it is evident that the rich are getting vastly richer, the poor are getting poorer and the middle class is being squeezed out of existence. The big secret is that we are not living with a democracy; we are under the foot of an oligarchy – big corporations and wealthy individuals that exercise their power to have the laws written to work in their favor instead of for the good of the average citizen.

PARTICIPATORY DEMOCRACY – RETURN POWER TO THE PEOPLE

This is so funny, I urge you to read it with both eyes, even the glass one. I really believe it can change our entire political system and electoral process.
With our new technologies, we can once again have town meetings. We have allowed politically motivated politicians to steal our democracy. They are bought and paid for by lobbyists, big corporations and powerful interests. We the people must be given the right to initiate the writing of the laws which govern us-not lobbyists. The adoption of this principle by the new political party, the Compassionate Conservative Party, will steam roll it into power to save capitalism and democracy. I suggest that those in existing parities who believe in most I have addressed here should get out of them and join the CCP. These should be individuals who want to represent the best interests of the American people and do not want to be put into the straight jacket of any political party. It is no wonder that so many Americans do not vote. We are not stupid. It is generally realized that both parties are about the same and that

once in office, they will "do their own thing" which amounts to doing the will of those who bought the election for them! There is really no need for any party other than the Compassionate Conservative Party (the CCP) which would exist only to facilitate the creation and smooth functioning of our **GOVERNMENT OF THE PEOPLE, BY THE PEOPLE and FOR THE PEOPLE.**

In actuality, we would not be voting for any party, but only for individuals who really represent us! This cannot become a dictatorship because there is wide latitude in choice and the ideas will be coming directly from the public and individuals. Besides, I am not proposing outlawing any party; that is for citizens to consider. Once the principles of the Compassionate Conservative Party take hold, we will see that all representatives will be concentrating only on what they consider to be good for the nation. Citizens who agree with their ideas, will vote for them. For a reasonable amount of time, citizens could send their ideas to the party or individual Congressmen they know really want participatory democracy or to the quickly created Compassionate Conservative Party (CCP) as a means of getting things moving. Candidates will be able to adopt their own positions by reference to polls or e- mails from the people they are expected to represent or they can determine their positions simply from their own convictions. Each candidate can establish his or her own website to state their positions and philosophies. From this, the Party can draw up a list of laws to protect our freedoms and national polls can get the opinions of citizens electronically. If there is no computer at home, we should be able to go to any library, school, coffee house or city hall to find and read these web-sites and become informed before voting. Both proposed laws and candidates can be voted on in this way. Our votes will finally count! WE THE PEOPLE would be originating many of our laws and the Congress could then consider them. Votes of Congressmen would, by law, be immediately available on their websites. All the details and safeguards, of course, need to be worked out by heads better than mine.

Fine, now how do we get away from our present anachronism? Simple, 'old chap! When it is time for elections – well before it would be best – any Congressman or individual could set up his own website and disclose his entire voting record, and/or what he or she proposes for the future. Any computer can be used by any properly identified citizen to record his or her choice. The days of spending millions of dollars on political campaigns would be ended just as multi-million dollar computers filling a room have been replaced by smaller, more efficient and much less expensive models that can even be worked on at home! Any citizen wanting to participate need only go to the nearest computer to be informed by the internet. All candidates running for office will have their names and websites listed. When it comes time for a vote on a candidate or a law, the one with the most "YES" votes carries the day or if it is very close or a tie, the casting of lots system may be called for. Naturally, I like the latter because it comes from the Bible. This is proof positive that there is some sense in the Bible.

To determine who is to be president and vice-president can be determined in a similar manner. All members of Congress wishing to be considered as a candidate for the presidency - and there can be many – a similar procedure can be followed. The one to receive the most "YES" votes will be the next president and the next runner-up will be vice-president. Accepting this "Town Meeting of the Air" idea for government I feel is the only hope we have of freeing the electoral process from the greedy hands of multi-billion dollar domestic and international corporations. That is another point. Many of our corporations are international behemoths who send lobbyists to Congress. Are they lobbying for American interests or for foreign interests? I know of no other way to force our representatives to represent voter's interests, the welfare of our country, and to stop them from pandering to special interests and big money which has been buying favors from the government that is supposed to be a government of the people, by the people and for the people. "The people" means all of the people, not only the rich that can buy influence with crooked politicians. Are you sick and tired of having a government that is bought and paid for? Do something! This is a country that should belong to all the people!

A major way to get us free of big corporate and special interests is through the use of initiatives and referendums. An initiative is a process whereby citizens gather enough signatures, using a petition to get an issue placed on a ballot. Once on the ballot, the voters can accept or reject it. It is a grass roots movement coming from the people. Now there may be a new bunch that may want to kill me. To the lawyers, lobbyists, extremist Muslims, right wing Christians we may now have to add big business moguls who may decide to hire the mafia! We certainly do have fun, don't we? Anyone know of a good body guard I can hire - how about a platoon of Marines?

On the contrary, a referendum originates with the legislature, it is put on the ballot for citizens to accept or reject. I would suggest a law, using an initiative from the people, to require all pay increases for congressmen to be presented in a referendum to the people who will be paying them! The people then could accept or reject such an increase. Serving this country should be considered an honor, not a means to great wealth. As matters now stand, politicians have voted themselves pay raises and benefits that are unbelievable. This is up to voters to investigate, not this author.

Perhaps we need to form a twenty-first century Continental Congress to draw up such a plan or platform. (Again, the "platform idea" has been dropped like a hot potato.) As you see, I have switched to laughing at myself by joking around. This is comic relief for me as I wonder who I think I am to try to remold our government. Well, I leave it to you to see if there is any merit or value to my efforts.

WE REFUSE TO BE SLAVES FOR BIG CORPORATIONS

Am I the only one on planet earth who is disgusted with automated answering machines that force you to use a menu to direct the call? There may be worse offenders, but I found that Bellsouth, now joined with AT&T, is the worst. To get to use Bellsouth Fast Access Internet Service, they sent me all the parts for me to connect. I pointed out that COMCAST installed such service for a friend and they came out and installed it for him, at no charge. When I complained, I was told they would send someone, but there would be an $80 charge. I told them I would not pay for it and that I was not going to be treated as a slave of a big corporation. If they wanted me as a customer, they needed to work for it and not ask me to do their job! The polite young lady, whom I believe was a fine black operator, conveyed my message to the supervisor as I had requested. She quickly came back and said there would be no charge and it would be taken care of. You see, I told you. There is a lot of good sense in the Bible. It says, "Ask and ye shall receive." It is time for the American public to stand up and demand some changes as suggested here. Demand to hear a human, breathing voice when you call a company; demand service; demand that work be done here in America by American workers. To confront a customer or prospective customer with a machine instead of a human voice waiting there to be of service, is a "public be damned attitude." We, the public, should not be considered to be the slaves of big corporations. If they want us to do business with them, they need to show a willingness to be of service. When confronted with an automated answering machine, find another company that respects the public and is willing to be of service. Let them know how you feel.

STAND UP TO BIG OIL –
it is time for AN EXCESS PROFITS TAX

The oil companies have never made so much money as now. The blame is put on the problems in the Middle East. True or not, the public should not be paying the consequences. The oil companies should be allowed to make no more in profits than they did prior to present difficulties and an average should be taken for a certain number of years prior to this. We should tax away excess profits to help pay the national debt caused partially by the war expenses. Do not expect present politicians to do this. They have, for the most part, been bought and paid for by the big oil giants. Remember the old American flag that showed a curled up snake that said: "DON'T TREAD ON ME!"? Act in this manner and changes will soon abound! We the people are the power, not the big corporations, not the politicians, not the lobbyists. We need to let them know what we want. Unless we act, nothing will change! You may refer back to CHAPTER 10 **DEMAND EXCESS PROFIT TAX**

* * * * * * * * *

I am against violence and for happiness. Thus I am including the following received via e-mail from an unknown source. This is proof positive that I am not the only one to come up with good ideas! At least I think they are good!

GET a BILL STARTED TO PLACE ALL POLITICIANS ON SOCIAL SECURITY. (I call it "Social Insecurity Plan. Use the town meeting of the air – the internet – and get a movement going. jk) Our Senators and Congresswomen do not pay into Social Security and, of course, they do not collect from it. You see, Social Security benefits were not suitable for persons of their rare elevation in society. They felt they should have a special plan for themselves. So, many years ago they voted in their own benefit plan. In more recent years, no congressperson has felt the need to change it. After all, it is a great plan. For all practical purposes their plan works like this: When they retire, they continue to draw the same pay until they die, except it may increase from time to time for cost of living adjustments. (Decided by them. jk) For example, Senator Byrd and Congressman White and their wives may expect to draw $7,800,000.00 (that's Seven Million, Eight-Hundred Thousand Dollars), with their wives drawing $275,000.00 during the last years of their lives. This is calculated on an average life span for each of those two Dignitaries. Younger Dignitaries who retire at an early age will receive much more during the rest of their lives. Their cost for this excellent plan is $0.00. NADA..! .ZILCH... This little perk they voted for themselves is free to them. You and I pick up the tab for this plan. The funds for this fine retirement plan come directly from the General Funds;"OUR TAX DOLLARS AT WORK!" From our own Social Security Plan, which you and I pay (or have paid) into every payday until we retire (which amount is matched by our employer), we can expect to get an average of $1,000 per month after retirement. Or, in other words, we would have to collect our average of $1,000 monthly benefits for 68 years and one (1) month - this is after retirement - to equal Senator Bill Bradley's reward for his years of work. This means we would have to live to the age of 133 to be on a par with the Good Senator (age 65, age of retirement + 68 years - forget the one month). Social Security could be very good if only one small change were made. That change would be to:

Jerk the Golden Fleece Retirement Plan from under the Senators and Congressmen. Put them into the Social Security plan with the rest of us. Then sit back and see how fast they would fix it.
Release Date: 9/22/2006 9:40 A.M

* * * * * * * * * *

With regard to the above, I would like to point out that our present system is in violation of the Fourteenth Amendment to our Constitution as it does not treat all citizens equally. Setting up politicians as a privileged class is not exactly part of the democratic philosophy as I see it! (jk)

I would add one other change that would help considerably. Assuming that the payroll tax cap is now $90,000 with nothing paid on incomes beyond that figure, I would require that the social security tax be paid on all earnings with no limit – into the millions if that is what is earned. This is for "we the people" to decide with no pressure from lobbyists, pressure groups or politicians. Our representatives in Congress were supposed to represent us, but today most of them vote for what is good for the very wealthy and the big corporations who helped pay for the election. We are not living in a democracy; it is an oligarchy - rule by the wealthy and powerful and the big corporations! Working through the internet, we can demand that our so-called representatives in Congress allow direct participation in the making of our laws as indicated in this book. We must vote against any who do not agree to support actual democracy as described here

LEGAL SYSTEM GONE BERSERK
END ELECTION OF JUDGES

Democracy is not perfect, but it is the best system we seem to have at the moment. This is about to change for the better if my observations bring about some needed adjustments. Voting for judges is democracy going to an extreme. It is like prescribing aspirin for a patient with bleeding ulcers. It does nothing to weed out incompetent or "off the deep end" judges on the bench who should, in some instances, be on the couch of a psychiatrist rather than on a bench in the court room! Our present American system of justice is an adversarial system, a game such as any sport in which the teams just seek to win. This system has lost sight of the requirement of a judicial system to seek truth, justice and equity. Now, what should be done? As one who believes that it is the responsibility of an individual to try to make this world a better place for future generations after he leaves it than it was when the Stork delivered him, I make the following proposals to clear the bench of incompetent or politically motivated judges:

1. A local commission of sitting judges should be empowered to select qualified lawyers who would then be selected by lot to attain status as judges. This commission should also be empowered to remove those whose decisions do not grant real justice. This should only be done upon the approval of the Justice Department of the State.
2. All new judges should be appointed from a list of qualified lawyers by the casting of lots as is proposed in the Bible. Remember, …I believe it is wise to use the wisdom that can be found in parts of the Bible.

"The lot causeth disputes to cease, and it decideth between the mighty'. (or in another version: "The lot causeth contentions to cease, and partith between the mighty")
Proverbs 18:18.

For more information on The Casting of Lots,

See jameslindlibrary.org on the internet.
Here is a perfect opportunity for "we the people" to take action against a sea of troubles and by opposing, end them! Shakespeare had it right all the time! That is what I told him when he wrote it!

You may help solve the out sourcing epidemic by sending a letter to all of your political representatives or use the internet as advised above. This is up to you. If you do not do so, I will not keep you after school, but do it!

CHAPTER 14

HOMOSEXUALITY –
THE NEW FOCUS OF HATE
FOR THE RELIGIOUS FASCISTS

If I may be so presumptuous as to speak as though I were a true believer, may I remind "said to be believers" that the command of Christ was the need, no - the command of Jesus - that we must love one another as He loved His disciples? Is it not evident that G-d has inflicted differences – in too many cases deformities – upon some of His children? Some He allowed to be born with minor differences such as height, weight or beauty and too many with dreadful afflictions such as the inability to hear or see, a propensity to have deadly diseases such as heart failure, cancer, sickle cell anemia or leprosy. Need I remind you that Jesus saw fit to heal a leper yet so many believers in Christ see fit to treat homosexuals as though they were lepers to be avoided and despised? Where is the love He commanded upon us? Have these so-called people of G-d no compassion for His creation who stutters, the hunchback, the lame or the one with little native intelligence? The essence of the teachings of Jesus was the need for love of one human for another and that is the corner stone of this book and the essential for creating world peace as well as harmony within a family and should be the basis of any religion worthy of being considered a religion. Think upon the above and draw your own conclusions.

I just thought of the following after reading about Rev. Pat Robertson on the internet. Pat Robertson once predicted Orlando, Florida could be hit by a meteor for flying the gay-pride flag. Is that a sane statement to make? Robertson said G-d told him during a recent prayer retreat that major cities and possibly millions of people will be affected by the meteor attack, which should take place sometime after September. Yes, of course, but September of what year? And Jesus will return on Robertson's next birthday! Sure He will! If G-d can talk to Robertson, He can talk to me, a closer relative to Jesus, and I am unanimous in this conclusion! G-d talks to me frequently throughout this book. When I told a neighbor about this, she asked how that could be since I say I am an atheist. I replied, "How many more centuries will it take people to understand that we are all G-d's children"? See, I told you. If religion can be irrational, why should not a non-religion be just as irrational? Robertson said G-d also told him that the U.S. only feigns friendship with Israel and that U.S. policies are pushing Israel toward "national suicide." I fear he is correct on this point. G-d told me the same thing! Robertson suggested in January 2006 that G-d punished then-Israeli Prime Minister Ariel Sharon with a stroke for ceding Israeli-controlled land to the Palestinians. This is not unlike Falwell's proclamation that AIDS is G-d's punishment for their life style. That style has been around since trees grew up straight (no pun intended) toward heaven. What took Him so long to create AIDS? How do these Bible thumpers explain why G-d allowed millions to die of the flu in 1918 just after He managed to kill off millions during World War 1? How can it be said that He is a loving G-d? I often jokingly say it is a matter of mismanagement at the highest level, but I do not blame our non-existent G-d for any of life's tragedies! As far as cataclysmic disasters are concerned, they happen because they happen as a result of divergent natural forces in motion. If I am wrong and G-d really exists, my apologies to one and all and to the Wizard behind the screen. I can assure you that I believe that Robertson and the other commercial religious zealots are full of "malarkey" or you know what! But it is the Gospel truth that G-d really did speak to me and asked that I explain to His creations (humans) that homosexuality should be welcomed as it is His merciful and loving way to control population rather than through disease, wars and famines. You see, in His old age, He has become more loving, more caring and more humanistic! Finally! I know you cannot wait to read my letter to Senator Santorum, a Holy Roller who believes the Bible is the exact, unalterable word of G-d. He sorely needs to read this book which G-d has commissioned me to write! Well, I will not allow you to read it, but I will tell you all about it! I assume Senator Rick Santorum believes himself to be a devout follower of Jesus Christ, but he has conveniently forgotten His teachings. Jesus is the man, or spokesman for God, who protected a harlot from the mob of zealots who were about to stone her to death as required by our loving Bible. The message was: "Let he who is without sin throw the first stone." Not a single stone was thrown. Why does Rick Santorum throw stones at a part of G-d's creation? To me, the above statement of Jesus means that the sinner must answer to God, not to the mob. Senator Santorum would empower the mob- read, the State – to judge and punish those who violate the thinking of the religious right. Again, Senator Santorum has forgotten that Jesus said: "Judge not that ye be not judged." But this self righteous Bible Thumper judges others and does not see the hump on his own back!

This sanctimonious, pontifical idiot –and I do mean Senator Santorum – would establish a Sex Police Force to enter bedrooms of both heterosexuals and homosexuals to see if any laws promulgated by a religious right court system were violated. I doubt if anyone would dispute the notion that the greatest impediment to democracy in Iraq is the presence of a large population of extremist Islamists who are in the same time warp, going back to the Dark Ages and back into unrecorded history, as our Christian religious right. If we allow this latter element to gain power in this country, we stand to lose our democracy and we will wind up with a theocracy and suffer the consequences as has been seen throughout history. I find that Senator Santorum does not wear a towel on his head, but his mentality is no different than that of the extremist Muslim Mullahs, Imams, Mommas and Pappas! We do not need these "Khomeiniacs" in Congress. A theocracy spells the end of democracy! Any time a politician evokes the word of G-d, you should expect something shady. As soon as our dearly beloved former and now deceased President Nixon ended his speech with "God bless you," I knew he was lying! After all, are we not taught that all can be forgiven? I am sure he had his fingers crossed just in case!

IN THE BIBLE JESUS PROCLAIMED
WE MUST LOVE ONE ANOTHER

I am confident he did not mean in the sense of horizontal recreation, but consider the following facts.

In both the First and Second books of Samuel we see the extraordinary love of Jonathan for David: I Samuel 18:1
"The soul of Jonathan was knit with the soul of David, and Jonathan loved him as his own soul."

I Samuel 18:3
Jonathan and David made a covenant because he (Jonathan) loved him as his own soul.
We see how Jonathan gave David his most personal apparel:

I Samuel 18:4
And Jonathan stripped himself of the robe that was upon him, and gave it to David, and his garments, even to his sword, and to his bow, and to his girdle.   There is no doubt about the intensity of this love:

I Samuel 19.2
Jonathan, Saul's son, delighted much in David.

I Samuel 20:4
Then said Jonathan unto David, Whatsoever thy soul desireth, I will even do it for thee.
And in case we are wondering how significant this love was, King David spelled it out:

II Samuel 1:26
Thy love to me was wonderful, passing the love of women.
Was their love more than platonic? Well, you decide…

I Samuel 20:41
…they kissed one another, and wept one with another, until David exceeded.

The Religious Tolerance Web Site states that, while the King James Version says "exceeded," the original Hebrew is actually, "David became large." When you love somebody as much as David loved Jonathan, you can imagine what "becoming large" means. Of course, most Sunday school teachers would rather not talk about this passage, and they either skip over it or say something like "David cried the most." It's clear that David loved Jonathan, and they hugged and kissed, and felt tender loving warmth for one another. And that love was beautiful because all love is beautiful. Love defines itself. It is the most powerful force there is because God is Love. In the New Testament we learn about G-d's love from His Son, and here, too, we learn that even the Son of G-d had a beloved friend:

Jn 13:23
Now there was leaning on Jesus' bosom one of his disciples, whom Jesus loved (John, the Beloved Disciple). Jesus made a special point about love. Love is not just permitted; it is required:

Jn 13:34
A new commandment I give unto you, That ye love one another; as I have loved you, that ye also love one another.

SOURCE: The Bible and UNKNOWN
If I may, my own comment on the above is that the unknown author read into it what he wanted, but what difference does it really make? Either kind of love is "a many splendored thing." Also, it is somewhat humorous.

A CHRISTIAN PREACHER OFF THE DEEP END!

Fred Waldron Phelps, Sr. (born November 13, 1929) is the highly controversial leader of the Westboro Baptist Church, an alleged cult based out of his home in Topeka, Kansas. Phelps is best known for preaching that G-d hates homosexuals and will punish both them and "fag enablers". He claims events such as the September 11 attacks and Hurricane Katrina are caused by G-d because of this hatred. He and his followers frequently picket various events, especially gay pride and funerals of gay men, feeling it is their sacred duty to impress their views upon others. Phelps is a self-described "fire and brimstone" preacher who believes that homosexuality and its acceptance have sentenced most of the world to eternal damnation, claiming true salvation can only be achieved through him. His group, which has roughly 100 members (90 of whom are related to him through blood or marriage), is built around an anti-homosexual core theology, with many of their activities stemming from a mantra that homosexuality is the lowest sin one can commit. He also refuses to use any word other than "fag" to describe homosexuals. Gay rights activists, as well as Christians of virtually every affiliation, have denounced him as a producer of anti-gay propaganda and violence-inspiring hate speech. Phelps rose to national prominence in 1998 when he and congregants from Westboro picketed the funeral of gay murder victim Matthew Shepard, delivering an obscenity laden sermon (with focus given to graphic descriptions of homosexual sex acts) informing the mourners that <u>Shephard</u> had gone to hell and that everyone in attendance would join him there. Ever since Phelps and Westboro have remained in the national limelight for their regular pickets of events ranging from gay pride parades to the funerals of soldiers killed in the Iraq War. He claims that these soldiers will go to hell because they were trying to protect our fag country. It seems that Fred Waldron Phelps, Sr. considers himself the new Jesus! (jk)

Laura Schlesinger, EXPERT ON G-D'S LAW

On Laura Schlesinger's radio show recently, she said that, as an observant Orthodox Jew, homosexuality is an abomination, according to Leviticus 18:22, and cannot be condoned under any circumstance. I am confident not all orthodox Jews hold to such a narrow and twisted view. The following response is an open letter to Dr. Laura, penned by a US resident, which was posted on the Internet. It's funny, as well as thought-provoking.

Dear Dr. Laura:

Thank you for doing so much to educate people regarding G-d's Law. I have learned a great deal from your show, and try to share that knowledge with as many people as I can. When someone tries to defend the homosexual lifestyle, for example, I simply remind them that Leviticus 18:22 clearly declares it to be an abomination... End of debate.

I do need some advice from you, however, regarding some other elements of G-d's Laws and how to follow them.

1. Leviticus 25:44 states that I may possess slaves, both male and female, provided they are purchased from neighboring nations. A friend of mine claims that this applies to Mexicans, but not Canadians. Can you clarify? Why can't I own Canadians?

2. I would like to sell my daughter into slavery, as sanctioned in Exodus 21:7. In this day and age, what do you think would be a fair price for her?

3. I know that I am allowed no contact with a woman while she is in her period of menstrual uncleanliness - Lev.15: 19-24. The problem is how do I tell? I have tried asking, but most women take offense.

4. When I burn a bull on the altar as a sacrifice, I know it creates a pleasing odor for the Lord - Lev.1:9. The problem is my neighbors. They claim the odor is not pleasing to them. Should I smite them?

5. I have a neighbor who insists on working on the Sabbath. Exodus 35:2.clearly states he should be put to death. Am I morally obligated to kill him myself, or should I ask the police to do it?

6. A friend of mine feels that even though eating shellfish is an abomination - Lev. 11:10, it is a lesser abomination than homosexuality. I don't agree. Can you settle this? Are there 'degrees' of abomination?

7. Lev. 21:20 states that I may not approach the altar of God if I have a defect in my sight. I have to admit that I wear reading glasses. Does my vision have to be 20/20, or is there some wiggle- room here?

8. Most of my male friends get their hair trimmed, including the hair around their temples, even though this is expressly forbidden by Lev. 19:27. How should they die?

9. I know from Lev. 11:6-8 that touching the skin of a dead pig makes me unclean, but may I still play football if I wear gloves?

10. My uncle has a farm. He violates Lev.19:19 by planting two different crops in the same field, as does his wife by wearing garments made

of two different kinds of thread (cotton/polyester blend). He also tends to curse and blaspheme a lot. Is it really necessary that we go to all the trouble of getting the whole town together to stone them? (Lev.24:10) Couldn't we just burn them to death at a private family affair, like we do with people who sleep with their in-laws? (Lev. 20:14)

I know you have studied these things extensively and thus enjoy considerable expertise in such matters, so I am confident you can help. Thank you again for reminding us that G-d's word is eternal and unchanging.

Signed, An adoring fan

MARRIAGE a la Bible!

About eleven states, due to religious conditioning (brain-washing) have changed their constitutions to outlaw gay marriages. Simply stated, they are attempting to write into the Constitution that marriage can only be between one man and one woman. Florida is now about to be running the risk of violating the civil and human rights of a good part of its population! As one who normally votes Republican, I am ashamed to say that it is largely extremist religious Republicans with Lilliputian minds who are supporting this constitutional change! Let us consider the Bible's thoughts on marriage! Now, if you're going to amend the constitution, let's make sure you do it right guys. The Presidential Prayer Team is currently urging us to:

"Pray for the President as he seeks wisdom on how to legally codify the definition of marriage. Pray that it will be according to Biblical principles. With many forces insisting on variant definitions of marriage, pray that God's Word and His standards will be honored by our government."

Any good religious person believes prayer should be balanced by action. So here, in support of the Prayer Team's admirable goals, is a proposed Constitutional Amendment codifying marriage entirely on Biblical principles:

A. Marriage in the United States shall consist of a union between one man and one or more women. (Gen 29:17-28; II Sam 3:2-5.)

B. Marriage shall not impede a man's right to take concubines in addition to his wife or wives. (II Sam 5:13; I Kings 11:3; II Chron 11:21)

C. A marriage shall be considered valid only if the wife is a virgin. If the wife is not a virgin, she shall be executed. (Deut 22:13-21)

D. Marriage between a believer and a nonbeliever shall be forbidden. (Gen 24:3; Num 25:1-9; Ezra 9:12; Neh 10:30)

E. Since marriage is for life, neither this Constitution nor the constitution of any State, nor any state or federal law, shall be construed to permit divorce. (Deut 22:19; Mark 10:9)

F. If a married man dies without children, his brother shall marry the widow. If he refuses to marry his brother's widow or deliberately does not give her children, he shall pay a fine of one shoe and be otherwise punished in a manner to be determined by law. (Gen. 38:6-10; Deut. 25:5-10)

Does any reader not believe that our human race has evolved a bit from these so-called words of G-d?

* * * * * * * * * *

Let us have a look at the claim of the men of the cloth, even if they do not wear checkered towels over their heads, that the acceptance of homosexuality can destroy marriage. Consider our political leaders in defense of marriage...

*Ronald Reagan - divorced the mother of two of his children to marry

Nancy Reagan who bore him a daughter only 7 months after the marriage.

*Bob Dole - divorced the mother of his child, who had nursed him through the long recovery from his war wounds.

*Newt Gingrich - divorced his wife who was dying of cancer.

*Dick Armey - House Majority Leader - divorced

*Sen. Phil Gramm of Texas - divorced

*Gov. John Engler of Michigan - divorced

*Gov. Pete Wilson of California - divorced

*George Will - divorced

*Sen. Lauch Faircloth - divorced

*Rush Limbaugh - Rush and his current wife Marta have six marriages and four divorces between them.

*Rep. Bob Barr of Georgia - Barr, not yet 50 years old, has been married three times.

Barr had the audacity to author and push the "Defense of Marriage Act." The current   joke making the rounds on Capitol Hill is "Bob Barr...WHICH marriage are you defending?!?

*Sen. Alfonse D'Amato of New York - divorced

*Sen. John Warner of Virginia - divorced (once married to Liz Taylor.)

*Gov. George Allen of Virginia - divorced

*Henry Kissinger - divorced

*Rep. Helen Chenoweth of Idaho - divorced

*Sen. John McCain of Arizona - divorced

Rep. John Kasich of Ohio - divorced

Rep. Susan Molinari of New York - Republican National Convention Keynote Speaker - divorced

So ... homosexuals are going to destroy the institution of marriage? Wait a minute.   It seems the Christian Republicans are doing a fine job without anyone's help!

Author unknown (Passed on by Dr. J. Knowname, a Devout Orthodox, homosexual, Jewish atheist – and G-D bless you whether He is there or not!)

FROM SPAIN, WHERIN FLOURISHED THE BLOODY INQUISITION, PRESENTS A PERFECT PROOF OF THE EVOLUTION OF HUMAN THOUGHT! I CAN ONLY SAY SHAME ON AMERICA, THE HOME OF THE FREE!

When the Spanish parliament ... took its historic vote legalizing both gay marriage and adoption of children by gay couples, Prime Minister Jose Luis Rodriguez Zapatero -- who put the full prestige of his office and party behind passage of the gay human rights legislation -- made probably the most remarkable speech in favor of full equality for those with same-sex hearts ever delivered by a head of government anywhere, in which he quoted two of the most illustrious gay poets in history. Here are excerpts from Zapatero's speech:

"We are not legislating, honorable members, for people far away and not known by us. We are enlarging the opportunity for happiness to our neighbors, our co-workers, our friends and, our families: at the same time we are making a more decent society, because a decent society is one that does not humiliate its members. In the poem 'The Family,' our [gay] poet Luis Cernuda was sorry because, 'How does man live in denial in vain / by giving rules that prohibit and condemn?'

"Today, the Spanish society answers to a group of people who, during many years have, been humiliated, whose rights have been ignored, whose dignity has been offended, their identity denied, and their liberty oppressed. Today the Spanish society grants them the respect they deserve, recognizes their rights, restores their dignity, affirms their identity, and restores their liberty.

"It is true that they are only a minority, but their triumph is everyone's triumph. It is also the triumph of those who oppose this law, even though they do not know this yet: because it is the triumph of Liberty. Their victory makes all of us (even those who oppose the law) better people, it makes our society better. Honorable members, There is no damage to marriage or to the concept of family in allowing two people of the same sex to get married. To the contrary, what happens is this class of Spanish citizens gets the potential to organize their lives with the rights and privileges of marriage and family. There is no danger to the institution of marriage, but precisely the opposite: this law enhances and respects marriage!

"Today, conscious that some people and institutions are in a profound disagreement with this change in our civil law, I wish to express that, like other reforms to the marriage code that preceded this one, this law will generate no evil, that its only consequence will be the avoiding of senseless suffering of decent human beings. A society that avoids senseless suffering of decent human beings is a better society.

"With the approval of this Bill, our country takes another step in the path of liberty and tolerance that was begun by the democratic change of government. Our children will look at us incredulously if we tell them that many years ago, our mothers had less rights than our fathers, or if we tell them that people had to stay married against their will even though they were unable to share their lives. Today we can offer them a beautiful lesson: every right gained, each access to liberty has been the result of the struggle and sacrifice of many people that deserve our recognition and praise.

"Today we demonstrate with this Bill that societies can better themselves and can cross barriers and create tolerance by putting a stop to the unhappiness and humiliation of some of our citizens. Today, for many of our countrymen, comes the day predicted by Kavafis [the great Greek gay poet] one century ago: 'Later 'twas said of the most perfect society / someone else, made like me / certainly will come out and act freely.'

(It may, indeed, be true that the U.S.A. is an underdeveloped and backward country as my French friends often told me! jk)

LOVE THY NEIGHBOR

I do hope we all understand that "Love Thy Neighbor" is equivalent to what I say many times in this book. It means: "Treat all human beings with consideration, respect, compassion and understanding no matter how different we may be." It has nothing to do with coveting thy neighbor's wife or "horizontal recreation of any kind!" But how do the Christian and Muslim right wing extremist fascists treat homosexuals? They certainly close their eyes and hearts to the words of Jesus and to the civilized part of the Koran. I say "civilized part" because it is over loaded with orders to kill infidels – not exactly in the minds of civilized people.

NO JEWS, DOGS or HOMOSEXUALS ALLOWED

Above is a sorry line in the history of mankind's refusal to heed the admonitions in "Love thy neighbor," but appropriate to remember here. It was the loving, Christian religious hypocrites who were responsible for the "NO JEWS OR DOGS ALLOWED" and "WHITE ONLY" signs to appear on clubs and hotels or simply practiced this as a policy. After Hitler's holocaust against the Jews, I guess Christians became ashamed to have such views against Jews anymore. They have now focused their rancor on homosexuals. It seems they are not happy unless they can find someone or some group to hate.

Several years ago, I took part in a march in front of the "Not-so-reverend" D. James Kennedy's church because of his condemnation of gays. I could not help but observe that representatives of right wing Nazi groups were across the street holding signs expressing their agreement with the church's position. It is, of course, well known that the Nazis sent homosexuals to the gas chambers along with the Jews as they, too, were said to be "Untermenchen" sub-human. Note the religious claim that homosexuality is an abomination in the eyes of the Lord!

May we take a lighter look at this for a moment? An unknown individual sent me the following:

"My mother took me to a psychiatrist when I was fifteen because she thought I was a latent homosexual. There was nothing latent about it.
~ Amanda Bearse

"It always seemed to me a bit pointless to disapprove of homosexuality. It's like disapproving of rain.... ~ Francis Maude

"The only queer people are those who don't love anybody.... ~ Rita Mae Brown

"The Bible contains six admonishments to homosexuals and 362 admonishments to heterosexuals. That doesn't mean that God doesn't love heterosexuals. It's just that they need more supervision. ~ Lynn Lavner"

The following factual story proves what a waste of human talent we are forced into by our religious bigots!

How 'Don't Tell' Translates
The Military Needs Linguists, But It Doesn't Want This One
By Anne Hull
Washington Post Staff Writer
Friday, June 18, 2004; Page A01

Glover recognized the sound instantly. It was the afternoon call to prayer coming from a mosque on Massachusetts Avenue. She held still, picking out familiar words and translating them in her head. She learned Arabic at the Defense Language Institute (DLI), the military's premier language school, in Monterey, Calif. Her timing as a soldier was fortuitous: Around her graduation last year, a Government Accounting Office study reported that the Army faced a critical shortage of linguists needed to translate intercepts and interrogate suspects in the war on terrorism. "I was what the country needed," Glover said. She was, and she wasn't. Glover is gay. She mastered Arabic but couldn't handle living a double life under the military policy known as "don't ask, don't tell." After two years in the Army, Glover, 26, voluntarily wrote a statement acknowledging her homosexuality. Confronted with a shortage of Arabic interpreters and its policy banning openly gay service members, the Pentagon had a choice to make which is how former Spec.Glover came to be cleaning pools instead of sitting in the desert, translating Arabic for the U.S. government. In at two year period, the Department of Defense has discharged 37 linguists from the Defense Language Institute for being gay. Like Glover, many studied Arabic. At a time of heightened need for intelligence specialists, 37 linguists were rendered useless because of their homosexuality. What a stupid waste brought on by imposing religious dogma! Historically, military leaders have argued that allowing gays to serve would hurt unit cohesion and recruiting efforts, and infringe on the privacy rights of heterosexuals. In 1993, at the urging of President Clinton, Congress agreed to soften the outright ban on gays in the military with a policy that came to be known as "don't ask, don't tell," which allowed them to serve as long as they kept their sexual orientation secret. On its 10th anniversary, "don't ask, don't tell" exists in a vastly changed nation. In 1993, there was no "Will & Grace," no gay Jack on "Dawson's Creek," no gay-themed Miller Lite commercials. In 1993, fewer than a dozen U.S. high schools had Gay-Straight Alliance organizations. Today, there are almost 2,000. In 1993, fewer than a dozen Fortune 500 companies offered health benefits to domestic partners. Today, nearly 200 do. This newer version of America is the one young enlistees leave behind when they join the military. On average, three or four service members are discharged each day because they are gay. Most are discharged for making statements about their sexuality, and most are younger than 25. "In the case of some, they get in the Army and they are traumatized by an awareness that the military is 20 years behind the societal curve," said Jeff Cleghorn, a former lawyer with the Servicemembers Legal Defense Network, a gay-rights group monitoring military justice. The Army says the discharged linguists were casualties of their own failure to meet a known policy. "We have standards," said Harvey Perritt, a spokesman for the U.S. Army Training and Doctrine Command at Fort Monroe, Va. "We have physical standards, academic standards. There's no difference between administering these standards and administering 'don't ask, don't tell.' The rules are the rules." (And the Bible thinks nothing is wrong with slavery! jk)

Of the discharges for the fiscal year that ended September 30, 2008, 410 were male and 209 were female, according to the figures obtained by the Globe from Pentagon personnel officials. That compares with a total of 627 discharges in fiscal year 2007; 612 in 2006; 726 in 2005;

and 653 in 2004. (Source: The Globe, by Bryan Bender May 19, 2009) Obama's national security adviser, James L. Jones, said in May he didn't know if the ban would be lifted. I guess Obama was just too busy increasing the national debt to worry about keeping his campaign promise to end the "don't ask, don't tell" policy. (jk)

Many military scholars agree that it's a matter of time before the ban is lifted. Said John Allen Williams, a professor of political science at Loyola University in Chicago and president of the Inter-University Seminar on Armed Forces and Society: " 'Don't ask, don't tell' is an interim step until the inevitable change. It's a useful speed bump." President Bush had made no move to reexamine the ban, despite the enormous strains placed on the military since the Sept. 11 attacks.

Alastair Gamble is one of the Arabic linguists discharged from the DLI. He was caught in his dorm room with his boyfriend, another linguist, during a surprise barracks inspection at 3:30 a.m. While several heterosexuals were also caught in the sweep, Gamble and his partner became the subjects of an investigation into homosexual conduct. Both were discharged. Gamble, an Emory University graduate who had also completed a nine-week intelligence course, assumed that his value to the Army would save him. "I developed a hubris about my ability," said Gamble, 24, who lives in Washington and works for an architectural design firm. "I believed I could do my job well and they would be foolish to separate me."

The Defense Language Institute, at the Presidio of Monterey, is the primary foreign-language school for the Department of Defense. For decades, Russian was the dominant language taught. But since Sept. 11, 2001, the size of the Arabic class has soared. Of the roughly 3,800 students enrolled at the DLI, 832 are learning Arabic, 743 Korean, 353 Chinese and 301 Russian, with the remaining students scattered in other languages. Many of the discharged gay linguists were studying Arabic or Korean, among the most rigorous taught at the DLI and most costly to the U.S. government. The DLI estimates the value of its 63-week Arabic language program -- not including room, board and the service member's salary -- at $33,500.

The Army gave Cathleen Glover a proficiency in Arabic, but it also typed the words "HOMOSEXUAL ADMISSION" on her official discharge papers. The best job she could find was cleaning pools. Glover looks like the standout soccer goalie she was in high school in rural Ohio. Her skin is tanned from a summer spent outdoors, her hair streaked blond by pool chemicals. Her backpack is crammed with books on Islam and the latest issue of The Army gave Cathleen Glover a proficiency in Arabic, but it also typed the words "HOMOSEXUAL ADMISSION" I would like to point out that Alexander the Great, who conquered most of the known world, was gay and a homosexual as well - or is it the other way around?. (jk) We will never know if prohibitions against gays in the military allowed the bombing of the Twin Towers in New York and of the Pentagon. What a waste! Just keep in mind a few of these points:

Military Would Gain 41,000 Recruits If Gay Ban Were Lifted
by Paul Johnson 365Gay.com Washington Bureau Chief Posted: July 25, 2005 5:00 pm ET

Over 1,200 Gays Discharged From Military
United Press International March 14, 2002 by Pamela Hess

A bill to end the controversial ban on gays is currently before Congress and has been languishing there in committee, as far as I can ascertain, since 2003. It is reintroduced each year. The Military Readiness Enhancement Act at one time had 90 bi-partisan supporters and was endorsed by eight retired military officers. "As a commander, I know that lesbian, gay and bisexual Americans have served our country with honor and distinction," said BG Evelyn Foote, one of the first women to achieve the rank of Brigadier General, upon the bill's introduction. "Our armed forces should be able to recruit every qualified, capable American to protect our homeland, regardless of their sexual orientation. 'Don't Ask, Don't Tell' is not only unnecessary and discriminatory; it is also detrimental to our military readiness. The law does not meet the common sense rule our military should abide by." The Government Accountability Office issued a report showing that 'don't ask, don't tell' has cost taxpayers more than $200 million since its inception in 1993.

More than 10,000 service members have been discharged over the last 10 years under the policy according to statistics from the "Service members Legal Defense Network." **©365Gay.com 2005** (It is now 2009 and the money wasted has certainly not decreased. jk) The "Don't Ask Don't Tell" policy of the military was drawn up by Colin Powel who was Secretary of Defense at the time. He was a native of Jamaica or of Jamaican extraction. I always had a special regard for Jamaicans and liked Colin Powell, considering him presidential material until I discovered how his mind had been twisted by religion! Jamaica is notorious for its anti-gay attitudes. Consider this out of the Jamaica Observer: "Christians and their God of fear keep up a constant verbal and physical abuse to people who dare to disagree, think differently or refuse to accept the doctrines and forms of the Christian Church or have a difference of opinion concerning the interpretation of the scriptures…" Several gay Jamaican men have been granted asylum in Britain over the past few years on the grounds that they were in danger here because of their homosexuality. Of the 25 countries that participate militarily in NATO, more than twenty permit gays to serve; of the permanent members of the United Nations Security Council, two (Britain, France) permit gays to serve openly, and three (United States, Russia, China) do not. Strange bed fellows "aye what?" The U.S.A is felt to be a nation build upon principals of religion while both Russia and China are largely anti-religion! Remember that too many followers of religions have the same attitude toward homosexuals as the Nazis. The main problem with "don't ask, don't tell," however, is that it violates the First Amendment's protection of free speech. In ruling that the policy is unconstitutional in 1997, U.S. District Judge Eugene Nickerson said that a military "called on to fight for the principles of equality and free speech embodied in the United States Constitution should embrace those principles in its own ranks." Gays already serving their country remain candidates for a dishonorable discharge even if they engage in private homosexual acts when off-duty. Steve Loomis, a lieutenant colonel who earned a Purple Heart and two Bronze Stars during a 20 year Army career, was dismissed in 1997 on charges of homosexuality only one week before he was set to retire.

By the way, I volunteered and served four years in the Navy during the Korean War. Being a devout orthodox atheist, I consider lying to be wrong, but I did lie about my sexual orientation because I felt and still feel the government has no business denying any citizen his or her right and obligation to serve the nation when needed in military situations. Besides, it is no one's business unless he or she is interested in having horizontal recreation with me! And I am unanimous in this, "godamn it"!

CONSTIPATION OF THE BRAIN!
(This book can sweep it all out!)

I was watching a legal battle on the TV about a school district and a student who wanted to wear a T-shirt declaring that gays were sinners and would go to hell. The judge asked if the principal would have been justified in allowing a student to wear a T-shirt saying that niggers should be put on boats and sent back to Africa. The student's lawyer sounded like a horse's "you know what" trying to answer that one! Of course, the lawyer tried to plead the First Amendment Right to express oneself! Only a religious nut could have such warped thinking! We have wasted enough court time on such idiotic nonsense. Let us just adopt the German law which outlaws hate speech or expression. (See NOTE 1)

PUT AN END TO HATE!

I sent the following to a minister, Mr. Rod Parsley, who said that "Will and Grace" was an abomination and declared that homosexuality was a learned behavior and an abomination. Being a Devout, Orthodox, homosexual, Jewish atheist, I cannot abide hearing other than the Gospel Truth! This bible-thumping idiot is making quite a bit of money out of selling hate, much as his kind filled their pockets for centuries by selling hatred of Jews.

TO: Mr. Rod Parsley
I watched a great deal of your TV program and feel it would be helpful
for you to read my letter sent to President Bush.

February 25, 2004

To: President George W. Bush

You are losing me as a long time supporter of the Republican Party.
But let me start on a positive note. It is not because of the Iraqi
situation. I believe that all intelligence departments around the world
were cleverly manipulated by Saddam Hussein to believe that he had
or was developing weapons of mass destruction not only to dissuade us
from attacking, but also to keep his own population under control.

You are losing me because it is becoming more and more apparent that
you are catering to the multibillion-dollar international corporations
and their officers; your immigration policy makes no sense; your Cuban
policy is only to pander to the Cubans in Miami; your handling of the
Haitian situation was inept and contrary to stated principles. How
could you claim to want to establish democracy in the Middle East
while allowing gangs of street thugs to force President Aristide, the
democratically elected leader of Haiti, out of office? I am offended by
the show trial of Martha Stewart who did what any other investor would
have done after learning that things were turning against a company
in which they had invested. Why are the real culprits, the liars and
thieves of Enron, WorldCom, etc. not in jail? I am sure it is because
they are your "buddies." Their ill-gotten wealth should be confiscated
and given to the workers who lost their jobs and to the stockholders
who lost hard earned savings because of their lies and thievery! If this
is not in the law books now, it damn well should be! You hypocritically
say you are working to create jobs, but this is so far from the truth that
it is laughable. You are doing everything to increase corporate profits
through the firing of workers, loss of overtime, out-sourcing and by
allowing companies to pick up stakes in this country to relocate in
a low wage foreign country! If you want to know how to bring jobs
back to this country, just ask me and I will be glad to explain it to you!
Ask for: "CAPITALISTS IN DEFENSE OF CAPITALISM." (See
CHAPTER 10)

The straw that broke the camel's back was your support of an amendment to the Constitution to forbid homosexual marriage. This is pushing me, and tens of thousands of other Americans, out of the Republican Party. I was forced to lie when I enlisted in the U.S Navy for four years of honorable service. When asked about my sexuality, I lied because I felt that my homosexuality was no reason for me to be denied my right and duty to defend my country! Homosexuals can be and often are responsible citizens in every realm of life. If it makes some happy to be married to one of the same sex, why not! Can you not just agree that America stands for life, liberty and the pursuit of happiness! What strange people these humans are: they give a medal to a man who kills a man, but despise a man who loves another!

Your support for the bill to make homosexual marriage unconstitutional through an amendment to the Constitution amounts to outrageous pandering to the religious fundamentalists and the religious right that have almost always been wrong. It seems to this poor soul (me) that the Constitution is supposed to confer rights, not take them away. Please be reminded that these Christian "Holier than thou" messengers of God, the Nazis and the extremist Muslims - the Khomeneiacs as I call them - hold the same views about homosexuals. These are the same types that used the Bible to support their position on slavery, the segregation of blacks, the burning of witches and the bloody persecution of Jews! Going back to my opinion that much religion can grow into a form of insanity, many brain dead religious idiots committed suicide to get to heaven on the tail of a comet or just killed themselves because they were in a hurry to float on a cloud in God's heaven!

Considering your support of such an amendment, what is to stop the religious right from going back to the days when interracial marriage was illegal? Note, the Bible, again, was used as an authority! I can understand that some religious folk may argue that marriage is traditionally between a man and a woman. This is so, but it was also traditional for thousands of years to accept slavery as a normal part of life.

We all know that there are many things that are offensive to many Muslims and that this book should be burned and my body parts should be fed into a blender and fed to the pigs, according to their extremists. But to Christian religious right extremists, it is offensive to use the word marriage rather than a union or domestic partnership in the case of two persons of the same sex seeking the same legal protections as are afforded to marriage between a man and a woman. But what difference should it make what we call it when two loving individuals want to go through life together devoted to one another! What happened to equal protection called for by the Fourteenth Amendment? This would be nullified by passing such a blatantly discriminatory amendment – a law that would engrave into stone a "caste system" in our country against a segment of the population that should be despised because of religious dogma! The Republican Party had best realize that it is a party for all of the people not just for the religious right – the blind leading the blind! The government is to protect rights, not to take them away! I will not accept "Khomeneiacs" in the White House!

If you really believe in G-d, you surely must believe that G-d gave us free will. Why should government be allowed to take away "what G-d hath given"? The same can be said for abortion. Government should not be allowed to enthrone a religious conviction onto the heads of those who do not agree with that dogma. If there is truly a G-d, it is for Him to decide if a sin had been committed. Man cannot take the place or role of G-d! And this is the Gospel Truth in my book! G-d and I are of one mind on this point. In your address, you hypocritically declared that America is a land of freedom and, then, in the next breath, supported a measure that would make lepers – second-class citizens – out of around 10% of the population! You have also proven yourself to be a hypocrite by expressing outrage at the interference of the judiciary. However, you did not object when it favored you in the election fiasco in Florida which put you into the White House. By the way, I voted for you and, for the first time in my life, sent a $25 contribution to the Republican Party, the one and only contribution I ever sent to any party. You may send me a check for this amount as I feel you have failed me! (I never did get a refund!)

The fear or claim that homosexual marriage would somehow destroy the concept of marriage is laughable. Marriage is already meaningless in more than half the nations in the western world. There are many reasons for this having nothing to do with homosexuality. One can logically claim that this all started with the emancipation of women! Shall we go back to the biblical concept that women should be subservient to men and be stoned to death if they commit adultery? Some Bible, eh what!

Yours very truly, for a FREE AMERICA, Dr. J. Knowname

P.S. When you said, "Let the voice of the people be heard," you were inviting tyranny by the majority. Is there any doubt that if such a course had been followed when black Americans had demanded civil rights that the majority would have voted them down? The purpose of the Court review is to prevent tyranny of the majority over the minority. You just do not seem to get it, Mr. President!

SIGNED: Dr. .J. Knowname, a teacher whose career and health were destroyed because he wanted a black child to succeed in school so that he could have a fulfilling life! (End of letter to President Bush)

* * * * * * * * * *

I would like to enlarge upon the subject of marriage mentioned in my letter above to George W. Bush. Considering the over 50% divorce rate of "normal couples," perhaps it is not normal for men to have only one wife. After all, in biblical times it was quite normal for men to have numerous wives. As is declared in (Gen 29:17-28; II Sam 3:2-5.) "Marriage…shall consist of a union between one man and one or more women. If the people involved freely agree to such an arrangement, why not accept it as legal? It may be wise to have a public debate on this issue. It seems that this would afford greater stability and support for children. Interesting thought, isn't it! Do you think that they need G-d in school or in their lives! Sorry, the children in Ireland, both Catholic and Protestant, were steeped in religion which simply gave them reason to kill one another because of the corrosion injected into their beings by religions only interested in power for themselves and not concerned with human beings.

Yes, I voted for George W. Bush in spite of me being one of those "girlyguys." I did so because I felt he did what had to be done in Iraq. Tragically, he did it very poorly. I felt that the safety and welfare of the country were the most important factors to consider, not my sexual orientation. But this guy worries me! Sometimes I wonder what he is drinking or smoking. His support for a Palestinian state next to Israel never made any sense since one never existed in the history of the world and the refugees were kept there by their own Arab brothers to eventually destroy Israel. I am sure Ariel Sharon was forced to accept the idea of taking Jewish settlements out of Gaza and some in the West Bank. This should have been welcomed by the Palestinians. If these Arabs were really desirous of living in peace, they would have welcomed his move and they would have stopped all violence. Perhaps they would have offered help to the Jewish families to resettle! Instead, Israel has been under almost daily bombardment. How can it be any different after the Palestinian state is created? It will simply develop into a failed but terrorist state hell bent on killing all the Jews in Israel and then taking all of Palestine. (I wrote this over two years ago. Now the dominant Palestinian terrorist groups are declaring this as their goal: to destroy Israel and take all the land.)

What got me on today's Bush bashing was listening to Adam Ereli (July 20, 2005), the State Department spokesman for the Bush administration. He said that Saudi Arabia is our trusted friend and partner in our struggle against terrorism. George (Bush) must really be up in his heavenly clouds to come up with such an idiotic conclusion. Is he smoking or drinking something really bizarre? Saudi Arabia is one of the main centers and financial backers of world terrorism. They have set up medrasses which teach Wahabbism, the extreme form of the Muslim religion which indoctrinates children to hate and kill Jews, Americans and anyone not a member of their particular sect. It is these medrasses which prepare children to be suicide murderers! How can anyone in his right mind declare that Saudi Arabia is our trusted "friend and partner in our struggle against terrorism"? George, you just did not do your homework or the mix of religion and alcohol are clouding your mind! I understand, George, you have oil on your brain, but this book contains the cure! I wish someone would tell George W.

Bush how he could regain my confidence – I know he is worried sick about what I think. When we understood we needed an atomic bomb or wanted to send a man to the moon, what did we do? We set up massive government agencies, with lots of money, to get to our goals – and we succeeded quickly. He should have done likewise to develop alternative energy so that we will one day be able to tell the Shieks of Arabie to drink their oil as we no longer need them. What a difference that would make in world events!

CHRISTIANS WHO ARE NOT CHRISTIANS

Dear President Bush:

Now that MY vote elected you, I am fearful that you will be drawn to an extreme by your religious beliefs. Since the safety of our country is more important than any other issue, I voted for you, but only because you were right to go into Iraq. On most other issues you are badly informed. I am writing a book on religion and on the harm it has done to humanity through the ages. Note the following and come to the realization that the American Religious Right, the Evangelicals or Fundamentalists are really hate groups. We need only consider their stand on slavery which they justified with the Bible and now they are trying to demonize homosexuals using the Bible again! I also remember when they put signs up: "No Jews or dogs allowed"! And remember how they loved the Indians - they loved them to death! These people have bigoted, Lilliputian minds and are a great danger to the country. They are trying to impose their religious dogma on the entire nation. This is unconstitutional. Since their religious rantings have become political statements, their tax-exempt status MUST be removed!

In case some readers object to me pointing out that religions are and have been used to foment hatred, remember the Inquisition, the burning of witches, the present push by extremist Muslims to convert or kill all "infidels" until they take over and create their Caliphate and remember the burning crosses used to intimidate negroes just a few decades ago! It seems to me that burning a cross was not exactly the Christian thing to do, but these Christians based their actions upon what is written in the Bible, the unalterable and forever correct word from G-d, according to their feeble minds! These same distorted minds now condemn homosexuals as an abomination in the eyes of the Lord! Again, their justification is direct from the Bible! Can you understand why I say that no tax money should be used to support religious education and that all religious institutions and property should be taxed as any other business?

A CURIOUS OBSERVATION

We give a medal to a man who kills another man; we shame one who loves another man.

True, in the first instance, it is in the context of war, but in the other it is a matter of living with the hand nature has given us. Homophobes should consider the maxim: But for the grace of G-d, there go I.

CHAPTER 15

THE END TIMES

Prof. Bernard Lewis, the great scholar of Islam and the Middle East offers the background in the *Wall Street Journal* on Aug. 8:

"In Islam, as in Judaism and Christianity, there are certain beliefs concerning the cosmic struggle at the end of time - Gog and Magog, anti-Christ, Armageddon, and for Shiite Muslims, the long awaited return of the Hidden Imam... Mr. Ahmadinejad and his followers clearly believe that this time is now, and that the terminal struggle has already begun and is indeed well advanced. It may even have a date, indicated by several references by the Iranian president to giving his final answer to the U.S. about nuclear development by Aug. 22. This was at first reported as "by the end of August," but Mr. Ahmadinejad's statement was more precise." (Of course, this was off the mark as all others were for centuries. jk)

The following statements certainly lend support to Prof. Bernard Lewis's above article in the Wall Street Journal.

Iran president paves the way for arabs' imam return
Nov 17, 2005

Ahmadinejad is on a mission to usher in the Twelfth Imam. He and his ten-million cult followers of death believe they can usher in the apocalypse. Ahmadinejad said that, "We must prepare ourselves to rule the world and the only way to do this is to wipe Israel off the map. I see a world without Zionism and America".

More mention of the end times:

"...As the millennium itself came and went, 40 percent or more of American Christians continued to tell poll takers in 2000 and 2001 that they expected the biblical prophecies of Armageddon and the end times to come true." (See NOTE 11)

* * * * * * * * * *

It is not only Christians who are obsessed with the idea of the End Days. Muslims have their Hidden Imam with a story somewhat like that of Jesus, but with a few variations. Consider what follows:

Hamas Issues Islamic Call For Genocide on Palestinian Authority (PA) Television by Ezra HaLevi Reported in DEBKAfile April 13, 2007

While Hamas has sought, since its Mecca Agreement with Fatah, to strike a moderate tone in order to renew international funding, it continues the calls for genocide of Jews. In a recent sermon on PA TV, Hamas spokesman Dr. Ismail Radwan reiterated Hamas's classic ideology that:

* The Hour of the Islamic resurrection and end of days is dependent on the killing of Jews by Muslims.

* The remaining Jews will unsuccessfully attempt to hide, but the rocks and trees will expose them, calling out "there is a Jew behind me, kill him!"

* "Palestine will be liberated through the rifle," meaning that Israel will be destroyed through violence. The Hamas spokesman ended his sermon with a prayer to Allah to "take" Israel and the USA.

I cannot understand how people with other than the minds of children can believe most of the religious fantasy lines that have been around for so many thousands of years. Tragically, they have been killing one another over this nonsense for centuries, and still are today, in spite of the fact that G-d said "Thou shalt not kill." No wonder G-d wonders what kind of idiots He created! I told Him not to worry; it will all be straightened out as soon as this book makes the rounds of the world. He was very pleased to hear this. I was happy to see a broad smile on His face.

AN EXAMPLE OF THE AUDACITY OF SOME RELIGIOUS LEADERS

Tim LaHaye and Jerry Jenkins:
"I think if Jerry and I were cut, we'd both bleed red, white, and blue... We believe that God has raised up America to be a tool in these last days to get the gospel to the outermost parts of the earth."
-Tim LaHaye

* * * * * * * * * *

The audacity, vanity and self-centered mentality of many Christian and other religious leaders are more proof that religion often borders on insanity. These people think the whole world revolves around them and America the Beautiful. This does not mean that I do not love our country. One of the main reasons for writing this book is to preserve the freedom of our country. (jk)

Here is an ad from a Tim LaHaye newsletter:
"...an online newsletter featuring Tim LaHaye, Jerry Jenkins, Mark Hitchcock and other End Times scholars. You also have access to **exclusive online message boards** where you can discuss these important issues with fellow Christians.

"It is our hope that by studying Bible prophecy and world affairs, those who believe will be bold in their faith and those who don't will begin to understand the link between **what is happening today and what was foretold in the Bible**." (These mental cases have been expecting the "End Days" for centuries! jk)

THE TRUTH BEHIND THE RESURRECTION?

Parents must, at some time, allow their children to know the truth behind the Tooth Fairy and Santa Claus. Religions have always borrowed myths and customs from one another and even from pagan customs and myths, but some are so strongly implanted that it can be disturbing to face up to reality. But be not afraid.

The tale of the "End Times" and the imminent return of Jesus Christ are tales designed to scare the "bejeebers" out of naive people to get them to join their religion and become paying customers. I realize that, at times, I seem to express contempt for religious beliefs. Were it not for the gruesome fact that we are now living in a world with WEAPONS OF MASS EXTINCTION, I would not be writing as I am in this book about religions because I understand they are very important in the lives of many people. Nevertheless, I do feel that religions are largely ludicrous, but I feel sorry for the entire human race which has not matured enough to understand just how foolish these beliefs are. How can you be angry or ridicule a child because he is afraid of the dark?

I emphasize that if a religion is needed for an individual because it gives comfort and a path for his life, there is nothing wrong with continuing with that faith as long as they have respect for the beliefs or non-beliefs of others. What is wrong is to try to force one's own faith onto others by proselytizing. Why is it written that they "go forth and spread the word"? Is it because they love us? Guess again! The individuals may indeed feel that emotion, but it is written because a new club or organization of any kind needs new paying members! Money makes the world go'round.

IT SEEMS THAT THE RESURRECTION OF JESUS IS THE MAIN CORNERSTONE OF THE CHRISTIAN FAITH and its main selling point. Just think about it. It is not unusual, even during recent centuries, for people to be buried alive because it was not known exactly how to determine death. I know for a fact that bodies have been exhumed from cemeteries in order to make room for needed construction or for other purposes. My father was responsible for moving whole cemeteries and he showed us pictures of bodies with the hair pulled out. Is this not clear evidence that the individual was buried alive? Believe me, I know my mother told dad to be sure she was actually deceased, gone out of this world before being placed in that proverbial box! Is it not possible that Jesus had been considered dead, but was really still alive when placed in the tomb? By the time he was removed from the cross, surely he must have been overheated by the sun and dehydrated. Is it not possible that he had been in a coma and how would the ancients have known that from death? Is it not reasonable to assume that as the "air conditioning" cooled him off on the cold slab, he may have been able to recover his energies enough to arise and find a way to roll the stone away from the cave opening? I found further evidence that this has happened. I read on the internet a theory on how certain sayings came about. Some originated as a result of the need to open coffins, for one reason or another. When reopening these coffins, 1 out of 25 coffins were found to have scratch marks on the inside and they realized they had been burying people alive. So the custom started of tying a string on the wrist of the corpse, lead it through the coffin and up through the ground and tie it to a bell. Someone would have to sit out in the graveyard all night (the graveyard shift) to listen for the bell; thus, someone could be saved by the bell or was considered "a dead ringer." Now, did that ring a bell!

No doubt Jesus did appear before His followers in solid form – not a ghost as the Bible makes so abundantly clear. But what happened to Him, one might wonder? Well, once a man has gone through the agony of crucifixion, do you think anyone in his right mind would stay around for a second go at it? He likely wondered away into the wilderness or to caves in which He finally died from His wounds. This is my common sense explanation to the story of His resurrection. Naturally, the resurrection of Jesus is the cornerstone of the Easter Holiday celebrations. By no means am I suggesting that this holiday be abandoned. It is not important if the story is correct or not, what is important – and should not be forgotten – is the message of love of all humanity. Besides, it gives joy to many people and that is one of the main reasons for writing this book. The actual origin of Easter is taken from pagan customs of celebrating the coming of spring at the time of the vernal equinox. I may have pointed out before that leaders of religions are usually good business people. To attract more customers they set the date for Easter to more or less coincide with the old pagan spring festival. There was nothing wrong with this as it was good to bring in more believers and a kind gesture. This is a perfect example of how life can be seen as a circle: in pagan times celebrations centered around the arrival of spring; with the development of Christianity, Easter, now celebrated at about the same time, became a celebration of the resurrection of Jesus, the Savior. Is spring not the resurrection of life after a frozen winter? This is life after death. In this age, there is no reason why we should not celebrate it in any way we wish and for any reason as long as it brings joy. These are beautiful holidays and traditions and should continue to be enjoyed.

By the way, I do not doubt that Jesus was sincere and really believed he was the savior. We are all a product of the age in which we live. The story of the arrival of a savior has been woven into many cultures for centuries and it is not unusual for people to become captive to such thoughts. Again, it is the message that is important. Surely Jesus would be happy with "**DO ONLY GOOD - DO HARM TO NO ONE!**"

* * * * * * * * * *

Otto Pfleiderer ("Urchristentum," 1887; "Die Enstehung des Christentums," 1905) argued that all the early Christian beliefs about Jesus' birth and resurrection originated from eastern pagan cults which spread widely throughout the Roman Empire. "

FROM: "TheFreeDictionary   **resurrection** [Lat., = rising again], arising again from death to life. The emergence of Jesus from the tomb to live on earth again for 40 days as told in the Gospels has been from the beginning the central fact of Christian experience and a cardinal feature of Christian doctrine (Mat. 28; Mark 16; Luke 24; John 20; Acts 4.2; Romans 6). It was the guarantee not only of Christ's mission and the seal of redemption but also of the resurrection of all men."

Was Jesus the only god to be resurrected? A resounding NO! Just type in "Religion and resurrection" into the address line at the top of your computer screen or ask in any library and you will find that resurrection is an age-old myth in many parts of the world. You see, Madison Avenue techniques of selling an idea were around long before, centuries before Madison Avenue was paved! Not unlike the Christian sales pitch is this one believed by most Muslims: The Twelfth Imam is still alive. (I would like to know if He and Jesus talk to one another!) He is in a state of occultation. He will reappear at a moment determined by Allah - or .will it be Ahmadinejad when he is ready with his atomic bombs? The Twelfth Imam is the Awaited One who will spread justice throughout the world - after slaughtering millions just as the Christians envision the Armageddon to annihilate millions so that Jesus will reign in peace and serenity. Can anyone now doubt that most religion has a touch of insanity about it? Remember, this is not to ridicule any one religion. Most religions are loaded with myths and irrational concepts that would put the believers in mental institutions if these beliefs were not associated with religions. Take the story of the Rastafarian religion which was founded in Jamaica. This Back to Africa movement believes that Haile Selassie of Ethiopia is God incarnate, the returned black messiah, come to take the lost Twelve Tribes of Israel back to live with Him in Holy Mount Zion in a world of perfect peace, love and harmony. Bob Marley, a convert to the faith, spread the message of Rastafari to the world. There are now estimated to be more than a million Rastafarians throughout the world. Too bad there was no Roman emperor to help them! Don't you think there are many Christians, Muslims and others who would consider these people to be stupid, idiots or insane? Of course not, not if it is based upon religion! Then again, they may think their religion is for morons or mental midgets! We need to look at the hump on our own backs! I wonder if the Rastafarians receive tax exempt status? In the following you will read about what others – even Christians - say about the "End Times."

Apocalypses: Prophecies, Cults, and Millennial Beliefs Through the Ages (Paperback)

by Eugen Weber (Excerpts taken) **From Publishers Weekly**

"...Surveying the field of millenarian beliefs, Weber (France: Fin de Siecle, etc.), professor of history at UCLA, contends that the apocalyptic "lunatic fringe" deserves more than the condescension typically doled out by scholars."

...By 1992, for instance, more than half of adult Americans expected the imminent cataclysmic return of Jesus Christ. What accounts for the persistence of such beliefs? Sifting through the historical record, Weber examines the utopian intent of much millennial thought. The Second Coming, after all, promises heaven on earth; even Engels noted the revolutionary potential of revivalist Christianity.... (This book cites many instances of religion causing insane acts, support for my contention that religion can cause insanity. How about the endless religious wars in Europe, the Salem Witch Trials, the Crusades during which they killed more on the way to Jerusalem than when they got there? etc. jk)

Below is my ANSWER TO apocalyptic "lunatic fringe" BELIEF THAT JEWS MUST ACCEPT CHRISTIANITY – This minister wrote: "MID-EAST STRIFE: RE-DISCOVERING THE BIBLE'S FORGOTTEN SOLUTION." In this typical Christian propaganda brief, he insists that Jews do not have the right to Palestine until they accept Jesus Christ as Lord. So new, what else is new? As is often the case, even Christians have widely divergent views of various portions of the same Bible. The interpretation I prefer is the one of the Evangelicals who believe that the present return of Jews to the Holy Land portends the imminent return of Jesus. I wrote this to the 'lunatic fringe' minister mentioned above: "It is sad and tragic that your interpretation of Christianity is still plaguing the world after over two thousand years. Using the Bible as proof that all Jews must convert to Christianity before they are to have the right to return to Palestine and create a Jewish state is part of your stale old sales pitch. Your insistence that Jews must be forced to flee into all four corners of the earth until they accept Christianity is not unlike the Muslim claim that all (including Christians) must accept Allah as the Only One True G-d or be killed. The extremist Muslims and Christians have about the same mentality, poor kids! When will they grow up! Is this not unlike children arguing in the school yard and insisting that "My God is bigger and stronger than your God, so there!"

Many Christian ministers (lunatic fringe ministers) whose minds are still mired in the Dark Ages quote passages out of the Bible, taking for granted that these are the exact words of the Lord and that everything in the Bible must be accepted as absolute truth. You will know better after digesting this book. Much of this book shows how so much of the Bible is full of nonsense! Keep in mind that I do not mean to disparage the Bible, but we must read it knowing that it was written by men with agendas both good and bad. And do not forget, there is wisdom in the Bible as well!

Do you remember me promising that I would likely insult most everyone? Well I feel I must if I am to drive home the point that the human race must grow up fast and come to its senses or our planet and humans are doomed. Let us look at the customs or requirements of some religions. They use incense and wave a light before the congregation probably to shoo away evil spirits and demons, they may go into a trance-like state or shout and roll on the floor, they play with prayer beads, they ring bells, they wear religious symbols, they create statues, they blow the shofar (the horn of a male sheep), they make the faithful partake of a wafer that is supposed to be the body of Christ and drink wine that is said to be His blood, they beat their backs until they bleed, they pray with black boxes containing biblical passages on their foreheads and arms, they place nicely adorned boxes containing the Ten Commandments on the door posts of their homes to keep away the Angel of Death and I am sure you may come up with other outlandish customs! As long as these customs do no harm, why not continue? If it is a comfort, why not!

Much lies in tradition and there is nothing wrong with it if people wish to continue as long as they do not tell others that if they do not do likewise and believe in the same things, they will go to hell and burn for an eternity. There is nothing dangerous in kissing a rabbit's foot or the Blarney Stone, but I never heard of anyone demanding that others do the same or die!

Now that so many are predicting that the End Times "approachith," there has been an enormous increase in mentioning the name Satan. I have heard more of this in the last fifty years, than in the preceding five thousand years, if I remember correctly! How do these magic machinations and beliefs differ from superstition, a rabbit's foot, touching wood for luck or witchcraft which many religions believe is a sin? All I can say, dear people of the world, grow up, enlighten yourselves and come back to reality! There is no Satan, there are no hobo goblins and no one is under the bed! (Should I say "Damn it!"?)

It is sad for me to have to bring into question the basis of one's faith as I know so many Christians take the Resurrection of Jesus literally and this really is the foundation of their faith. But there are many Christian leaders who have open minds and have come to the same conclusion as I did decades ago. Two who have openly admitted this are Bishop John Shelby Spong, the retired <u>Bishop</u> of the <u>Episcopal</u> <u>Diocese of Newark</u> and <u>Bishop</u> <u>John A.T. Robinson</u> reject the historical truth claims of some Christian doctrines, such as the <u>virgin birth</u> (Spong, 1992) and the bodily resurrection of Jesus (Spong, 1994). Bishop John Shelby Spong has written several books on what he calls the New Christianity. . Apparently they agree with me that religion needs to reinvent itself. Good for them, men of the Twenty-first Century! (See Note 8)

My own sense is that if people still need to go to a house of worship, they should use it as a means of doing good to others, to the community, a place to meet and make friends, a place to have all kinds of celebrations and a place to discuss serious issues of the day. As I say elsewhere in this book, if your religion, whichever it may be, gives you comfort and you are happy with it, go on believing as long as you do not try to spread it to others. This is where good Christians should stop trying to spread Christianity to Muslims or any other group. They rightfully take offense, since in essence, they are saying that the Muslim religion or what other faith they may have is defective and has no merit. This is like telling someone he is stupid! Please pass this on to our present Pope and help welcome him into the twenty-first century! By the way, it is unfortunate that the Pope who now dictates what is right is worlds apart from our last one, Pope John Paul II. I did not agree with all of his views, but he was a man who showed love and human kindness. The important basis of Christianity and any other religion worthy of being considered such is love and caring about others and this is exactly what this book is all about – not that I am giving any religion my stamp of approval, you understand, and it is not needed! You should do and believe what is best for you as long as it does no harm. All that the world really needs is love!

Now that I have declared that it is not good to tell someone he is stupid, what follows may seem like a contradiction. It is not. The beliefs of most Christians come from over two thousand years of brain washing from the "Greatest Story Every Told." Who can blame them! It is a beautiful story that is a comfort to most, but beware. The concept that Jesus was or is the son of G-d and that he was a king (King of the Jews) was a yarn that goes back to ancient cultures reaching back into the haziness of antiquity! I am sure most readers realize that even into relatively modern times, kings were considered as Gods. I regret having to express so many negative opinions regarding most if not all religions, but I know I must if we are to have a chance of saving the lives of believers and non-believers from applying the finger to a self-destruct button! Forgive me for being so brutal, but a shock treatment may be needed for some readers! (Sorry if this kills the business of the TV evangelists – no I am not sorry, damn it!) Most religious beliefs are quite fanciful, borrowed and blended with more ancient cultures to attract business and keep them coming back for more. The Resurrection Story, the nonsense surrounding Mary, his mother - and, no doubt, a fine Jewish mother - really has to take the cake, and I love cake, even sponge cake! It is especially tasty with applesauce on the top. You may add whipped cream if you like. Permission granted! You see, I told you I never miss a chance to play on words or joke! Thanks for your patience! But, did you get it: Bishop Spong - sponge cake?)

See: NOTE 3 "SOME CONVOLUTED THINKING" at the end of the book, if it is where I left it!

CHAPTER 16
END POVERTY

Money is not everything, but it sure can buy a change of misery! Now you know I just made up this line! Some readers may think I am crazy to suggest the ideas which follow, but just how sane is it to declare that a piece of paper can replace the value of gold? I suspect there may be some doubt. In 1955, the words "In God We Trust" were added. No one will admit it, but I know this was done because it is widely known that the government cannot be trusted; so what is wrong in trusting G-d! No doubt, someone in government must have dreamed up this idea. If it makes people happy, good! In this age of the Obamanation Government which is spending money as though it were just paper, we surely need trust in something!

The ILLUSION of MONEY

In a country in which athletes and CEO's are rewarded with salaries, options and other perks which amount to earning millions upon millions of dollars, I do not understand how we can accept poverty for anyone. Now, please allow me to make a brilliant statement. Poverty, I say, can be ended with money. But what is money? Yes, I know. It is evil, but I would not mind having some more evil! Seriously, let us read on to see what it really is.

AN INTERESTING VIEW OF MONEY

Facts taken from Paul Tustain

Austin Report Editors Note: We often warn readers about the potential disaster that awaits fiat paper money, especially the U.S. Dollar. But, only when you can see the foolishness from a different perspective, can you appreciate the risk we all take holding paper currencies. Our thanks to Paul Tustain for reminding us all of how history repeats itself.

Charles II was king of England from 1660 - 1685, when wooden sticks were being used as a form of money until the system collapsed. The story has obvious parallels to the modern world. Here it is. While the Pilgrim Fathers were busy founding America their English puritan brothers were also shaking off religious oppression. By 1650 Oliver Cromwell had taken power for the people, chopped off the king's head, and in a familiar pattern was lording it over a parliament which he dissolved when it threatened to oppose him. He died passing power directly to his feeble son, apparently untroubled by charges of hypocrisy. With Cromwell gone England decided that if it were going to have a king it ought to be a proper one. So Charles II was sought out and granted a restored throne in 1660, 11 years after his father's beheading. The new king's powers were diminished. Much of what he needed to do now depended on the co-operation of parliament, so an uneasy truce prevailed. In particular the royal tax raising privilege had been lost, leaving Charles forever begging taxes from his new governing partners. Legislating a tax was one thing, collecting it quite another. There were few useful records, there was no internal revenue service, and it was a job which would certainly require both local knowledge and the occasional use of force, now under the control of parliament too. So tax collection was enabled by a combination of privatization and delegation. Parliamentarian intermediaries were allocated a region, and then would gather the money in that locality through their own initiatives. For their efforts they received a healthy cut, which helped to motivate them to keep authorizing new taxes.

But there remained a problem of Charles' cash resources. Parliament met rarely, and the logistics of tax collection caused long delays. He was still struggling to pay the bills. At about this time the financial development of London was getting underway. The goldsmiths - whose traditional role was the fabrication of jewelry and plate - were emerging from a number of potential candidates as the trade group which would evolve into modern bankers. Their success grew from the safekeeping role of their vaults through the uncertain period of the civil war, and also from the strength of London's position within growing European trade, with its frequent requirement to exchange foreign coin. They soon found themselves able to lend as well, and from this they became the middlemen in a developing market in government debt. It worked like this. Armed with parliamentary permission to raise taxes, Charles immediately cashed in by selling specific future tax receipts to the goldsmiths, at a discount to the face value. The goldsmiths needed to be able to honor their private accounts, and unable to distribute the royal debt were rapidly insufficiently liquid to lend the king more. So it was arranged that the debt redemption would in fact be paid not specifically to the original goldsmith lender but to any bearer of the debt, thereby enabling the original lender to sell the debt on and replenish his cash, ready for the next royal loan. The next problem was how to ensure the new bearer of the debt - not being the original borrower - could reliably identify the authenticity of the bearer debt. And here nature offered an ancient solution.

A piece of wood split down the middle will only match perfectly with its other half: so wooden sticks became a key component of English currency. The government's debt office took a nice looking hazel stick and notched across it various symbols which denoted monetary amounts borrowed and lent. The stick was then split down the middle, with each side showing one end of the notches. One side - which had a wooden handle known as a 'stock' - was held by the king's treasury, while the other was given to the goldsmith, who also got a piece of paper describing the date and circumstances of redemption. The system was simple and effective. The goldsmith-bankers proved trustworthy. They generated liquidity by trading what were by now being called 'stocks' between themselves, and they solemnly placed all the wooden sticks in their own vaults, next to the gold and silver. They had good reason to remain honest as they were well placed in a profitable and rapidly growing market. For their part the wooden sticks thoroughly outwitted the forgers, and the king was the ultimate and trusted guarantor of all the debts.

It was the perfection of the system which ultimately caused its downfall, because it led to a market far bigger than was ever healthy. To begin with the supply of cash came from the goldsmith bankers themselves. Then, with caution, they let out a little of the money they held on private current accounts, knowing that their own personal credit would get them sufficient cash if ever they needed it to repay their depositors. Then they realized they could do better still by offering interest on private accounts held at notice, because the notice period would eliminate unanticipated cash calls. By paying interest they accumulated more public cash, and these funds were lent on to the king at an increasing rate. Charles soon found he no longer needed to bother with parliamentary approval to raise taxes before issuing stocks, because he could sell it anyway, and from about 1668 it became generally accepted that the state's borrowings were secured by unspecified future taxes on the nation; an assumption which remains with us today. The parliamentary brake on the speed of issue of this new monetary medium had now been sidestepped, and before long half of London was booming on credit evidenced by valuable broken wooden sticks. This was when things started to get harder. As each tier of willing private depositors dried up it took another notch up the interest rate scale to squeeze out more of the public's cash. The goldsmiths could only offer to the king discounts which they could finance by attracting deposits, and by 1670 the king was having to accept as much as 10% per annum discount on the face of his 'stock' debts. Depositors were by now receiving 7% and the middlemen the rest. By 1671 the system was hardly benefiting the king at all because redemptions were consuming all the cash subsequent issues could raise. He had sucked in all the private money he was going to get, so when at the year's end he demanded still more vital cash for his navy the bankers couldn't get it - at any price. Annoyed, Charles conveniently remembered that the bulk of the loans which he had recently taken out had been at rates above the 6% limit permitted by his own usury laws. He declared the debts illegal and his own exchequer's payments stopped. This temporary action was enacted on 2nd January 1672, was extended after one year for another two, and after those two (subject to a few carefully chosen exceptions) it became indefinite.

The effect - often repeated since - was that those who lent to the state turned out to have accidentally provided all their carefully accumulated personal wealth as voluntary taxes. The goldsmiths were blamed. They were caricatured as greedy opportunists and damned by their once enthusiastic depositors. Eleven of the biggest 14 failed, leaving their chiefs variously (i) ruined, (ii) bankrupted (iii) on the run (iv)jailed or (v) dead. The humble wooden stick never regained any credibility. It was doomed to lose out to its close cousin - paper.

More articles by Paul Tustain can be found at http://www.galmarley.com/ See NOTE: 10

* * * * * * * * *

The following taken from: **Shell Money: Past and Present: moneyc.html**

Shell currency has been around for over 4,000 years and was, in its heyday, the most widely used currency in the world. Even today, there still exist minor currencies based on certain shells.

Some examples of shells' uses in trade are:

Cowrie shells (*Cypraea annulus* L., and *C. moneta* L.), Collected loose in bags or strung into strands, were the earliest forms of currency used in many countries. The Chinese, so far as we know, were the first people to use cowries as currency. Here, cowries have been found in prehistoric Stone Age sites. Examples of other country's native money-strands are the **diwara** in New Guinea, **rongo** in the Melanesian islands and **sapisapi** in Africa. The image of the cowrie as a type of currency was so strong that the first oval metal coin minted in the Greek colony of Lydia around 670 B.C. was modeled after that shell. By the eighteenth century, approximately 400 million cowries were being traded per year mostly for the purchase of black slaves. By the middle of the nineteenth century, it could take up to 100,000 cowries just to buy a young wife. Inflation, it seems, was the main demise of the cowrie currency.

Hard clamshells and whelks were the shells used to make the North American Indian **wampum**. Eastern Indians also used the tusk shell ***Dentalium pretiosum*** Sowerby (collected on Vancouver Is.! (Canada)) Sowerby, as a trade shell. Wampum continued to be used as money through the first half of the eighteenth century when it finally died out due to counterfeiting and mass production. (Does this worry you? Just think. Our money is being counterfeited in many places in the world that we are not told about. Not even G-d told me, but I am guessing. I have read that a lot of it is done in North Korea, but I would not swear to it, and as you know it is against my non-religion religion to swear! And then the second point, "mass production of Wampum" that killed its usefulness as a means of exchange or money. Is this happening to our dollar as the Federal Reserve prints more money? We have nothing to worry about if my other ideas for cutting spending will be effectuated. Sorry, chaps, I am not an economist even though I graduated from the Wharton School of Finance and Commerce. (jk)

Mercenaria mercenaria
(Linnaeus, 1758)
Hard clamshells, Northern Quahog

Dentalium (Antalis) pretiosum

Indian-money Tusk, I"o*qua shell

I believe that what I have been pointing out here is justification for declaring that the value of money, or what it is, derives from man's mind and his imagination. Not much different from religion and G-d, is it?

I wonder, come to think of it. Is this why we have come up with the expression of worshiping money? They say the poor will always be with us, but we can put our minds together to change this. I am sure I am not smart enough to discover all of the answers to this unfortunate situation, but I am hoping that by reading some of my thoughts, some brains in a Think Tank or a group of economists can take my thoughts as mentioned below and come up with their own answers or perhaps find that I may just be on the right track with some ideas presented below.

1   Often we see stocks that go up in value to heights that make no sense. The tech wreck was a perfect example of prices going up to outrageous levels, but before they broke, many investors cashed in and pocketed the money. That was money created out of thin air. Stocks often go up to unrealistic levels simply because of the greed, hopes, dreams and imaginations of the stock buyers! In effect, this is illusory money, but real to those who take it to the bank! Just how different is this from money printed by the Treasury Department?

2   Those who are old enough may remember the economic miracle of post World-War II Germany. This largely came about because the United States created the Marshal Plan which pumped I do not know how many millions or billions of dollars into their economy. The Marshal Plan money, of course, came from the printing presses of our Federal Reserve or the Treasury Department. Money created out of thin air! This was money very well spent because it created prosperity in Germany and helped get the world economy going in the right direction. They had cities, roads and just about everything else to rebuild. As they rebuilt, workers were paid and they then were able to purchase whatever they needed to make a life for themselves. In effect, prosperity was created, again, by illusory money created by our printing presses! Seeds were planted and a harvest produced!

When I write about ending poverty, I am serious in spite of the natural question of where the money would come from to pay the bill for this humanitarian idea. It does not need to come solely - or perhaps not at all - from the printing presses. As explained in this book, billions can come from dropping the disastrous fake war on drugs; by limiting incomes of the top earners or encouraging them to contribute voluntarily to the needed fund for ending poverty. Consider how many CEO's and athletic professionals earn millions of dollars that they could never live long enough to enjoy, often even if they were to live ten normal lifetimes. How about asking them to donate funds to make it possible to grant a normal yearly income to citizens who may be in need? It is great to see that there are now many very wealthy CEO's and wealthy individuals who do just that. They donate great sums of money to improve society in many ways. I feel the government should not force this on citizens who are responsible for the great creation of wealth in our country. On the contrary, I urge that the extremely wealthy gather together to discuss how they can voluntarily help toward this goal.

A great and valid source of income to help the poor and the country in general would be to drop federal tax exempt status from religious enterprises – church property included, to be sure. As long as their income and property are not taxed we would remain in our present violation of the Fourteenth Amendment which requires that all citizens be treated equally. Coming into compliance with this Amendment alone may make it unnecessary to ask the extreme wealthy to volunteer their funds for the purposes mentioned here. There is no logical reason for granting special treatment for churches and their many businesses. They are selling everything but the Man in the Moon: books to promote their concocted stories, cruises on which they can preach, cemeteries in which they can bury only those of their faith, (this has changed somewhat in recent years), etc. The main things they are selling are "everlasting life" and the "saving of souls." By their very nature, they have to amount to fraud as there is no way of proving that they can deliver what they promise. By relieving them of paying taxes, the government is shifting the burden on to all other citizens, many of whom are not believers and work hard for what they receive. We are forced to pay for what is actually or very close to being superstitions and utter nonsense. Since psychologists must pay taxes, why not religions which, in reality, are selling "psycho-babble" under the pretense of being religion?

Believers or non-believers, most sensible people would rather see the money used to help the poor, to pay down the national debt, to support social security, to pay for quality education through the voucher system, to help pay for better health care, to help with providing affordable housing, to promote science that can save lives, save the environment, develop alternatives to oil and relieve the tax burdens heaped upon working people. Once tax exemption privileges are removed, can you imagine how many so-called religions would vanish into thin air? Considering how many TV and radio shows flood the public airwaves, imagine what fruitful money makers these religions are! Would it not be interesting to investigate and disclose the growth in private wealth of televangelists through their years of delivering "the word"?

With regard to CEO's being given more money than makes any sense, I would like to call attention to a headline, dated December 15, 2006, stating that the CEO of Morgan Stanley was given a $40 million bonus on top of his regular salary! Don't go away, it gets worse. Median 2005 pay among chief executives running most of the nation's 100 largest companies soared 25% to $17.9 million, dwarfing the 3.1% average gain by typical American workers, USA TODAY found in its annual analysis of CEO pay. At poor-performing companies, some boards are ignoring performance guidelines to reward executives. Sun Microsystems, down more than 90% from its 2000 peak, gave CEO Scott McNealy a $1.1 million "discretionary" bonus last year, even though Sun failed to meet income or earnings targets. The board cited a "one-time need" to recognize McNealy's performance. McNealy gained $11.8 million exercising options. Already Sun's largest individual shareholder, McNealy also received fresh options worth $7.6 million. "There's a point where a board should tell the CEO, 'You have enough to incentivize you,' " says Paul Hodgson, pay analyst for The Corporate Library, a governance watchdog group..."But it's still business as usual at most companies. It's all about keeping up with the Joneses. There's still a disconnect between paying for performance and actually delivering it. There's no shame factor." Above Posted 4/10/2006 2:43 AM ET
There is really no point on sighting any more statistics on the outrageous incomes, perks, stock options, bonus's, etc. showered upon CEO's while workers have a struggle to get a slight raise or are put out of a job

so that the company can downsize or outsource to a foreign country. This is all too well known. I would rather spend more time on the solution than on the problem. If volunteer funds are not sufficient, why not print money for this purpose just as we did for the Marshal Plan or the countless billions we create out of thin air to spend foolishly on a fake drug war! Drop it, for G-d's sake – O.K. for the sake of the poor among us and for the sake of the all too many blacks in jail because they were pursuing the free enterprise system. Where there is demand; someone must be free to provide the supply. We do believe in capitalism, don't we?

It is interesting to note that once alcohol prohibition was ended, many "bootleggers" became wealthy entrepreneurs in many different businesses, aside from just alcoholic beverages. I discuss elsewhere in this book why we must stop pouring money down this bottomless black pit to try to stop what people obviously do not want to stop! Let me repeat a line from Chapter 11 "END FAKE WAR ON DRUGS": "Our $40 billion-a-year war on drugs has created more prisons, more criminals, more drug abuse and more disease." Ending the fake war on drugs would provide about $40 billion-a-year to go toward providing a stipend for those who need it! Add to this the money coming from formerly untaxed religions and we would all be able to go out and play golf!

As one of my ideas to end poverty, I am suggesting that any citizen in need would have the right to ask for and receive a stipend or living wage if he or she needs it. Whether a reason should be given or not is up to citizens, voters. This would mean the end of poverty, welfare, food stamps, soup kitchens, and the costs of administering these programs. No need to sell drugs to make a living! Individuals would have money to pay for private medical insurance in case my plan in this book is not accepted. These recipients would then have money to spend as they see fit and the economy would then boom as it did in Germany. Think what it would mean to the economy to make sure that all citizens had decent housing at a reasonable price! This would create jobs and jobs create other jobs! As a result, fewer citizens would have to ask for a living wage or stipend. If the government accepted the ideas proposed in this chapter, I am confident there would be plenty of money for all that is needed and so often neglected. By just declaring the "War on Drugs" won so that we can stop throwing our money down a bottomless sink hole and by taxing all religion based institutions, including taxes on their property, there would be countless billions to solve real needs and problems facing people be they believers or non-believers.

I know there are good people who are trying to provide housing for the poor, Habitat for Humanity is one. I have seen their ads and it seems that the families usually have several children. Does no one see that this is one of the main reasons for poverty? China has stopped their yearly death tolls from famine by requiring that families have no more than one child. The poor all over the world need to know about this, especially in Haiti and Africa as well as in our country. I saw another show on TV in which we are providing the most fuel efficient housing for the poor. The speaker emphasized that these are people who need most to save. The father, and I do not remember any mention of a wife or girl friend, but this father said he knows that he really must save – as his full set of gold teeth gleamed in the sun! I guess the public schools and no one in his "family" ever taught him a sense of responsibility! And how many more children is he going to have? Where is the mother or where are the mothers of the children he paraded in front of the camera? The natural question arises, is it good to just give hand-outs to the poor? We do it anyway in the form of welfare benefits, rent subsidies and food stamps. It seems to me that much of this is a costly, bureaucratic maize. What I am proposing here would cut out the red tape and what we pay for its administration would be given to those in need. Should we require some work for the stipend given out upon request? My guess is "yes," if the recipient is physically able. The work done can be good for the public in general and they could become used to getting to work on time and doing a respectable day of work. But, as I readily admit, I do not know all the answers – just most of them. Oh, boy, do I like to have fun! Why not! It is my book; I should be able to do what I want with it! I know the Bible states that the poor will always be with us. Would it not be nice to prove the Bible to be wrong once again!

CHAPTER 17
HMO's are KILLING US!

HMOs have been created by government to fill the pockets of big corporations so that they can take control of our lives while hiding the fact that it is really the government that is dictating to us, the citizens. It is an abandonment of our capitalist system of free enterprise in which citizens can make their own decisions about what is in their best interests. This is one of the main reasons why health costs have been like a balloon reaching toward the clouds. Please keep one thing in mind. HMOs can only increase profits by cutting service or by letting us die. How many readers are aware that HMOs are buying out other HMOs and why are they making so much money that they can afford to do this? What happened to the idea of competition? With fewer and fewer to choose from, is there not less competition? Are they depriving "we the people" of decent medical care and service to fill their own pockets? I am sure it is clear to any fifth grader that as a corporation becomes larger by buying out another, the profits of the buyer usually increase so that the CEO can steal more from Medicare run by the government and paid for by us, the taxpaying suckers. The bigger the corporation becomes, the higher the salary of the CEO can go. So what happened to competition? It vanishes just as the human voice on the telephone has vanished. But these devious CEOs are clever, tricky and smart as well. The company that is bought out is often allowed to keep its old name so that the public has no idea that the concept of competition is as gone as the old five cent cigar or nickel cup of coffee!

(You need not take up a collection for me: I go to my Bank United for a FREE cup of coffee which I can still afford.)

But do not lose sleep over loss of competition. So much money is being made that more HMOs are popping up like crocuses in the spring to get their hands on more of our money in a competitive way, maybe! In other words, government is allowing the money of hard-working people to be taken out (stolen?) from Medicare to set up corporations (HMOs) that are not cutting costs of medical care as was intended (as they told us they would). They are rationing and cutting care. The money that is taken out of Medicare is our money. It is not coming out of the pockets of investors or from those put in charge. This is a great reason for getting rid of both political parties because the "Demorats" want to put the government in charge of our lives; the "Republirats" want to turn us over to big corporations so that they can fill their pockets with money we sent to Medicare. (Review CHAPTER 13)

How in the world do they amass so much money that they are able to buy other HMOs other than by killing us off or cutting down on needed care to its members? In effect, they are using the tax money of American citizens that flow into Medicare and then on into those greedy pockets. After all, who checks up on them? Obviously, it is not the likes of the **Insurance Commissioner of Florida.**

Anyone who is not demented knows very well that government must follow the desires of the big corporations because that is where the politicians get their money for their election or reelection. This is exactly why our government, hog tied to big business, has set up more big corporations called HMOs to dole out medical care to us peasants. One way to correct this is for the public to demand that all congressmen, elite senators and compliant representatives who no longer really represent "we the people" must receive the same level of medical care as we peasants! It would be fun to see how fast the entire situation would change. Who knows? They may even comprehend the utterly brilliant ideas in this book.

Amazing, amazing, amazing, but I have written letters to congressmen asking what the salaries of these HMO CEOs might be and how much, if at all, did they increase as the benefits to the public diminished, as co-pays increased and service became worse. Strange, no answers! Would you believe it? This must be TOP SECRET since these newly anointed corporate executives of the HMOs are now more BIG money people beholden to the government! I thought there was a "Freedom of Information Act." After all, they are using our money. We should know how it is spent. No?

Let's face it, **the HMO bureaucracy is a rationing system imposed upon the American public by our government.** We the people must take back the government from the politicians. The bureaucrats of the HMOs, these non-doctors, are charged with making medical decisions that can mean life or death for the patient. This is just another government boondoggle as Social "Insecurity," public housing and public schools that so much of the public, black and white, dare not use! I have news for you; there are no easy solutions unless enough people are willing to accept what I propose below. Some of what I suggest may sound cruel, but I consider nothing crueler than having some 45 million American citizens unable to pay for reliable medical treatment. NOTE: I did not say "unable to pay for insurance." For the most part, I believe insurance companies should have nothing to do with health care. This lost business can be more than made up if my idea of establishing private retirement accounts as a replacement or adjunct to Social Security. I suggest a major role for them in providing investment insurance for all private individual retirement accounts. This can be accomplished by using the relatively new concept for annuities which now can guarantee the base value of the account (or fund) no matter how the market performs. This means that at the anniversary date of the insured fund the higher value would become the base value below which the fund can never go. Even if the market drops, the value of the fund upon death of insured cannot go down. It is important for the protection of the insurance companies and to keep premiums as low as possible to limit investments for such Private Retirement Accounts to high grade bonds, treasury certificates or government bonds and stocks of solid corporations with a long history of paying and even increasing dividends. Wiser heads than mine need to determine who and when allocations for above should be made or changed. It could be the insurance companies themselves, but it may be better for individuals owning the accounts to select and pay for investment advisors to provide this service.

It is important for the economic health of the nation to encourage private savings. The above is a means of doing this and, by creating a salary ceiling for CEOs and officers of companies, they would be encouraged to pay out more in dividends rather than continuing with the present insanity of paying many millions of dollars to top executives while leaving all others in the dust. If these executives are not fully satisfied with their salaries, they would have <u>an incentive to grow the business and pay out more in dividends.</u> They then could buy more stock and collect those dividends to increase their own personal income. It is not in my pay grade to determine the proper ceiling for said salaries, but one might consider a range of $250,000 to $1,000,000 as reasonable. There are CEOs today who are within that range and I know of one who accepts only one dollar - I assume he must own a great deal of stock in the company. It would be helpful to get ideas and advice from wealthy executives themselves to determine the best range, but my guess is that most could skimp by on a $1,000,000 yearly salary. This is another area in which Think Tanks can do some thinking! I have come around to this suggestion because it should be obvious that extremes of wealth are not good for anyone in the long run. Keep in mind the French Revolution was brought about by the statement of Marie Antoinette that if they do not have bread…"Let them eat cake"! Our social and economic elites should not be saying: "Let them eat sushi!"

The same holds true for labor unions that have ruined GM and other companies with their extortion tactics to get as much as possible out of the companies. If the workers feel they would like to earn more, they should try to save and buy stock in the companies for which they work. This would be an incentive to help keep the company profitable so that dividends might be maintained or even grow. Doing the above would go a long way toward enhancing a major part of the stock market due to what was learned in Economics 101 mentioned above: increased money flowing in increases demand and thus prices. In this manner Wall Street can become a safe and sound place for savings and income and will take away the casino aspects of much of the market making it safe for Main Street. This can be the **ROAD BACK TO PROSPERITY. <u>It can be a major step toward saving retirement accounts now bleeding from the gills!</u>**

The existence of insurance itself is a major part of the problem. Does any reader doubt that the insurance industry is big business, very big business? How many citizens realize that some HMOs are owned by insurance companies? The more insurance there is, the more money becomes available and the higher the costs will go. Can anyone find out or guess how much insurance companies paid into political campaigns and for what purpose? I will leave it to your imagination or personal research and pure logic. Insurance increases the demand and provides the money to pay for it. Economics 101 takes over as price becomes what the market will bear when there is no one watching how the money is spent. With a Medical Allotment Plan, the consumer would be a watchdog on every penny spent because he would be entitled to all money at the end of the year that has not been spent! The funds left over would be added to a personal retirement savings plan not to be available until official retirement. This idea can go a long way toward solving our problem of an extremely low savings rate in our country. May we call this a collateral benefit? Under a Medical Allotment Plan, each citizen would choose his own doctor according to convenience, cost and/or reputation. Each consumer of medical care would be careful to check bills to make sure they are honest and correct. Unnecessary and expensive procedures would be avoided if agreed to by the doctor and the patient. Under our present system, no one really gives a "you know what" because they think it is the insurance company that pays. Wrong, wrong, wrong. This is a big factor in today's high costs. I will not even discuss the fraud that is often brought to light. With each consumer shedding light on everything that is done, there is bound to be much less fraud. I trust you are beginning to see the solution. To continue, end the HMO nonsense and place that money into a Medical Allotment Plan (MAP) for every American citizen. To bring in the MAPs, we must close our borders to illegal immigrants. To do otherwise would be ludicrous. If we do not have the guts to do this, kiss good-by to the USA as we have known it! Most immigrants are coming here because they have so over populated their own countries that it is no longer possible to earn a living there! **They will create the same environment here that existed in the homeland from which they fled!**

I heard a comment on the TV that we just cannot expel 20 million illegal immigrants. Not necessary! Just pass a law that anyone found to be in the country illegally, would be sent to prison and hard labor for five years and then returned to his country with empty pockets! Any employer found to be hiring illegal immigrants would face a heavy fine and a mandatory five to ten years in prison under hard labor. But if you put them into prison, that must cost a lot of money. Wrong again. My friend, Al Smith, proposed the idea of outsourcing prisons by paying Mexico a fraction of what it costs to house and feed illegal immigrants in this country. It would provide some income to Mexicans. This is something to be considered if Mexico is receptive to the idea. If not agreed to, no problem. We can set up tent cities to house prisoners. There would be no need for fancy prisons. Remember how early legal immigrants who went west to build a better life for themselves by crossing in their covered wagons lived. If our troops can sleep on the ground under tents with no heat, air conditioning, TV or other amenities that many American citizens cannot afford, so can illegal aliens. They should have to work at least ten hours a day on meaningful public works projects, such as clearing brush from forests so that we will have fewer catastrophic forest fires. How about plowing the fields to prepare ground for planting crops? Let this be widely known well in advance and I believe there would be a rush to the border to get out.

In all fairness, we cannot hold employers responsible until we have a viable and reliable National Identification Card in place. Once this is accomplished we will see an end of illegal immigration and a rush to the borders! They would soon find their way back to whence they came just as easily as they found their way in! No more need for border patrolling, a huge savings right there! Forget the building of walls and fences along the border, another great savings. A double ring of barbed wire with rottweilers roaming about would keep the prisoners in the tent prison. Problem solved.

Aside from the obvious stupidity of paying for medical costs of lawbreakers - illegal immigrants - there is a not so evident reason for "encouraging" them to leave the country. HMOs have been forcing hospitals to toss patients out prematurely and have done everything possible to stop from placing patients in hospitals in the first place because of the outrageous expense. The cost of a hospital stay has run off the chart because those who can pay or who have insurance are paying for those who do not have the money or insurance. Most illegal immigrants would fall into the latter category! **WE ARE NOW PAYING THE MEDICAL COSTS FOR LAW BREAKERS!   I remind you that this is the fault of both political parties.**

Here is a Benjamin Franklin type of statement from your author, me. **An illegal immigrant is very much like a street person forcing his way into your home and then insisting that you feed, clothe, house and educate him and his entire family and PAY FOR THEIR MEDICAL CARE! It is known that hospitals have been forced into bankruptcy or nearly so because of this.**

And now back to the all-important Medical Allotment Plan (MAP). Statisticians can find the average cost NOW of medical care. Cut that by a given percentage determined by brilliant men, perhaps in a "think tank", say by 30% to 50%. The balance would be paid into an account for each citizen. No money would be given to the citizen (patient). The doctor would bill his MAP Once that fund is empty, a Catastrophic Insurance Plan, paid for by Medicare or covered by a special government health fund would take over. If citizens and/or Congress agree, insurance companies may be granted the right to make a competitive bid for writing such insurance, if we take this route. In the first few years, it may be necessary to agree to a reasonable profit margin for the carriers. If the carriers are unable to reach a given profit level, the government may have to supplement their income as it is a bit unfair to expect them to know exactly what to charge without statistical evidence under an MAP system. Under no circumstances should this government subsidy be continued beyond a reasonable number of years. I personally feel it would be best having only the government provide this coverage since all decisions would be made by the patient up to the point at which costs go well over the allotment. The savings will show up for the entire system up to the point at which the allotment to the Medical Allotment Plan contribution for the year is used up. Remember, the consumer has every incentive to be frugal and wise in the way in which this is spent since all that remains will go into his retirement account. It may be that we can discontinue the Medicare deductions from pay checks and terminate the program. Brighter heads than mine, the boys in the "Think Tank," will have to give this a lot of thought.

Each patient would have the right to choose his own doctor and decide upon his treatment with his doctor. Under today's HMO system, a government bureaucrat dictates to us! This is not compatible with a free society in which individuals are expected to make decisions for themselves. The MAPs give us back our freedom and allow free enterprise to bring down costs! I understood that was what built this country and what we are supposed to believe. I am confident the above will be less costly than what we are now paying for in one way or another, but if more funds are needed, there will be ample to go around if we end the fake war on drugs, end tax exempt status for religion and use the money for Medical Allotment Funds, for financing the creation of vouchers for private education and billions would most likely be left over to pay for national defense and toward reducing the national debt! To your health, my friends! Never forget! HEALTH IS WEALTH!

JUST HOW BAD ARE HMOs?

They are absolutely perfect if you do not get sick. Once you are sick, beware. For those who have had to deal with them, I need not waste time by recounting how bad medical service has become since it is well known. From my experience, I would conclude that the HMOs make doctors take on so many patients that they cannot really give the patients - "we the people" - the care required. No doubt this is done so that doctors can make a living on the pittance paid them by the HMOs. To top it off, they are apparently understaffed because they cannot afford to hire more help to handle the bureaucratic paper work! No wonder they do not answer the phone, do not return phone calls, do not do what they know must be done. If Medicare is really paying the bills, why were the HMO'S set up as middlemen? This is the $64 question or is it the $64 billion or trillion or a lot of money question or did I answer it above?

Just think of all the trees cut down to provide all the paper needed to accommodate the growing need for paperwork engendered by HMOs? Most of these bureaucrats must think that paper grows on trees. I know, it does, but this is certainly planet unfriendly. Over the years, I have switched from one HMO to another because of various failings, often not answering telephone calls or responding to messages. Eventually, I discovered it was just jumping from the frying pan into the fire as they are all facing the same problems. I do not blame the doctors; it is the system.

My first really serious medical problem started a few years ago. I started going to my primary care physician in the first week of December with some symptoms that were unusual for me. Not too many years ago, when the USA had real medical care, I would have been placed in a hospital for a day or two to undergo all needed tests. Not in this age. Using the HMO, outpatient testing was done from the first week of December to the end of February - almost three months. I had to wait until the HMO was ready. I was obliged to make some ten doctor and outpatient hospital visits, paying $20 for each doctor's visit. (I remember when a visit to a doctor's office was $5.00.) A number of these visits were unnecessary, as I already knew their findings from prior visits. It is just a ruse used by some doctors to milk the insurance providers, Medicare and the HMOs. The results indicated a 95% chance of it being cancer of the left kidney.

In the good old days, this would have been known in the first or second week of December while in the hospital, not three months later because of HMO bureaucracy. NOTE: delay can be deadly in cancer. Can anyone deny that by denying or delaying prompt medical care, especially to the elderly and seriously ill, HMOs ARE KILLING US OFF TO SAVE MONEY! If you do not believe this, I have a famous bridge in Brooklyn I can sell you, cheap! Do you agree with me that killing off the elderly and seriously ill is un-American and inhumane? Tell that to your political leaders! By the way, months ago I was again diagnosed as having another type of cancer. I was first sent to an orthopedic surgeon instead of an oncologist! So much for our governmental educational system! I was finally, after months, told to go to the correct surgeon (I guess), but he would not be able to see me for a month. By that time, I believed more cancerous areas were beginning to show up, but I had to wait about a month to find out or to get needed treatment. In the meantime, they kept growing. This convinced me to change my HMO again.

I met with the salesperson for this new HMO, Humana, and he assigned me to a primary care physician who was far from my home. I pointed this out and he said I could change the next month. I could not convince him that this would be adding to expenses and a waste of time for the HMO and for me. He assured me I had to go to the one assigned – another loss of freedom in our said-to-be free country. Agreeing to sign up with them anyway, I immediately called the office of the HMO and pointed out that they would be wasting their (taxpayers') money by forcing me to wait yet another month to go to the primary care provider close to home as the new PCP would have to go through the same routine of testing and waiting to see past medical records. I explained that it would be best if they were to change my PCP before anything was done. Again, nothing sank in with the brilliant administrators at Humana - thus another month of delay. Delay with cancer can mean death. No matter, rules are rules! I told them even Popes can make exceptions. That rang no bells or even chimes! On one occasion, there was so much delay, my urine was reeking to high heaven. It smelled as though I was rotting from the inside. All this due to a government-mandated dictatorship called HMO's. **It is a rationing system trying to save money by killing off the seriously ill and elderly (seniors).** Perhaps this is not the intent, but it is the result. I suggest you ask your Congressmen if they would like to be subjected to the same slow death process or if they would like this for members of their families. Ask them and then let them know you expect a personal, signed, written response letting you know what they intend to do about it. No such response means no vote for them!

Unfortunately it will not be so simple to make the needed changes without **REFORM OF OUR DEMOCRACY TO REPRESENT THE COMMON MAN RATHER THAN BIG MONEY INTERESTS THROUGH THE LOBBY HUCKSTERS WHO CARE ONLY ABOUT WEALTHTY CORPORATIONS and their own wallets. As matters now stand, OUR GOVERNMENT IS BEING BOUGHT AND PAID FOR BY BIG CORPORATIONS!** (Chapter 13 spells out in a concise way how this can be corrected – or "rectified" if you like a $64 word.

After first being seen by my new PCP from Humana, I decided to stay with him even though it was a good ride from home. A few weeks later, I contacted his office to request a referral to see an eye specialist who had successfully treated a condition a year before. He asked me to return after one year and it was then time to have a follow up visit. Since I had been in and out of HMOs, I called to verify with doctors to see if Humana would be acceptable to the eye specialist and find out if the referral had been faxed to him. I started doing this checking weeks in advance. Close to the appointment time, I checked again only to be told by a number of offices that I had been dropped by Humana and therefore there was no one to give me the needed referral. Humana had never notified me that I had been removed as a member. I did not learn that HUMANA had cancelled my coverage with them until late Friday, just before the Monday appointment with the eye doctor. I did not know what to do or which way to turn. Since I had a number of serious medical problems, some of which needed immediate attention, I went to NORTH BROWARD MEDICAL CENTER to try to get advice from an administrator or a social worker, but no one was available. Since I have a blood condition that could kill me if not attended to, I was told to go to the ER room. I was there most of Saturday. The day before, I had tried to talk to someone at HUMANA to ask why I had been dropped with no notification to me, but was confronted with an automated machine that went on long enough for me to have read GONE WITH THE WIND plus LADY CHATTERLY'S LOVER over and over again. Usually, these infernal machines give you the option of dialing zero to get to speak to an operator, but HUMANA does not even allow this relief. I believe I am right when I say this is a clear indication of a "devil be damned" attitude toward their trapped members.

Apparently, professionals in the medical business have a secret number to get to talk to a human being in such uncaring bureaucracies as HUMANA. The hospital had such a number and thus found out that I had not been dropped – contrary to what I had been told by two doctor's offices – but that the inhuman HUMANA had just changed my primary care provider with absolutely no notice to me. I was told that is their normal procedure. This still left me in mid-air as I had no way of knowing who this new provider was or his telephone number which I would naturally need to arrange to see him. I guess my health care provider was not able to figure this out. By the way, about my statement above that there exists secret numbers not given to the pubic which depends on them to remain alive, I called CARE PLUS which I had to leave because of similar, but different insane irregularities covered in another document, but their living operator was kind enough to give me a secret number. I called it and a machine asked if I were a member of Humana. Once I declared I was, the MACHINE told me to call the number on the back of my Humana membership card. That is the very number that never answered and I was not ready to read GONE WITH THE WIND and LADY CHATTLEY'S LOVER over again. Now the key question is WHY DOES HUMANA use those infernal impersonal answering machine devices rather than have a human operator available as is the case with CARE PLUS and most other humane organizations? The answer, my dear Watson, is that HUMANA's CEO is apparently more concerned with the growth in profits - his bottom line – rather than to serve the sick and elderly. It is from this bottom line that he is able to raise his own salary rather than pay for telephone operators. He cannot be too stupid since he had brains enough to take advantage of our present system to make enough money to buy another HMO (I heard it is Care Plus which I renamed Care Less). I fled from HUMANA years ago because they refused to grant permission for me to see a dermatologist who said it was necessary to see me again to look out for other cancer spots. Just as a matter of interest, I very recently had a cancer operation on my face, having to cut through a number of layers to clear it out.

I went back to HUMANA, hoping they had grown up and became more responsible to human needs as their false name implies. It should be renamed: "INHUMANA." I did not have much of a choice since I had experienced many other problems with all of the other HMOs I had used. They are all no good and a burden on the backs of the American people. I just do not have the money to travel to Cuba or Russia for medical care; so on it goes.

I am glad to report that recent experience with Humana has been very good, but this does not negate the need to replace them as prescribed here. Good care such as recently provided to me by HUMANA could be received by replacing HMOs with the Medical Allotment Plan (MAP) as explained in this book and at a lower cost.

On February 18, 2008, I wrote to our Insurance Commissioner of Florida to tell him of my experiences with HMOs. My letter was never answered. This gives you a good idea of how "caring" (irresponsible) our governmental officials are. This is just one more indication that our elected officials are beholden to our very wealthy corporations and this includes HMOs, of course.

SOLUTION: GET RID OF THE HMOs
AND THEIR OVERPAID CEOs.
IF NOT HMOs, THEN WHAT?

There must be a brainy think tank out there that can refine the concepts I am suggesting here for the Medical Allotment Plan. Here are the basic ideas I have, but I am sure wiser people can refine this to get us out of our present mess. By the way, I call myself a "Devout Orthodox

Capitalist (or DOC), but if we leave matters stand as they are now, I fear we may have to go to Cuba or to Russia to get proper medical care!

Finally, here are my positively brilliant ideas: I propose that the government set aside X number of dollars for each citizen (not for illegal immigrants) for medical care for the forthcoming year. If at the end of the year, the entire fund is not spent, this money can be added to his personal social security retirement account which will be owned by the citizen, but not available until retirement. This means people should be allowed to set up privately funded retirement accounts, putting in a given amount of money each year. This would be an incentive for each consumer of medical services to not over use the system and to seek doctors to accept a reasonable fee for what needs to be done. This is called competition. Remember that capitalistic word?

It would stop unnecessary testing which doctors now feel compelled to use to protect themselves from law suits. The patient need only sign a paper that he, along with the advice of his doctor, decided the test was not necessary and he would not pay for it and the patient understood that the doctor would not be later held liable for not taking the test. This is called personal choice, competition and a bit of common sense. For extraordinary medical expenses, an insurance pool should be set up to provide a catastrophic illness coverage for which insurance companies may charge a fee that may have to be supplemented by government or have the government provide this fund without insurance companies. I see the need for some health insurance as just stated, but the overuse has been one strong factor in the stratospheric rise in the cost of health care. This comes about because of an age-old economic principle that a price will rise to what the market will bear. The more insurance money available, the higher the price can go! The consumer - the patient - does not care; it is the insurance company that pays the bill – so he thinks! By establishing a national Medical Allotment Plan, the patient will look carefully before spending willy-nilly! He will have reason to make sure he is not being charged for services not rendered. Fraud would be much less likely. Money saved can go to his retirement fund.

This is another plan that we the people can force the government to put up to a national vote – referendum – so that no "honest politician" need worry about pressure from the lobbyists and pressure groups. Can you imagine the position insurance companies would take! Without a change in the political system as suggested here, such a plan would go over like a led balloon. (Refer back to CHAPTER 13)

I happen to believe in the free enterprise system and believe that a Medical Allotment Plan would be much cheaper and of greater service to all concerned rather than the two bureaucracies we have now - Medicare and the HMO superimposed on top of that one. It is not "double your pleasure"; it is doubling the inefficiencies of having two governmental agencies wasting money in their own peculiar ways.

"HOLY" AS PART OF A NAME SHOULD MEAN JUST THAT

Here is a true story which clearly demonstrates how uncaring and irresponsible some members of our medical profession have become. I want this to become widely known so that hospital CEOs will learn that their first responsibility is the health and well-being of the patient. This needs to be priority number one!

My letter to:
Mr. John Johnson, CEO   (I delivered it myself to his office.)
June 13, 2005
Holy Cross Hospital
4725 N Federal Highway
Fort Lauderdale, Florida 33308

BELOW IS LETTER TO WHICH I HAD NO RESPONSE
My letter to Mr. John Johnson (actual name)
Mr. John Johnson, CEO
Holy Cross Hospital
4725 N Federal Highway
Fort Lauderdale, Florida 33308
June 1, 2005
Dear Mr. Johnson:

Discharge, May 5, improper?

All other names changed to protect privacy. Any resemblance to their real names is purely intended – sometimes.

Persons involved: Discharge nurse was, "Nurse Mendelah"
      Dr. Silverlining
      Dr. Chewawa
      Dr. Fooler (According to Dr. Chewawa who said he assisted at the procedure)

At around 2 P.M., "Nurse Mendelah" came to my bed and announced that I was to be discharged from the hospital that afternoon. I asked her how that could be since Dr. Chewawa, the physician who performed the operation, told me he would visit me that afternoon. She said that Dr. Silverlining had discussed it with him and both agreed I could be discharged. I did not believe her; so I asked if he had signed the discharge paper. She replied that only Dr. Silverlining had to sign. Again she said that Dr. Chewawa knew all about it. I asked what would happen if I were to refuse to leave as I felt it was wrong for me to leave without first seeing Dr. Chewawa, the doctor who had done the procedure. She replied that I would lose my insurance. I felt I was being forced to leave, as I could not be without insurance. After arriving home, I called Medicare and was told that she had lied! Any patient has the right to refuse discharge and the insurance would be valid until the appeal had been decided. Obviously, I was improperly discharged because of the ignorance of that discharge nurse – "Nurse Mendelah"!

I did not want to leave without first seeing Dr. Chewawa, as he had agreed to see me that afternoon. He should have signed any discharge paper in front of me if he had really agreed to it. I felt I was not ready to leave because of continuing pain that was supposed to last one to three days. That pain had lasted well into the eighth day. I felt I was entitled to an explanation. I copied the following from my medical records:

"The 10mm balloon trocar was subsequently placed. Inspection of the retroperitoneal space **unfortunately** revealed that the superior aspect of the balloon dissection, the peritoneum had been **widely** entered. A 5mm port was placed posteriorly as well as one anteriorly. Eventually both of these ports were changed out for 10 mm ports." (I found out later that this was a nice way of saying that there was a little mishap that could have caused the pain.) I could not afford to lose my insurance; so I allowed them to force me out. The last minute, the nurse arrived to change my wound dressings. This was the first time in eight days that this had been done! This action set the pain nerves in action and I was back in excruciating pain. I asked for pain medication while still in my hospital room and again several times of many passersby for a pain pill as I sat in a wheelchair at the front door, waiting for the "get-away" van! It was always refused! Even the nurse from my room came down to explain that they were not permitted to give me pain medication once discharged. If they were afraid I might go out to the street to try to sell it, all they had to do was see it go down my throat with a glass of water! But why not while I was still in the room! Was it because of indifferent nurses or an uncaring administration that simply made up rules without considering consequences?

I have a great deal to say about my stay in Holy Cross Hospital. I find it to be a disgrace to this country and to the Catholic religion. I always admired the fact that Catholics had built so many excellent hospitals to help those who are ill and need help. What has happened? The most caring attendant I found was a young black man named "Ben" who was the only one who ever noticed that I was out of water and had the initiative to ask me if I wanted some. I believe he may have been in training. I am not religious, but I intuitively wanted to and did say "God bless him" to myself! He is a real caring individual. I do not fault the other nurses. They were not sitting around filing their nails or chatting, as far as I could see, and many of them were very nice, but seemed quite harried. I do, however, fault the administration. The nursing staff was obviously overworked and understaffed! Many times I struggled between trying to get to the telephone or the nurse buzzer to call for help for one thing or another. Once being successful in that chore, I often had to wait so long I could have read a good part of Gone with the Wind!

Here is an example of the kind of nursing service I saw and experienced at Holy Cross. A few days after my arrival, the empty bed next to me was given to a diabetic patient who had to expectorate a great deal. He was either never given any tissues or ran short of them. His mouth was full when a nurse passed and he asked her if she could bring him some tissue. She gave him a mean look, said NOTHING, and walked away! In case no one in the hospital knows, it would have been proper if she had smiled and said something like: "Please give me a moment and I will bring you some." Not much to ask, is it? She needs retraining and I suggest you find that patient and have him identify the nurse. Please do not tell me you cannot find the name of that patient! If that is the case, you are even more mismanaged than I suspect! In fact, I INSIST that you find him and have him contact me (my telephone number) if he wishes.

What I just recited above may perhaps be behind my sudden departure! **YOU NEED TO INVESTIGATE!** The above gentleman waited so long to see a tissue that he finally spit it out on the floor in disgust, yelling that they did not hear the end of this incident and that I (the gentlemen in the next bed, as he stated it) would be a willing witness! Could it be that some nurses got together to see that I would not be around to be his witness? Interesting thought. That is for you (Mr. Johnson) to find out. And, I mean find out!

After getting home, Dr .Chewawa called and told me his secretary told him I did not understand why I had been discharged without his agreement. I had not seen his signature on any form! He said he was not aware of my discharge. He then added that my cousin Janet had called to tell his secretary that she was quite irate over my premature discharge. I paused to think! I told him that if he had not told me that Janet had called, I might have believed him, but under the circumstances, I feel that the hospital administration needs to fully investigate this matter, **IMMEDIATELY!** I explained that Janet knows a slew of lawyers and is very adept at slaying the giant if it needs to be done. She has good experience in this realm and probably intimidated Dr. Chewawa into lying about knowing anything about my discharge. The discharge nurse assured me several times that Dr.Silverlining had full agreement from Dr. Chewawa for my discharge. It is quite apparent, even to an apprentice Dr. Sherlock Holmes, that someone is lying. Is it Dr. Silverlining, Dr. Chewawa or the discharge nurse Ms. Pozo (Millie) or a combination thereof? I call for an **IMMEDIATE INVESTIGATION**, and that means now.

Dr. J. Knowname

No response to above; hence the following:

My letter to: Mr. John Johnson, CEO

(Again, taken by me to his office.)   June 13, 2005

Holy Cross Hospital

4725 N Federal Highway

Fort Lauderdale, Florida 33308

Dear Mr. Johnson:

I have a very strong suspicion you are ignoring my letter to you dated June 1. Just in case the lady at the front desk did not deliver it to you, a copy will be at the bottom. I am giving you the benefit of the doubt. This matter will be resolved. It would be best for Holy Cross if you were to take care of it. To save you, personally, a great deal of embarrassment, I strongly insist you send me a telegram by Friday, June 17 to inform me you will have full answers to my questions by Friday, June 24. A telephone call will not be satisfactory…

Respectfully yours,

Dr. J. Knowname

Below is my follow-up letter.

July 6, 2005

Dear Sir:

Please excuse me for not entering the addressee line. I am exhausted. I am overwhelmed by poor health and related matters that have taken this off my front burner, but I will never stop until this is brought to a just conclusion. Note that my letter to the CEO of Holy Cross Hospital was June 1 and the issues have been unceremoniously ignored. I have a great deal of respect for those with sincere religious beliefs. My step-mother, whom I loved deeply, was Catholic. She would turn over in her grave if she knew the details spelled out below.

Mr. John Johnson needs to be reminded that he is representing a Catholic Hospital. I presume it is Catholic as there are crosses and statues of Jesus very much in view. I think this faith is beautiful, if sincere, but for a Catholic institution to ignore serious problems brought to the attention of those responsible and to allow the acceptance of lying on the part of key personnel amounts to hypocrisy. It is wearing one's religion on one's sleeve. I do not think Jesus would be pleased with this! I trust you will see to it that the questions I have asked will be fully answered as they are causing me a great deal of anguish.

Above is my first letter to the CEO of Holy Cross Hospital. It was ignored.
The second letter dated June 13 was also ignored.

IS THIS WHAT AMERICAN HEALTH CARE HAS COME TO?

I happen to have been fighting for my life; it may be your turn next! Do we really have to suffer hospital administrators who overlook lying on the part of staff or totally ignore cries for help from a patient who was just confronted with the prospect of having cancer? What has happened has destroyed my trust in three doctors and in Holy Cross Hospital. I am most likely in need of another operation or procedure, but I dare not return to the one who did the first procedure. My appointment with him was for June 30, three days later! (Because of inaction on the part of Mr. Johnson, I felt forced to cancel the appointment and start with an entirely new team of doctors!) Although I clearly stated in my letter below that a telephone call would not be acceptable, Ms Debbie Saylor, Senior VP of Nursing, called to explain that Mr. Johnson (CEO of Holy Cross Hospital) was out of town and may not return until Monday (June 20). (Oh, how I would love to see absolute proof of this!) This would make it impossible for him to comply with my stipulation that I must have a telegram from him no later than June 17. We had a long conversation in which I made it quite clear that I needed **a complete answer to all concerns spelled out in the letter below.** Ms. Saylor agreed that our conversation would be immediately followed by a letter confirming our conversation and all matters would then be investigated.

Apparently, I am a sucker for the smooth voice of a female who sounded like a real lady. I actually believed she would send me a letter of confirmation of our discussion! As it turns out, she is yet another liar! We spoke on June 16 and it is now June 27. (Date this letter was first put together.) Does anyone consider eleven days to be "immediate"? Still no response! I do not understand how the Catholic Church can allow this to go unnoticed! This remains to be seen!

I sent the entire disgraceful story to the Bishop of Miami on July 6, 2005. The result was about the same as one might expect by placing a note into a hole in the Wailing Wall. NOTHING from the main keeper of souls for believers!

I hope a reader will think of a way of teaching hospital CEOs that their first concern must be the health and welfare of their patients. Use the town meeting of the air – the internet – and get a movement going. I wanted to sue Mr. Johnson and Holy Cross Hospital, but I had too many medical problems and felt it more important to finish this book.

Who is going to be brave enough to clean out these HMO leaches and parasites and allow true free enterprise to flourish by the creation of a well structured Medical Allotment Plan which would empower individuals to make their own choices and decisions without being dictated to by government? It is up to us – WE THE PEOPLE, but there is one major problem, the very rich do not have to settle for HMOs, but the wealthy along with us peasants having humanist values, I hope, will step up and take action for the rest of us. Are you going to lie back and let them walk all over you and your children or are you going to flood the mail boxes of your so-called representatives. DO SOMETHING. IT IS YOUR LIFE!

MORE HISTORICAL OR HISTERICAL DOCUMENTS THAT SHOULD BE KNOWN BY THE PUBLIC.

TO: Senator XYZ (a shortened version)
November 23, 2007

To keep matters simple, I will seek help in only one of three complaints against CARE PLUS, my HMO provider. I tried to call the Insurance Commissioner of Florida for help and found that they only had a toll free number, apparently only for Tallahassee, as a machine told me that the one given on the internet was not valid in my area, Pompano Beach, Florida. I then sent an e-mail on September 20 and had no response...

As I understand it, we pay our Medicare taxes to the government and Medicare then pays the HMOs. Am I naïve to think that they should spend our money prudently as any individual with half a brain would? Would such a person be stupid enough to pay for a service or product that cannot be of use? CARE PLUS has forced this upon me by paying for work done on new glasses which are useless because they did not prepare them correctly. They insist that this causes me to lose my right to receive a new pair of glasses. I am forced to walk around half blind! This is the basis of my complaint as explained below.

The following is the applicable portion of that message I tried to get through to the Insurance Commissioner of Florida:

"I went to Dr. R S, one of Care Plus's providers for new eye glasses. They had only the cheapest available under their plan. I chose one I thought might be satisfactory, but when I told the assistant that they did not fit and I did not see how they could adjust them since they were made of plastic, I was assured they would be able to do so. When delivered, I found that they slid down to the end of my nose seconds after I put them on. An adjustment was tried with no success. Worse yet, when I compared the vision with the old glasses, I found that the latter were much better than the ones they had made up for me. I finally returned them and prevailed upon them to refund what I had paid. "I then called Care Plus to find out if they had cancelled payment to Dr. S's office. They had NOT and I was told they could not get a refund for what they had paid. It seems to me that in the normal course of human events if unsatisfactory work is done, it should not be paid for. Does this mean that in the case of an HMO they are obliged to pay even if the service is unsatisfactory to the consumer? Does it also mean that I have lost my opportunity to receive free glasses for the year or time period required? In other words, have I used up my benefit because the bureaucracy has forced payment for something I returned and cannot use? I have been unable to get a satisfactory answer to this question!"

And now to continue. I now have the answer which confirmed my suspicion. I went to another eye doctor and w y as told Care Plus refused to pay for new glasses as a result of the above. It is not my fault that Care Plus engaged the services of a providing physician who could not do the job either because of poor training or defective equipment. At the time I requested a return of the money I had paid to Dr. S, I immediately called Care Plus and asked to see another doctor for a second opinion. They ordered me to return to the same doctor even after asking to speak to a supervisor and after much arguing. I could not convince them that the meaning of a "second opinion" means going to another doctor, not the same one found to be unsatisfactory. AM I CORRECT IN THIS MATTER? When I returned as ordered, to Dr. S, she claimed that the glasses she provided were perfect. Did the idiots at this HMO really expect her to admit to an error or that her testing equipment was not properly calibrated? I discussed all of the above with Medicare and they could be of no help even though they are paying my tax money to this HMO.

Can someone in our government explain to this taxpayer why we must accept and pay for an inferior product to replace one that is perfect?

I happen to believe in the free enterprise system. Sadly we lost this years go as we allowed government into controlling our lives. This is just one of many myths. We are quickly losing freedoms we once had. I believe that a Medical Allotment Plan would be much cheaper and of greater service to all concerned rather than the two bureaucracies we have now - Medicare and the HMO superimposed one on top of the other. It is not "double your pleasure"; it is doubling the inefficiencies of having two governmental or semi-governmental agencies wasting money in their own peculiar ways.

If citizens were allowed to take care of themselves by the creation of a Medical Allotment Plan, unsatisfactory work would not have to be paid for and we would simply go to another doctor rather than having to depend on the people at an HMO who most likely were not adequately educated in a government run public school. I was a teacher in that governmental system, but once I saw the harm they were doing, I spent decades advocating free enterprise via a voucher system!

This has been dragging on since June 20. At this point I can hardly see because a few weeks ago I left my old glasses (the ones that are perfect) on the back seat of a car provided by CARE PLUS to take me to a dermatologist. This transportation was provided because CARE PLUS did not have a dermatologist near my home. As soon as the driver drove me back to my house, I quickly realized I had left the glasses in the car. I called CARE PLUS immediately and asked them to try to retrieve them for me. Weeks later I am still waiting!

Can you tell me how much longer I will have to go around half blind in our growing socialist state?

Thank you sincerely,
Dr. J. Knowname

NO RESPONSE FROM MY REPRESENTATIVE IN CONGRESS or THE INSURANCE COMMISSIONER OF FLORIDA

This gives you a good idea of how "caring" (irresponsible) our governmental officials are. This is just one more indication that our elected officials are beholden to our very wealthy corporations and this includes HMOs, of course, and they are in some cases associated with big insurance companies.

The Medicare/HMO twins have turned out to be a sad, tragic joke on the American public.

Am I wrong in thinking that most of us are like sheep, standing around just waiting to be sheered? If this book does nothing else, I hope it will move some of my readers (if there are any) to not accept the status quo if it is stupid and self-destructive and to stand up and speak up for what is good and just and, above all, to THINK. One of several purposes of this book is to encourage readers to THINK, THINK and THINK AGAIN.

OUR "MONEY-OCRACY" needs to be replaced by TRUE DEMOCRACY and REAL FREE ENTERPRISE, not just lip service.

BOOK POSTSCRIPT

Now that you have read, absorbed and fully understand this entire book, you may be thinking I should have my head examined. Sorry, you are too late. After experiencing severe headaches for too long a time, my doctor sent me for a brain scan, pet scan or dog scan – I forget which. As soon as the results came in, the specialist showed me the pictures and explained that the large white areas indicated memory loss. So what else is new, my friends have known this for years, I thought. He further explained that the white areas also indicate that my brain cells are shrinking. I immediately asked him how long it took him to get his license to practice medicine. He replied, "Eighteen years." "O.K doc," I said, "since I am a bit retarded, it will take me twenty years, but I will go to medical school (I a was then 78 going on 100), become a research scientist and discover how to regenerate new brain cells and then you and I will be able to cure everyone." He was thrilled to hear this and then told me: "Take this pill in the meantime." He said it would not cure me, but would most likely stop its progression.

I started taking them and discovered that G-d had performed yet another miracle for me. The doctor was wrong. I now no longer forget a thing – unless I can't remember it! Well, G-d bless you' all, whether

He is listening or not! I even love people of religion as long as their teachings do not promote hate. I do not hate them as I know hate is wrong and it is against my non-religion religion. Above all, remember that the solution to all our problems is "Universal Love" and you will not need a pill to remember that!

IN APPRECIATION

I am very grateful to Rosabella Torres for her help in preparing this book for publication. I told her I was not exactly a wizard with the computer and became stymied in certain aspects of clearing up the text and placing of the pictures. She knew how concerned I was in getting the book out there to hopefully do some good and perhaps prevent someone from pushing the self-destruct button for our world. I instinctively sense that Rosie is a person of deep faith, yet even knowing my circumstances and thinking, she volunteered to get over these road blocks for me. The world needs more people like Rosie. I profoundly appreciate her assistance.
By Dr. J. Knowname

BOOK EPILOGUE
TO ANY READERS STILL ABOARD!

I wish you all health, wealth and happiness regardless of your religion or non-religion! All I have written here is the Gospel Truth, according to Matthew, Mark, Luke, John and Jack...and I am Jack, the last of the Apostles or the Fifth, of course! And, most sincerely, may G-d bless you whether He exists or not! Naturally, I have an eye

Out for a bolt of lightening!

More importantly, I wish to thank G-d for saving my life three or four times (I forgot how many exactly) so that I have been able to finish this book on atheism and make His world a happier place!

FIN

NOTES

NOTE 1: Germany's treatment of hate speech, which, on the whole, exemplifies the position taken by most European countries and by international law, hate speech must be effectively eliminated.

U.S. court decisions have strongly supported the First Amendment in cyberspace, even when the speech is hateful -- and have suggested that the U.S. has no duty to enforce contrary European law. I do not understand how our reluctance to amend or declare an exception to the First Amendment in view of the principle that we should not be allowed to yell fire in a crowded theatre when there is no fire! "Shouting fire in a crowded theater" has come to be known as synonymous with an action that the speaker believes goes beyond the rights guaranteed by free speech, reckless or malicious speech, or an action whose outcomes are blatantly obvious.

NOTE 2: For a full understanding of what I mean by "Left Leaning Liberal Lunatics," a term I enjoyed making up, may I suggest you read "TREASON" by Ann Coulter. Enjoy it; it is an education in itself. I agree with what she has to say about the "Left." This is not to imply that I appreciate all of Ann Coulter's positions.

NOTE 3: Go to stevefaithweb.com to witness more CONVOLUTED THINKING found in the Bible. This is about Mary and immaculate conception. It is further proof of my opinion that much of religion is just plain silly. I have said nothing about it myself, but I certainly made my feelings known about so much else that is silly in religion – all of them! Please recall that I would not say these things in normal times, but in this age, we must grow up fast or we children (humans) will destroy our entire civilization if we continue to play with fire. Religion is the fire that has set the world ablaze over the centuries.

NOTE 4: The VOICE of the MARTYRS, P.O. Box 443, Bartlesville, OK 7405-0443 or e-mail = the voice@vom-usa.org

NOTE 5: DEBKAfile Type DEBKAfile into address bar and you will be able to contact them. This is a wonderful source for news from the Middle East.

NOTE 6: To receive articles by Mike Evans, intelligence reports from Iraq, and to receive notices of scheduled showings of the television documentary, *The Final Move Beyond Iraq, go to your internet address line and type in "The Jerusalem Prayer Team." Leave out the quotation marks.*

Jerusalem Prayer Team, P.O. Box 210489, Bedford, TX 76095, FAX: 817-285-0962
1-800-825-3872
http://jerusalemprayerteam.org

NOTE 7: TO GET YOUR COPY OF *THE AMERICAN PROPHECIES*, GO TO: AMAZON.COM Jerusalem Prayer Team, P. O. Box 210489, Bedford, TX 76095.

NOTE 8: John Shelby Spong (born 16 June 1931 in Charlotte, North Carolina) is the retired Bishop of the Episcopal Diocese of Newark (based in Newark, New Jersey). He is a liberal theologian. Bishop **John Shelby Spong** is the retired Bishop of the Episcopal Diocese of Newark and Bishop John A.T. Robinson reject the historical truth claims of some Christian doctrines, such as the virgin birth (Spong, 1992) and the bodily resurrection of Jesus (Spong, 1994).

NOTE 9: Fred Gielow gielow@youdontsay.org This is loaded with views worth considering.

NOTE 10: The following two sources were a great help: www. BullionVault.com and paul.tustain@BullionVault.com

NOTE 11: American Theocracy, Kevin Phillips

NOTE 12: The not-so-reverend Martin Luther did not first vote for the Jews and then vote against them. Instead, he loved them as he tried to convert them and then hated them when he had no success! He did such a good job of then killing them and preaching against them that Hitler often referred to him. Life is funny and not so funny isn't it!

I remember when Luther started his ministry, he tried to get Jews to accept Jesus as Savior. Being quite unsuccessful, he started writing about the Jews saying that their homes should be destroyed, their synagogues burned, money confiscated, and liberty curtailed. During the Nazi era, 1933-1945, his ideas were revived and given widespread publicity by the Nazis in Germany. I know I do not have to remind any Jewish readers that this is no reason to feel anger or hatred against any Lutheran or German. If the world is to become better, we must let horrors of the past lie in the past. We need to follow the precepts in this book to work together to create a happier world now and in the future.

NOTE 13: On July 26, 1956 Egyptian president, **Gamal Abdel Nasser**, nationalized the **Suez Canal**. The canal had been owned by the Suez Canal Company, which was controlled by French and British interests. In August, British oil and embassy officials were expelled from the country. Israel had been denied passage through the canal since 1950 and having suffered repeated border raids from Egypt, Israel, with French and English air support, invaded Egyptian territory on Oct. 29, 1956. Within a few days France and Great Britain sent armed forces to retake the Suez Canal. Criticism and lack of support from our President Eisenhower brought on intervention by the United Nations. There was an armistice in early November, and a UN emergency force replaced the British and French troops; Israel suffered the consequences. The United Nations had been charged with guaranteeing free passage of vessels through the canal, but Egypt prevented Israeli ships from using the waterway. The canal was closed by Egypt during the Arab-Israeli War of 1967. In Oct. 1973, Egyptian troops crossed the canal and attacked Israeli forces on the east bank of the canal; Israeli units crossed the canal to the west and eventually encircled the Egyptian Third Army. In early 1974, Israel was forced to sign an agreement with Egypt that led to Israeli withdrawal from the Sinai.

NOTE 14: "Convert to Wahabbism now lest you die infidel pigs."
This is a friendly message from **Sheikh Usama ibn Akhmed** who is a
professor of Wahabbism at Drexel University in Philadelphia, PA, the
City of Brotherly Love. He is also the president of Wahabbism Now for
America. Go to Google, type in (**Wahabbism Now for America),** no
brackets, and you will get the whole story, so help us Allah, Schmallah,
Challah!

BE SURE TO GIVE A COPY TO THE DEMOCRATS and
similar fools who want us to walk away from Iraq! NB - I am not
calling all Democrats fools. Some must realize that we need to defend
ourselves! By the way, the founder of the Muslim religion, Mohammad,
had nine wives. Did they have something like Viagra at that time?

NOTE 15: It is only because I know our country and the planet are in
great danger that I allow myself to say so many negative things about
our President George W. Bush. I hope he will forgive me, but I know
that much of what he has done is very dangerous, but deep down inside
I really like the man. He has just been naïve and uninformed with
regard to consequences and historical realities.

His idea of creating a never before in existence Palestinian state on land
that the entire world, through the League of Nations, declared should
be set aside as a homeland for Jews is one of them. No doubt this has
to do with the fact that his feet are stuck in the oil patch and his head
is in the clouds, if I may say so! I just said so.

The other is his brainstorm idea of having faith based initiatives -
another explosive issue that can lead to no good. We are already paying
for the building of Mosques through tax exempt status for religion and
now, due to this latest gimmick, taxpayers are funding money going
toward Muslim charities that often pay the families of suicide bombers
to kill us. Do not forget, the Muslim religion has been largely taken
over by the lunatic fringe that teaches they should kill Christians,
Jews and even Muslims who do not agree fully with their version of
Mohammad's Laws in the Koran, which is largely a hate book whose
goal is to lord it over the entire world through a world Caliphate. (I
am sure decent, modern day Muslims decry this, but they are not in

control!) We have already been funding similar hate groups, namely churches, which preach that homosexuals are an abomination in the eyes of the Lord! Harmless, you think? Ask the families of homosexuals who have been killed by these twisted minds! If you are not aware of this, come back to planet earth and read old newspapers!

NOTE 16: We cannot understand or cope with what we are facing with the Muslim extremists or with our economic debacle if we do not give our youth a solid education. I firmly believe we are in serious political trouble now because our children have not been taught about the philosophy behind the founding of our country and learned little, if anything, about our Constitution. I was originally concerned with the poor education received by black children and fell for integration and affirmative action as a means to change this for the better. Unfortunately, I found that this weakened the entire educational system and destroyed lives and futures of so many black children. I am convinced this is the main reason for the outrageous number of deaths of black youth.

They see no future for themselves with such an inferior education. I took three trips to stand across from the Liberty Bell in Philadelphia to expose the public fraud of our public schools and to encourage the establishment of a voucher system to get government out of education. My sign read: APOLOGY DUE FROM NAACP for ruining public schools and killing black children. No one objected and I had nothing but praise and thanks from blacks who read my material and they ran from street people to college educated and even many college professors. A plan I created to totally change from government to private education will be posted in my web-site or BLOG and I will try to have it in the media.

Of course, it is the entire world that needs to be educated about the need for a feeling of universal human brotherhood - the innate morality of treating all with respect and care no matter how different we may be. This is, perhaps, an area in which the WORLD PEACE ASSOCIATON may be of help. Considering the gang killings in our country, this is instruction needed as well in our schools.

NOTE 17: Just type in "Brazil imports of oil, alternative fuel" in the SEARCH line and you will get an education on what can be done to free us from dependence on oil from hostile countries.)

NOTE 18: Sheldon Drobny in The Huffington Post, "Organized Political Parties: Another Form Of Religion" Posted July 2, 2007 | 12:38 PM (EST) George Washington's Farewell Address

NOTE 19: From GLOBAL POLICY FORUM E-Mail: gpf@globalpolicy.org Website: www.globalpolicy.org

Sudan has been torn by war since independence in 1956. The civil war between North and South has left some 2 million people dead and many more that have fled their homeland.

.